Spirituality

Sayyid Ali Al-Hakeem

TRANSLATED BY MOHAMED ALI ALBODAIRI

Author: Sayyid Ali Al-Hakeem

Translated by: Mohamed Ali Albodairi

© 2021 The Mainstay Foundation

ALL RIGHTS RESERVED. No part of this work covered by the copyright may be reproduced or used in any form or by any means – graphic, electronic, or mechanical, including photocopying, recording, taping, web distribution, information storage and retrieval systems, or in any other manner – without the written permission of the Mainstay Foundation.

Printed in the United States.

ISBN: 978-1943393916

To our guide. To our hope. To our salvation.

To our Prophet (s).

Contents

About the Author ix
Translator's Preface xi

    Introduction 1
    Spiritual Methods 5
    Between this World and the Hereafter 21
    Why do we Lack in Worship? 39
    Love of the World 59
    Whim 71
    Austerity 89
    Piety 103
    Rectitude 121
    Perseverance in Self Struggle 131
    Fasting and Strengthening the Will 147
    Worship and Happiness 161
    Remembrance of God 187
    Guidance and Misguidance 205
    Ill Outcomes 223
    Seeking Closeness to God 243

Translation Note 269
Referenced Works 271

ABOUT THE AUTHOR

Sayyid Ali Al-Hakeem is an esteemed Muslim scholar, lec-turer, and researcher, residing in Dubai, UAE. Sayyid Al-Hakeem spent ten years studying at the Islamic seminaries of Qum, Iran. There, he completed his Advanced Seminars (a Ph.D. equivalent in Islamic seminaries) in Islamic Jurisprudence and Thought. He also received a Master's degree in Islamic Thought from the Islamic University of Lebanon. Sayyid Al-Hakeem has dedicated the past twenty-two years of his life to service of the Muslim community in different capacities. He serves as a resident scholar in the Imam Hassan Mosque, Dubai. He is the chair of the Religious Committee and the religious supervisor of the Charitable Deeds Committee of the Ja'afariya Endowment Charitable Council of Dubai.

Translator's Preface

Amongst all of God's creations, humanity was given both body and soul. The purpose of our creation is to reach closer towards perfection. God Almighty created perfect beings such as angels, yet His wisdom dictated that a more perfect being be made. That being – us – can reach higher than the angels when we choose to act in accordance with virtue and excellence. So, while the angels are perfect, a human that chooses perfection is greater because that perfection came out of free will and volition.

Thus, we were endowed with moral agency. We were created on this Earth and given the ability to choose and act. We are also faced with trials and test where we are tasked with putting our free will into action. Our lot is to make the best choices and reach closer towards perfection.

God's justice dictates that whoever utilizes their free will and passes these tests be rewarded accordingly. Similarly, those who abuse their free will, transgress against others, and fail these tests should be punished. For that, God dictated that our actions be reflected in the realm of the hereafter, and that all mankind be resurrected and judged.

God's grace also dictates that we are not left alone on this path. Rather, we are given guides and signs throughout this journey. Chief amongst those guides are the Holy Prophet Muhammad (s) and his blessed progeny. They did not only instruct their followers on how to tread through this world, but led us through their noble examples.

God also appointed for each individual a personal guide to accompany them on this journey. This guide – human reason by which we interpret the world, evaluate choices, and make judgements – will always tug us towards the right path. It interprets the enumerable signs that God placed on our path, all pointers towards the right way.

Thus, we are moral agents blessed with free choice and tasked to strive ever closer towards perfection. Our goal is to safeguard our souls and ensure for them the best abode in the eternity of the hereafter. We are provided with guides, both internal and external to ourselves, that help us navigate this path.

The reader will now see the gravity of the subject matter of this book. Spirituality is the endeavor of connecting with the divine to achieve salvation. But how does a person go about tying the reins of their spirit to divine will? How do I align my heart with divine guidance?

The answer lies in metaphysical incentives and divine love. Any believer knows that there is a lot at stake in their hereafter – either the punishment of Hellfire or an eternal home in the gardens of Paradise. We must keep in mind the fleeting nature of this world and the everlasting nature of the next one. Orienting the heart and mind to the true consequences of every action and decision will take a person a long way on their journey towards God.

A true believer will be drawn even closer to the Almighty through the power of divine love. How does a person instill the love of God in their heart? You cannot love what you do not know. So, the first step in attaining that love is to know more about God. Study His attributes and reflect on His signs. Read His word and follow His guides.

Once that knowledge is attained, it must be put to work. Knowledge, if left unpracticed, will either flee the mind or be distorted by time. But knowledge when put into practice will enter the heart and shape it like clay. This is the importance of pious work on our spiritual journey. From prayer and fasting to repentance and remembrance, acting on divine commands roots love deep in the heart.

This formula may sound simple, but it is much simpler to say than to accomplish.

Spirituality cannot be achieved simply by reading books and engaging in theoretical discussions. Spirituality requires action and sustained practice. Just as physical health cannot be attained by reading a book on physiology but through sustained healthy practices, the same is true with spirituality. We cannot promise the reader that they will be a more spiritual person once they put this book down. Yet we are confident that it will change your perspective and provide invaluable wisdom that will aid you on your journey.

I know this because I have personally benefitted from this book and its author.

I met Sayyid Ali al-Hakeem through his son Sayyid Hassan, one of my close friends and colleagues. When I first met Sayyid Ali, his humility and wisdom left an impression on me. We sat in his humble home with a delegation of scholars. He did not speak much but gave everyone his attention. He made conversation with every person in the gathering, asking them how they were doing and how their travels have been.

I had a greater opportunity to benefit from Sayyid al-Hakeem's knowledge and wisdom upon reading his books (and translating a few). What is most remarkable about his work are the clarity and simplicity with which he delivers the most valuable wisdom.

He delivers nuggets of wisdom through using simple and practical traditions from the Holy Prophet (s) and Immaculate Imams (a) as clear guiding principles. Three examples come to mind – though there are many others – all of which come from the Holy Prophet (s).

- "This world is the farmland of the Hereafter"[1] – a reminder that we will simply reap in the hereafter what we sow in this world.

- "[The path to] Paradise is filled with troubles and [the path to] hellfire is filled with [satisfaction of] desires"[2] – a reminder that even though doing good might not feel

---

[1] Al-Ihsa'ei, *'Awali al-La'ali*, 1:267.
[2] Al-Radi, *Al-Majazat Al-Nabawiyya*, 387.

good, it is still the right thing to do and should be done with the goal in mind.

- "Virtue is a habit, and vice is an incessant [habit]"[3] – a reminder to do good even if it were out of habit, and to avoid sin even if it were only once because it may become a habit.

The reader will see from these examples the practicality of Sayyid al-Hakeem's advice. This book is meant to be just that – a set of practical solutions to the common problems that may hinder our spiritual growth. From balancing between this world and the hereafter, to practicing piety and rectitude, to seeking closeness to God, each chapter in this book provides a set of actionable and practical takeaways that will help you on your spiritual journey.

Above all, I pray that the reader will pick up this book with an open heart. Listen to its wisdom and practice its advice. At the end of the day, we are all making this journey together. And just as I have personally benefitted from its morals and lessons, I pray that you do too.

Mohamed Ali Albodairi,

The Mainstay Foundation's Editorial and Translation Team

---

[3] Al-Rayshahri, *Mizan al-Hikma*, 4:2770.

Introduction

In the name of God, the most Beneficent, the most Merciful

Mankind lives in this world surrounded by temptation and desire. Many of us fall into complacency – becoming more and more attached to this world, while not paying much attention to the hereafter. God sent His messengers and scriptures to call mankind to avoid the temptations of this world and seek the eternal life of the hereafter, setting out on a journey towards an everlasting Paradise.

God created a system in which our free will and choices can lead us towards the greatest of spiritual heights, to be the greatest of His creations. This spiritual journey is not a small or trivial matter. We cannot approach the task of spiritual advancement without first equipping ourselves with the proper tools and understanding.

This book is a compilation of lessons in ethics revolving around specific discussions on man's relationship with God and the effects of our actions on that relationship. The topics discussed here range from the methodology for self-betterment to building a relationship with the Creator. It is an effort to provide some practical wisdom for anyone seeking to reach nearer to the Almighty.

The teachings of Islam have one unequivocal goal – to allow followers to pursue excellence. From that perspective, Islam places great emphasis on knowledge and learning. The Holy Quran gives knowledge a special status that is unique when compared with other human virtues. God says, "Say, 'Are those who know equal to those who do not know?' Only those who possess intellect take admonition."[1] God also says, "Only those of God's servants having knowledge fear Him."[2]

A firm warning or reprimand.

The traditions of the Holy Prophet (s) and his Progeny (a) contain numerous similar admonitions as well. It is also narrated that the Commander of the Faithful Ali ibn Abi Talib (a) once said,

> Oh people! Know that excellence in faith consists of seeking knowledge and acting in accordance to that knowledge. Indeed, seeking knowledge is a higher obligation for you than seeking sustenance. Your sustenance is pre-ordained and guaranteed. Your Just Lord has divided it amongst you and promised to deliver it to you. Surely, He will keep His promise. [On the other hand,] knowledge is protected by its keepers. You were commanded to seek it from its keepers, so go forth and seek it.

---

[1] The Holy Quran, 39:9.
[2] The Holy Quran, 35:28.

Introduction

Islam did not stop at admonitions and theories about knowledge and learning. Instead, it created opportunities and enabled conditions that would foster learning, research, and study. Amongst these was the establishment of Friday prayers – God says in the Quran, "O you who have faith! When the call is made for prayer on Friday, hurry toward the remembrance of God, and leave all business. That is better for you, should you know."[3] One of the important pillars of this ritual is the sermon, where the prayer leader must convey Islam's teachings, in addition to addressing all other relevant worldly and other-worldly matters.

Dear reader, this book is based on a compilation of Friday sermons that I have delivered over the years, as well as lectures I have given at a number of commemorations and celebrations. Throughout such gatherings, I have been able to address and speak on a wide array of issues relevant to the Muslim community.

At the insistence of a number of dear brothers, I compiled my notes to publish a series of books with the hopes that God will accept the work and that the benefit will spread to believers. I tried to maintain the conversational tone of the original sermons, in order to make the books more reader-friendly. After a series of these books were printed in the original Arabic, a group of believers then insisted on having the work translated into English so that English-speaking audiences may benefit as well.

---

[3] The Holy Quran, 62:9.

I thank God, the Exalted, for His infinite support and favor. I must also thank everyone who participated in making this book a reality.

I ask God, the Almighty, to take this work as an act of devotion for His sake and to accept it by His grace; He is surely the All-Kind and Magnanimous.

Ali Al-Hakeem,
Dubai, United Arab Emirates

Spiritual Methods

In the Name of God, the Most Beneficent, the Most Merciful

إِنَّا خَلَقْنَا الْإِنسَانَ مِن نُّطْفَةٍ أَمْشَاجٍ نَّبْتَلِيهِ فَجَعَلْنَاهُ سَمِيعًا بَصِيرًا

Indeed, We created man from the drop of a mixed fluid so that We may put him to test, so We endowed him with hearing and sight.[1]

The process of developing and training the spirit is not something that can be approached haphazardly. It requires a methodical approach, relying on precise scientific foundations. Without such an approach, any attempt to improve the soul will likely not yield the intended result.

We can say that the science of ethics is the study of the proper ways through which to achieve virtues and avoid vice. Through ethics, we can find the proper methods and means to reach our goal of spiritual attainment and moral excellence. Indeed, this is one of the greatest reasons for which God Almighty sent his messengers and apostles. Prophet Muhammad (s) said:

---

[1] The Holy Quran, 76:2.

إنّما بعثت لأتمّم مكارم الأخلاق

Indeed, I have been sent to complete the best of morals.[2]

METHODOLOGY

It should come as no surprise that spiritual attainment requires a properly prescribed course and method. It is clear that in other areas of life, an individual needs similarly to follow a properly prescribed method to accomplish a particular goal. When it comes to physical training and fitness, for example, we see that an individual who exercises rarely and inconsistently will not attain the goal of physical fitness. Conversely, an individual who puts too much strain on their body will end up causing unexpected ailments and harm their body, instead of developing it.

Since the human spirit is much more sensitive than the body, we must make sure to follow the proper methodology through which we can attain our goal of spiritual development. We must look for the method that was prescribed to us by God Almighty so that we can attain our goal of developing closeness to Him.

The process of spiritual development and the practice of ethics cannot be reached solely through theoretical discussion and study. A person will not start behaving in a certain way simply because he or she studied its merits. A behavior must be practiced before it becomes habitual and part of the individual's character.

---

[2] Al-Majlisi, Bihar al-Anwar, 16:210.

A person cannot become brave simply by studying the attribute and believing that it is a valuable course of action. He or she must act with bravery, whenever possible, before he or she can become a brave individual. Simply speaking of bravery or acting bravely on one or two occasions does not translate into an internalized characteristic. The same is true with all other virtues. Only with continuous application of virtues will an individual achieve them as characteristics. They become attached to the individual and an inseparable part of them. Otherwise, the individual becomes a manifestation of the following holy verse:

مَثَلُ الَّذِينَ حُمِّلُوا التَّوْرَاةَ ثُمَّ لَمْ يَحْمِلُوهَا كَمَثَلِ الْحِمَارِ يَحْمِلُ أَسْفَارًا ۚ بِئْسَ مَثَلُ الْقَوْمِ الَّذِينَ كَذَّبُوا بِآيَاتِ اللَّهِ ۚ وَاللَّهُ لَا يَهْدِي الْقَوْمَ الظَّالِمِينَ

The example of those who were charged with the Torah, then failed to carry it, is that of a mule carrying books. Evil is the example of the people who deny God's signs, and God does not guide the wrongdoing lot.[3]

We should also note that practicing virtue and refraining from vice does not alone provide the most complete results in terms of the development of the spirit. An individual also needs to maintain true and sincere belief. Islam sees an inseparable link between belief and action: neither is complete without the other. An individual of sound belief will be driven towards virtuous deeds and towards building a virtuous character. An individual of faulty beliefs is more easily swayed towards vice. As God Almighty says,

---

[3] The Holy Quran, 62:5.

SPIRITUALITY

> وَالْبَلَدُ الطَّيِّبُ يَخْرُجُ نَبَاتُهُ بِإِذْنِ رَبِّهِ ۖ وَالَّذِي خَبُثَ لَا يَخْرُجُ إِلَّا نَكِدًا ۚ كَذَٰلِكَ نُصَرِّفُ الْآيَاتِ لِقَوْمٍ يَشْكُرُونَ

The vegetation of the good land comes out by the permission of its Lord. As for that which is bad, it does not come out, except [sparsely.] Thus do We paraphrase the signs variously for a people who give thanks. [4]

(margin note: Tiny / Dispersed / scattered)

And just as virtuous character and behaviors stem from a sound belief system, such character is also a major factor in preserving and maintaining faith. God Almighty says:

> مَن كَانَ يُرِيدُ الْعِزَّةَ فَلِلَّهِ الْعِزَّةُ جَمِيعًا ۚ إِلَيْهِ يَصْعَدُ الْكَلِمُ الطَّيِّبُ وَالْعَمَلُ الصَّالِحُ يَرْفَعُهُ ۚ وَالَّذِينَ يَمْكُرُونَ السَّيِّئَاتِ لَهُمْ عَذَابٌ شَدِيدٌ ۖ وَمَكْرُ أُولَٰئِكَ هُوَ يَبُورُ

Whoever seeks honor [should know that] honor entirely belongs to God. To Him ascends the good word, and righteous conduct elevates it. As for those who devise evil schemes, there is a severe punishment for them, and their plotting shall come to naught. [5]

Conversely, engaging in vice has its effect on a person's faith and belief. God says:

> ثُمَّ كَانَ عَاقِبَةَ الَّذِينَ أَسَاءُوا السُّوأَىٰ أَن كَذَّبُوا بِآيَاتِ اللَّهِ وَكَانُوا بِهَا يَسْتَهْزِئُونَ

---

[4] The Holy Quran, 7:58.
[5] The Holy Quran, 35:10.

> *The fate of those who committed misdeeds was that they denied the signs of God and they used to deride them.*[6]

So, there is a strong relationship between knowledge and faith on one end, and character and conduct on the other. Sound belief and knowledge will drive an individual to adopt good traits and act virtuously. Unsound beliefs and lack of knowledge will draw an individual deeper and deeper towards vice and deviance. Righteous conduct will help to preserve sound beliefs, whereas vice and misdeeds will undermine sound faith.

With this introduction in mind, we can now address the different methods which scholars of ethics have laid out for sound spiritual development.

Temporal Incentives

One theory – discussed by early philosophers and adopted to a greater extent by modern and contemporary philosophers – proposes that man will act virtuously so long as there are physical and emotional incentives that will drive him towards that end. Similarly, an individual will refrain from vice so long as there are adequate physical and emotional disincentives to fall into vice. For example, so long as acting virtuously is a means to achieve monetary rewards, recognition, and praise, an individual will act virtuously. So long as engaging in vice will result in monetary loss and harm to the individual's reputation, the individual will refrain from vice.

---

[6] The Holy Quran, 30:10.

This theory is not entirely accepted by Islam. It is true that someone who does good should be rewarded and praised, but there are conditions.

The temporal rewards earned by acting virtuously are just that – they are limited by time and space and will cease at some point in time. What value is praise to an individual who has died and departed this world? Even when an individual is alive, what value do praise and admiration really carry for the individual?

Additionally, praise can be a cause for vice just as well as it can be an incentive for virtue. A person who is continuously praised will develop a sense of arrogance and conceit. Their action would simply become a façade by which they seek only more praise. Once the praise stopped, so would the virtue.

Thus, Islam does not accept this approach completely. Imam al-Rida (a) said,

من لم يشكر المنعم من المخلوقين لم يشكر الله عز وجل

> *Whoever neglects to praise a good-doing creature has neglected to praise the Almighty Creator.*[7]

Praise is a means to incentivize the doing of good and to spread virtue within society.

At the same time, Islam rejects egotism, arrogance, and duplicity. Praise can sometimes lead to such vices; therefore, Islam recommends that we deal with it cautiously. The Holy Prophet (s) said,

---

[7] Al-Sadouq, *'Oyoun Akhbar al-Rida*, 1:27.

أحثوا في وجوه المادحين التراب

Throw dust in the faces of flatterers.[8]

Accordingly, praise should not turn to flattery and feed the ego to the point of arrogance.

Thus, praise is appropriate in many circumstances, including:

1. To incentivize virtue and push people to compete in this regard. God Almighty says, "For such let the viers vie."[9]
2. To remember the virtuous individual by his good traits and have that as a cause for the believers to pray for him.
3. To bring joy to the believer's heart by assuring him that his actions are accepted by God Almighty. We see that the Holy Quran praises the believers by mentioning their virtues, and such praise reflects God's acceptance of their deeds.
4. To strengthen social ties and community relations between believers.

These are appropriate so long as praise does not lead to the deterioration of another virtue, or drive the individual into a vice, such as arrogance or duplicity.

METAPHYSICAL INCENTIVES

The second approach to ethics looks at the metaphysical consequences of an individual's actions and what they mean for them

---

[8] Al-'Amili, *Wasa'el al-Shia*, 12:132.
[9] The Holy Quran, 83:26.

in terms of their life in the hereafter. Although this is somewhat like the previous approach – both rely on a system of incentives – there is a great difference in terms of the desired incentive. In the first approach, the incentives for action or inaction were limited to the physical realm. In the second approach, the incentives are wholly metaphysical. This difference translates into a great difference in results. Whereas a physical result is fleeting, a metaphysical one is everlasting. More specifically, we can list the differences between the two approaches as follows:

First, the result in the second approach is everlasting. It is not something transitory, such praise or wealth. Rather, it is an everlasting life in the gardens of Paradise. God Almighty says:

فَإِن تَابُوا وَأَقَامُوا الصَّلَاةَ وَآتَوُا الزَّكَاةَ فَإِخْوَانُكُمْ فِي الدِّينِ ۗ وَنُفَصِّلُ الْآيَاتِ لِقَوْمٍ يَعْلَمُونَ

Indeed, God has bought from the faithful their souls and their possessions for paradise to be theirs: they fight in the way of God, kill, and are killed. [This is] a promise binding upon Him in the Torah and the Evangel and the Quran. And who is truer to his promise than God? So, rejoice in the bargain you have made with Him, and that is the great success.[10]

Imam Ali (a) also says:

إنه ليس لأنفسكم ثمن إلا الجنة فلا تبيعوها إلا بها

---

[10] The Holy Quran, 9:111.

Your souls are as valuable as Paradise. Do not sell them for any other price![11]

Worldly rewards are limited and fleeting, whereas the rewards of the hereafter are everlasting.

Second, metaphysical rewards are conditioned on sound faith. Virtuous actions do not deserve a metaphysical reward unless they are undertaken with the right intent and belief. The second approach is different from the first approach, which does not give any regard to the individual's faith.

Third, the second approach looks at the soundness of an individual's actions, both internally and externally. This is because the soundness of an action is contingent on the soundness of the factors that drove the individual to undertake the action. God, who will reward the individual for his actions, is omniscient: He knows and assesses the individual holistically and completely, internally, and externally. This too, is contrary to the first approach, where the individual is assessed only externally.

Fourth, the second approach is more just, as God does not let any virtuous action go unrewarded. God Almighty says:

فَاسْتَجَابَ لَهُمْ رَبُّهُمْ أَنِّي لَا أُضِيعُ عَمَلَ عَامِلٍ مِّنكُم مِّن ذَكَرٍ أَوْ أُنثَىٰ ۖ بَعْضُكُم مِّن بَعْضٍ ۖ فَالَّذِينَ هَاجَرُوا وَأُخْرِجُوا مِن دِيَارِهِمْ وَأُوذُوا فِي سَبِيلِي وَقَاتَلُوا وَقُتِلُوا لَأُكَفِّرَنَّ عَنْهُمْ سَيِّئَاتِهِمْ وَلَأُدْخِلَنَّهُمْ جَنَّاتٍ تَجْرِي مِن تَحْتِهَا الْأَنْهَارُ ثَوَابًا مِّنْ عِندِ اللَّهِ ۗ وَاللَّهُ عِندَهُ حُسْنُ الثَّوَابِ

---

[11] Al-Radi, *Nahj al-Balagha*, 4:105.

I do not waste the work of any worker among you, whether male or female; you are all on the same footing. So those who migrated and were expelled from their homes, and were tormented [for following] My way, and those who fought and were killed – I will surely absolve them of their misdeeds and I will admit them into gardens with streams running in them, as a reward from God – and the best of rewards are with God.[12]

God Almighty also says:

$$\text{فَمَن يَعْمَلْ مِثْقَالَ ذَرَّةٍ خَيْرًا يَرَهُ وَمَن يَعْمَلْ مِثْقَالَ ذَرَّةٍ شَرًّا يَرَهُ}$$

So, whoever does an atom's weight of good will see it, and whoever does an atom's weight of evil will see it.[13]

No individual will lose out in the end, as all actions will be rewarded. Thus, each will work knowing that they will be rewarded justly by God. This is contrary to the first approach, where the rewards are conditioned on the assessment – whether just or unjust – of other individuals and society at large.

This second approach is adopted by Islam, just as it was adopted by the previous divine messages. The duties of the prophets and messengers were to warn and give glad tidings to their nations. They are the ones who give glad tidings of Paradise and warn of Hellfire. God Almighty says:

---

[12] The Holy Quran, 3:195.
[13] The Holy Quran, 99:7-8.

Spiritual Methods

$$\text{يَا أَيُّهَا النَّبِيُّ إِنَّا أَرْسَلْنَاكَ شَاهِدًا وَمُبَشِّرًا وَنَذِيرًا وَدَاعِيًا إِلَى اللَّهِ بِإِذْنِهِ وَسِرَاجًا مُّنِيرًا}$$

O Prophet! Indeed, We have sent you as a witness, as a bearer of good news and as a warner and as a summoner to God by His permission, and as a radiant lamp.[14]

Divine Love

This third approach, which relies entirely on divine love, is mentioned in the Holy Quran. In fact, as Allama Tabatabaei mentions in *al-Mizan*:

> *This third approach is found only in the Holy Quran and is not contained in what we find of the Holy Scriptures or the teachings of the past prophets. Neither is it mentioned in the teachings of the spiritual philosophers. It consists of nurturing the individual in both character and knowledge through disciplines that leave no room for vice. In other words, it is the removal of vicious characteristics through elevation rather than through revulsion.*[15] — A sense of disgust and loathing

The discussion of divine love is a lengthy and complex one, requiring a detailed analysis of many precise intricacies. But in

---

[14] The Holy Quran, 33:45-46.
[15] Al-Tabatabaei, *al-Mizan*, 1:358.

general, this third approach relies on two main pillars – knowledge and pious works.

The first pillar – knowledge – requires the individual to dedicate him or herself to the realization of pure monotheism. Before an individual can work on attaining virtue and avoiding vice, he must first attempt to know God sincerely. As our narrations mention, the basis of religion is knowledge of God. Once the individual attains sincere knowledge of God, there will be no room left for vice.

If we wish to understand how true and sincere knowledge of the divine eradicates any room for vice, we must ask: "Why do we act in a certain way? And why do we refrain from certain actions?"

When it comes to actions we undertake, we can see that they stem from an aspiration to achieve a certain result. A person may excel at their job to get a promotion. Another may become proactive and act with bravery to receive honor and recognition. On the flip side, we refrain from certain actions because there is some force or result that we fear. A person may drive at the speed limit for fear of getting a traffic ticket. Another may work hard to recieve a high grade in a class because they fear that they might disappoint their parents.

Thus, the roots of our behavior can be found in two mental processes – aspiration and fear.

If we understand this premise, we can see why a true and sincere knowledge of God eradicates any room within us for vice. All of our aspirations then flow from our knowledge of God's mercy,

SPIRITUAL METHODS

magnanimity, and benevolence. All of our fears flow from an understanding of God's just retribution. Thus, all of our actions are rooted in knowledge of God Almighty and are aligned to His will. As God says:

$$\text{وَمِنَ النَّاسِ مَن يَتَّخِذُ مِن دُونِ اللَّهِ أَندَادًا يُحِبُّونَهُمْ كَحُبِّ اللَّهِ ۖ وَالَّذِينَ آمَنُوا أَشَدُّ حُبًّا لِّلَّهِ ۗ وَلَوْ يَرَى الَّذِينَ ظَلَمُوا إِذْ يَرَوْنَ الْعَذَابَ أَنَّ الْقُوَّةَ لِلَّهِ جَمِيعًا وَأَنَّ اللَّهَ شَدِيدُ الْعَذَابِ}$$

> *Among the people are those who set up [idols] besides God, loving them as if loving God. Yet the faithful have a more ardent love for God. Surely, the wrongdoers will see, when they see the punishment, that power, altogether, belongs to God, and that God is severe in punishment.*[16]

No one has any power to fulfill their aspirations, except through the sole and absolute power of God. A person who knows God knows that only He has real power and honor. This knowledge will erase all vice and leave no room for them to act in any way except for His sake.

The second pillar – pious works – cannot be achieved without that first pillar of knowledge. Once an individual attains that knowledge, they must work in accordance with it. This can only be maintained through dedication of love to God.

An individual who loves another individual or thing will focus their dedication on that object of love. The beloved will hold

---

[16] The Holy Quran, 2:165.

sway over the lover and the lover will fall under the spell of the beloved, to an extent that may even turn into worship. Allama Tabatabaei says:

> *If a servant increases in faith and belief, his soul and mind are drawn towards his Lord. He will reflect on His Most Beutiful Names and beautiful attributes, which are impeccable and above any lack or fault. The soul will continue to be drawn and elevated until he begins to worship God as if he sees Him, knowing that God sees him. The individual will see the manifestations of this dedication and love, and that love will continue to grow, due to the innate human drive to love all that is beautiful.*[17]

An individual who genuinely loves a thing will love everything associated with it. Whoever loves God will love everything which manifests God's attributes. Who manifests the attributes of God better than the prophets and messengers who were sent to us by Him – chief among them being the Holy Prophet Muhammad (s)? That is why God Almighty says:

$$\text{قُلْ إِن كُنتُمْ تُحِبُّونَ اللَّهَ فَاتَّبِعُونِي يُحْبِبْكُمُ اللَّهُ وَيَغْفِرْ لَكُمْ ذُنُوبَكُمْ ۗ وَاللَّهُ غَفُورٌ رَّحِيمٌ}$$

> *Say [O' Prophet Muhammad], 'If you love God, then follow me; God will love you and forgive you your sins, and God is all-forgiving, all-merciful.'*[18]

---

[17] Al-Tabatabaei, *al-Mizan*, 1:374.
[18] The Holy Quran, 3:31.

Spiritual Methods

The bottom line is that the two approaches of metaphysical incentives and divine love, with all their overlap, are both adopted by the religion of Islam. God Almighty has called mankind to perfect themselves through these methods. This is the meaning of the narration in which Imam al-Sadiq (a) is reported to have said:

العباد ثلاثة: قوم عبدوا الله عزوجل خوفا فتلك عبادة العبيد وقوم عبدوا الله تبارك وتعالى طلب الثواب، فتلك عبادة الاجراء، وقوم عبدوا الله عزوجل حبا له، فتلك عبادة الاحرار وهي أفضل العبادة.

> *People are of three types. There are those who worship God Almighty out of fear, and that is the worship of slaves. There are those who worship God Almighty in aspiration of reward, and that is the worship of laborers. And there are those who worship God Almighty out of love for Him. That is the worship of the free and it is the best of worship.*[19]

---

[19] Al-Kulayni, *al-Kafi*, 2:84.

Reflections:

① Better to make small steps and turn into habits, consistently.

② Do actions & Refrain for the love of God, as opposed to "tit-for-tat" mindset.

③ Distance / Lack of Spirituality may have stemed from not enough reading / listening RE Allah SWT. "Basis of religion is knowing God".

BETWEEN THIS WORLD AND THE HEREAFTER

In the Name of God, the Most Beneficent, the Most Merciful

مَّن كَانَ يُرِيدُ الْعَاجِلَةَ عَجَّلْنَا لَهُ فِيهَا مَا نَشَاءُ لِمَن نُّرِيدُ ثُمَّ جَعَلْنَا لَهُ جَهَنَّمَ يَصْلَاهَا مَذْمُومًا مَّدْحُورًا وَمَنْ أَرَادَ الْآخِرَةَ وَسَعَىٰ لَهَا سَعْيَهَا وَهُوَ مُؤْمِنٌ فَأُولَٰئِكَ كَانَ سَعْيُهُم مَّشْكُورًا كُلًّا نُّمِدُّ هَٰؤُلَاءِ وَهَٰؤُلَاءِ مِنْ عَطَاءِ رَبِّكَ وَمَا كَانَ عَطَاءُ رَبِّكَ مَحْظُورًا

> *Whoever desires this transitory life, We expedite for him therein whatever We wish, for whomever We desire. Then We appoint hell for him, to enter it, blameful and spurned. Whoever desires the Hereafter and strives for it with an endeavor worthy of it, should he be faithful, the endeavor of such will be well-appreciated. To these and to those – to all We extend the bounty of your Lord, and the bounty of your Lord is not confined.*[1]

Mankind lives in this world surrounded by temptation and desire. Generally, people largely fall into complacency – becoming more and more attached to this world, while not paying much attention to the hereafter. God Almighty verifies this observation when He says in the Holy Quran,

---

[1] The Holy Quran, 17:18-20.

$$\text{كَلَّا بَلْ تُحِبُّونَ الْعَاجِلَةَ وَتَذَرُونَ الْآخِرَةَ}$$

> *Indeed, you [mankind] love this transitory life and forsake the Hereafter.*[2]

God Almighty tells us about how we give in to temptation and desire, even though He has promised us great rewards in the hereafter. He says,

$$\text{تُرِيدُونَ عَرَضَ الدُّنْيَا وَاللَّهُ يُرِيدُ الْآخِرَةَ وَاللَّهُ عَزِيزٌ حَكِيمٌ}$$

> *You desire the transitory gains of this world, while God desires [for you the reward of] the Hereafter.*[3]

There are many similar verses that clearly call for mankind to avoid the temptations of this world and seek the eternal life of the hereafter. Indeed, one of the most important missions of the prophets and messengers was to remind people of the hereafter and guide them towards an everlasting Paradise. We find this to be clear in the words of our Immaculate Imams. We also find that pious individuals are always looking towards the hereafter and seeking God's promised rewards therein.

There is a clear preference towards the hereafter over this transitory life. So, why do so many people continue to be attached to this world and seem to work tirelessly for it, while putting little thought and effort into the hereafter? What explains the persistence in being attached to the transitory life while neglecting the eternal one?

---

[2] The Holy Quran, 75:20-21.
[3] The Holy Quran, 8:67.

There are many points that can be made in answering these questions. However, the most important point – and the main subject of this chapter – is the lack of true understanding of the two worlds.

If we observe how people around us look at this issue, we find that there is much confusion in distinguishing between the two. In other words, many people usually look to the hereafter in the same way that they look at this world. Due to our shortsightedness, we analyze and value the realities of the hereafter the same way we analyze and value them in this world. We attempt to use our understanding of the physical world to judge and place a priority on the metaphysical.

Yet, there are those who have been blessed to realize the priority of the hereafter. They are attached to eternal life and strive to gain its greatest rewards. They do so because they have a true understanding of the hereafter, one that does not rely on their limited physical observations and sensations. Instead, they gain their understanding from the words of God in the Holy Quran and the traditions of the Holy Prophet (s) and his Immaculate Household (a). The hereafter is part of the unseen realms that we cannot observe or fully understand. Therefore, we must turn to the divine to provide us with a true vision of the hereafter and clarify for us its distinguishing characteristics.

Therefore, we must attempt to understand the reality of the hereafter and the differences between it and this transitory life. We must approach this topic with a practical outlook – our study and understanding of these differences is not meant to be theoretical, but is intended to have a real and practical impact on our mindset and behavior. As you read the rest of this chapter, ask yourself the following questions:

How have I been looking at the hereafter? Do I understand the differences between the hereafter and this transitory world? What do these differences mean for me? How can I change my day-to-day habits and behavior so that they reflect a more accurate understanding of these two worlds?

YOU REAP WHAT YOU SOW

One of the main differences between the two worlds is that the physical world is meant for action, while the hereafter is where we reap the consequences of our actions. Think of this world as your farm. The more seeds you sow and nurture, the greater your harvest will be. If you sow bitter seeds through sin and deviance, you will reap the evil that you sowed. This very same analogy was given by the Holy Prophet (s) to his companions when he said,

الدنيا مزرعة الآخرة

This world is the farmland of the Hereafter.[4]

Thus, this world is the world of action, while the hereafter is the world of consequences. You reap in the eternal life what you sow in this transitory life.

---

[4] Al-Ihsa'ei, *'Awali al-La'ali*, 1:267.

This understanding provides us with a lens that we can use to draw further conclusions about the two worlds and change our habits and behaviors accordingly.

Firstly, we must understand the importance of utilizing this world to sow the greatest amount of good. In fact, it is our only chance to sow and prepare for the harvest. The more we sow in this world, the greater our chances of reaping a higher level of eternal happiness in the hereafter. That is why the narrations of the Immaculate Imams emphasize the need to invest our time in this world properly. The opportunities to invest that are available to us now might soon diminish or fully disappear. As the Commander of the Faithful (a) said:

عِبَادَ اللهِ، الْآنَ فَاعْمَلوا، وَالْأَلْسُنُ مُطْلَقَةٌ، وَالْأَبْدَانُ صَحِيحَةٌ، وَالْأَعْضَاءُ لَدْنَةٌ، وَالْمُنْقَلَبُ فَسِيحٌ، وَالْمَجَالُ عَرِيضٌ، قَبْلَ إِرْهَاقِ الْفَوْتِ، وَحُلُولِ الْمَوْتِ

> *O' servants of God, work now [for the Hereafter] while your tongues are free, your bodies are healthy, your limbs are active, the area of your coming and going is vast and the course of your running is wide; before the loss of opportunity or the approach of death.*[5]

Secondly, we may come across some words of disparagement towards this world in the Holy Quran and noble traditions. But when we approach this world as an opportunity to prepare for

---

[5] Al-Radi, *Nahj al-Balagha*, 2:171, Sermon 196.

the otherworldly harvest, it becomes clear that this disparagement is no longer applicable. In fact, we find that the Holy Quran and the noble traditions praise this world when it is approached as the means of gaining the rewards of the hereafter. In one narration, Imam al-Baqir (a) was asked about the verse,

$$وَلَنِعْمَ دَارُ الْمُتَّقِينَ$$

The abode of the Godwary is surely excellent.[6]

He replied, "This world [is the excellent abode of the Godwary]."[7] In another narration, Imam al-Baqir (a) relays that God Almighty said to Moses,

$$هي دار الظالمين إلا العامل فيها بالخير فإنها له نعم الدار$$

[This world] is the abode of the unjust, except for those who act righteously in it; for them, it is a good home.[8]

The position of the Divine Legislator towards this world is based on the position we take towards it. If we treat this world as an end, it becomes disparaged as an evil home, as it will be the downfall of whomever strives toward it. However, if it is treated as a means to achieve the great promises of the hereafter, it becomes a good home. In fact, there are narrations that forbid us from cursing this world. The Holy Prophet (s) is reported to have said:

---

[6] The Holy Quran, 16:30.

[7] Al-Majlisi, Bihar al-Anwar, 70:107.

[8] Al-Majlisi, Bihar al-Anwar, 70:104.

> لا تسبوا الدنيا فلنعم المطية للمؤمن فعليها يبلغ الخير وبها ينجو من الشر
> إنه إذا قال العبد: لعن الله الدنيا قالت الدنيا لعن الله أعصانا للرب

> *Do not curse this world, for it is a good vehicle for the believer. Through it, he will do good and avoid evil. If a servant says, 'May God curse this world,' the world replies, 'Surely, God will curse whomever is more disobedient of our Lord!'*[9]

Thirdly, the hereafter is the world of consequences and rewards. Once a person arrives at that world, they can no longer change their position. The opportunity – rather, the many opportunities – given in this world will be gone. Once a person ungratefully allows all opportunities to pass them by, God will not give them further chances to correct their mistakes. The Commander of the Faithful (a) says:

> وَإِنَّ الْيَوْمَ عَمَلٌ وَلاَ حِسَابَ، وَغَداً حِسَابٌ وَلاَ عَمَلَ

> *Today is the day of action, when there is no [divine] reckoning. Tomorrow is the Day of Reckoning, when there will be no [opportunity for] action.*[10]

A person can continue to live in this world with the opportunity and hope of someday changing their habits and behavior for the better. However, once their life in this transient world ends, they will not be able to live in that hope. A person will reap only what they sow. That is why the Holy Quran tells us about the situation

---

[9] Al-Majlisi, *Bihar al-Anwar*, 17:388.
[10] Al-Radi, *Nahj al-Balagha*, 1:93, Sermon 42.

of an individual who missed these opportunities and about how they will beg to be returned to this world so that he can correct their mistakes. God Almighty says:

$$\text{حَتَّىٰ إِذَا جَاءَ أَحَدَهُمُ الْمَوْتُ قَالَ رَبِّ ارْجِعُونِ لَعَلِّي أَعْمَلُ صَالِحًا فِيمَا تَرَكْتُ ۚ كَلَّا ۚ إِنَّهَا كَلِمَةٌ هُوَ قَائِلُهَا ۖ وَمِن وَرَائِهِم بَرْزَخٌ إِلَىٰ يَوْمِ يُبْعَثُونَ}$$

When death comes to one of them, he says, 'My Lord! Take me back, that I may act righteously in what I have left behind.' 'By no means! These are mere words that he says.' And before them is a barrier until the day they will be resurrected.[11]

God Almighty – who created us and knows best what we harbor in our hearts – describes mankind as liars, even in that cry described in the verse above. God tells us that even if we were returned to this world, we would just go back to the way we were. He says:

$$\text{بَلْ بَدَا لَهُم مَّا كَانُوا يُخْفُونَ مِن قَبْلُ ۖ وَلَوْ رُدُّوا لَعَادُوا لِمَا نُهُوا عَنْهُ وَإِنَّهُمْ لَكَاذِبُونَ}$$

Indeed, what they used to hide before has now become evident to them. But were they to be sent back, they would revert to what they were forbidden, and they are indeed liars.[12]

We must realize that the only opportunity we have to better ourselves and seek eternal happiness is in this transient world. We

---

[11] The Holy Quran, 23:99-100.
[12] The Holy Quran, 6:28.

must use this realization to drive change within ourselves, so that our habits and behaviors conform to this reality.

A Fleeting Life and an Eternal One

Another of the important differences between the two worlds is the nature of their existence. This physical world is only transient – its existence will last for a set period. This world is characterized by change. In it, each individual has the ability to change him or herself and their surroundings and to be changed by people and circumstances.

The ever-changing nature of this world has allowed us to develop habits through which we cope with and make use of the circumstances we face. Every day, we live our lives without giving much thought to days past. We may face some trouble in this world, but we always have hope that things will change for the better.

However, because we have developed these habits in this world, we tend to superimpose them – whether consciously or not – on to the life of the hereafter. We think that even when our time in this world ends and we move on to the next, we can expect to change our lot and move on. We think that even if we face some punishment or retribution in the next life, it will be temporary and fleeting.

Yet if we read the words of the Holy Quran, we find that it places a great emphasis on the everlasting nature of the hereafter. The Holy Quran tells us that a person who is rewarded with Paradise will forever live honored therein and whoever is deserving of

Hellfire will also take it as an eternal home. The Day of Judgement is described in the Holy Quran:

يَوْمَ يَأْتِ لَا تَكَلَّمُ نَفْسٌ إِلَّا بِإِذْنِهِ ۚ فَمِنْهُمْ شَقِيٌّ وَسَعِيدٌ ۚ فَأَمَّا الَّذِينَ شَقُوا فَفِي النَّارِ لَهُمْ فِيهَا زَفِيرٌ وَشَهِيقٌ خَالِدِينَ فِيهَا مَا دَامَتِ السَّمَاوَاتُ وَالْأَرْضُ إِلَّا مَا شَاءَ رَبُّكَ ۚ إِنَّ رَبَّكَ فَعَّالٌ لِمَا يُرِيدُ وَأَمَّا الَّذِينَ سُعِدُوا فَفِي الْجَنَّةِ خَالِدِينَ فِيهَا مَا دَامَتِ السَّمَاوَاتُ وَالْأَرْضُ إِلَّا مَا شَاءَ رَبُّكَ ۖ عَطَاءً غَيْرَ مَجْذُوذٍ

The day it comes, no one shall speak except by His leave. [On that day,] some of them will be wretched and [some] felicitous. As for the wretched, they shall be in the Fire: their lot therein will be groaning and wailing. They shall remain in it for as long as the heavens and the earth endure – except what your Lord may wish – indeed, your Lord does whatever He desires. As for the felicitous, they will be in paradise. They will remain in it for as long as the heavens and the earth endure – except what your Lord may wish – an endless bounty.[13]

Indeed, the Holy Quran makes it clear that no one will be able to escape Hellfire after being sentenced there through God's divine judgment. God Almighty says:

وَأَمَّا الَّذِينَ فَسَقُوا فَمَأْوَاهُمُ النَّارُ ۖ كُلَّمَا أَرَادُوا أَن يَخْرُجُوا مِنْهَا أُعِيدُوا فِيهَا وَقِيلَ لَهُمْ ذُوقُوا عَذَابَ النَّارِ الَّذِي كُنتُم بِهِ تُكَذِّبُونَ

As for those who have transgressed, their refuge will be the Fire. Whenever they seek to leave it, they will be

---

[13] The Holy Quran, 11:105-08.

turned back into it and told: 'Taste the punishment of the Fire which you used to deny.'[14]

On the other hand, those granted Paradise are meant to stay there for eternity. God says,

$$\text{وَالَّذِينَ آمَنُوا وَعَمِلُوا الصَّالِحَاتِ سَنُدْخِلُهُمْ جَنَّاتٍ تَجْرِي مِن تَحْتِهَا الْأَنْهَارُ خَالِدِينَ فِيهَا أَبَدًا ۖ لَّهُمْ فِيهَا أَزْوَاجٌ مُّطَهَّرَةٌ ۖ وَنُدْخِلُهُمْ ظِلًّا ظَلِيلًا}$$

As for those who have faith and do righteous deeds, We shall admit them into gardens with streams running in them, to remain in them forever. In them, there will be chaste mates for them, and We shall admit them into a deep shade.[15]

The people of Paradise will be constantly engaged in merriment and pleasure. God says:

$$\text{إِنَّ أَصْحَابَ الْجَنَّةِ الْيَوْمَ فِي شُغُلٍ فَاكِهُونَ هُمْ وَأَزْوَاجُهُمْ فِي ظِلَالٍ عَلَى الْأَرَائِكِ مُتَّكِئُونَ لَهُمْ فِيهَا فَاكِهَةٌ وَلَهُم مَّا يَدَّعُونَ سَلَامٌ قَوْلًا مِّن رَّبٍّ رَّحِيمٍ}$$

Indeed, today the inhabitants of paradise rejoice in their engagements – they and their mates, reclining on couches in the shades. There they have fruits, and they have whatever they want. 'Peace!' – a watchword from the all-merciful Lord.[16]

Thus, the nature of the hereafter is one of constancy. Change is the exception rather than the norm. There are instances when a

---

[14] The Holy Quran, 32:20.

[15] The Holy Quran, 4:57.

[16] The Holy Quran, 36:55-58.

person may enter Hellfire for only a temporary period. Those are the individuals who died with true faith, but whose sins do not allow them to enter Paradise. For them, Hellfire will be a temporary period meant for purification, after which they are shepherded into Paradise.

Still, this does not mean that we can take the punishment of Hellfire lightly. Although there is a chance that it will be temporary, even that is a great burden to bear. Imam Ali (a) said in one of his sermons:

وَاعْلَمُوا أَنَّهُ لَيْسَ لِهَذَا الْجِلْدِ الرَّقِيقِ صَبْرٌ عَلَى النَّارِ، فَارْحَمُوا نُفُوسَكُمْ، فَإِنَّكُمْ قَدْ جَرَّبْتُمُوهَا فِي مَصَائِبِ الدُّنْيَا. أَفَرَأَيْتُمْ جَزَعَ أَحَدِكُمْ مِنَ الشَّوْكَةِ تُصِيبُهُ، وَالْعَثْرَةِ تُدْمِيهِ، وَالرَّمْضَاءِ تُحْرِقُهُ؟

You should know that this thin skin cannot tolerate the Fire [of Hell]. So, have pity on yourselves, because you have already tried it in the tribulations of the world. Have you ever seen the crying of a person who has been pricked with a thorn, or who bleeds due to stumbling, or whom hot sand has burnt?

فَكَيْفَ إِذَا كَانَ بَيْنَ طَابَقَيْنِ مِنْ نَارٍ، ضَجِيعَ حَجَرٍ، وَقَرِينَ شَيْطَانٍ؟! أَعَلِمْتُمْ أَنَّ مَالِكاً إِذَا غَضِبَ عَلَى النَّارِ حَطَمَ بَعْضُهَا بَعْضاً لِغَضَبِهِ، وَإِذَا زَجَرَهَا تَوَثَّبَتْ بَيْنَ أَبْوَابِهَا جَزَعاً مِنْ زَجْرَتِهِ؟!

How would he feel when he is between two frying pans of Hellfire with stones all round and with Satan as his companion? Do you know that when Malik [the guardian of Hell] is angry with the fire, its parts begin to clash *with each other [in rage], and, when he scolds it, it leaps between the doors of Hell crying on account of his scolding.*[17]

THE WORLD OF PLAY AND THE WORLD OF LIFE

In this world, we constantly interact with many creatures of various types. Some creatures are living and thinking like us – other human beings. There are other creatures that are also alive, but that do not have the faculty of reason, like animals and plants. There are also some creatures that we perceive to be inanimate, like roads and buildings.

Throughout our lives, we give the most attention and care to other living, thinking beings – other individuals. We do not give that same care to animals and inanimate objects. We care about how other people perceive us, but we do not care about the perceptions of our pets and walls. That is why we may not sin in the company of other people, but we do not hesitate to do so in the presence of an animal or an inanimate object.

This observation – which is fully reasonable within the bounds of this world – does not hold true once we steer our vision towards the hereafter. We find that the Holy Quran describes how inanimate objects come to life in the hereafter and testify to what they witnessed in this world. Even our body parts will be granted a life of their own so that they can give their testimony against the soul inhabiting the body. God Almighty says:

---

[17] Al-Radi, *Nahj al-Balagha*, 2:113, Sermon 183.

$$\text{وَقَالُوا لِجُلُودِهِمْ لِمَ شَهِدتُّمْ عَلَيْنَا ۖ قَالُوا أَنطَقَنَا اللَّهُ الَّذِي أَنطَقَ كُلَّ شَيْءٍ وَهُوَ خَلَقَكُمْ أَوَّلَ مَرَّةٍ وَإِلَيْهِ تُرْجَعُونَ}$$

They will say to their skins, 'Why did you bear witness against us?' They will say, 'We were given speech by God, who gave speech to all things. He created you the first time, and you are being brought back to Him.[18]

God also says:

$$\text{الْيَوْمَ نَخْتِمُ عَلَىٰ أَفْوَاهِهِمْ وَتُكَلِّمُنَا أَيْدِيهِمْ وَتَشْهَدُ أَرْجُلُهُم بِمَا كَانُوا يَكْسِبُونَ}$$

Today We shall seal their mouths, and their hands shall speak to Us, and their feet shall bear witness concerning what they used to earn.[19]

Indeed, the hereafter is the realm of true life. God says:

$$\text{وَمَا هَٰذِهِ الْحَيَاةُ الدُّنْيَا إِلَّا لَهْوٌ وَلَعِبٌ ۚ وَإِنَّ الدَّارَ الْآخِرَةَ لَهِيَ الْحَيَوَانُ ۚ لَوْ كَانُوا يَعْلَمُونَ}$$

The life of this world is nothing but diversion and play, but the abode of the Hereafter is indeed Life [itself], had they known![20]

Realizing this truth can mean so much for each one of us. We must understand that everything around us is perceiving what we do and witnessing our conduct. This realization can become a driving force for us to change our habits and behaviors. Yet,

---

[18] The Holy Quran, 41:21.

[19] The Holy Quran, 36:65.

[20] The Holy Quran, 29:64.

because we do not realize this, we continue in our sins and deviance, despite having witnesses all around us. Since we do not realize how observant and perceiving the physical objects around us are, it is no wonder that we don't pay heed to the fact that we are always perceived from beyond the world of matter. If we cannot heed the perception of our own limbs, how can we heed our all-witnessing Lord?

A Social World and an Individualistic World

We believe that there is a direct relationship between our behaviors and their consequences. In other words, there is no difference between our actions and the rewards or punishments associated with them. We see this in some verses of the Holy Quran, like the one speaking about oppression of the orphans. God Almighty says:

$$\text{إِنَّ الَّذِينَ يَأْكُلُونَ أَمْوَالَ الْيَتَامَىٰ ظُلْمًا إِنَّمَا يَأْكُلُونَ فِي بُطُونِهِمْ نَارًا ۖ وَسَيَصْلَوْنَ سَعِيرًا}$$

Indeed, those who consume the property of orphans wrongfully, only ingest fire into their bellies, and soon they will enter the Blaze.[21]

The act of oppressing the orphans and the act of ingesting flames are the same – except that we do not directly observe the latter in this world.

---

[21] The Holy Quran, 4:10.

We do not observe and realize that the direct consequence and punishment of our misdeeds is due to the social nature of this world. Our righteous deeds and the righteous deeds of others around us protect us from being instantly punished. God Almighty says,

$$\text{وَمَا كَانَ رَبُّكَ لِيُهْلِكَ الْقُرَىٰ بِظُلْمٍ وَأَهْلُهَا مُصْلِحُونَ}$$

Your Lord would never destroy the townships unjustly while their inhabitants were bringing about reform.[22]

Imam Ali al-Rida (a) also said:

$$\text{إن لله عزوجل في كل يوم وليلة مناديا ينادي: مهلا مهلا عباد الله عن معاصي الله، فلولا بهائم رتع، وصبية رضع، وشيوخ ركع، لصب عليكم العذاب صبا، ترضون به رضا}$$

Every night, God has a caller call, 'Wait! Wait, O' servants of God, and refrain from disobeying God. Surely, if it were not for the free-ranging cattle, suckling infants, and prostrating elders, punishment would have surely befallen you and you would surely be thrashed a [dire] thrashing.'[23]

We do not see a direct and instantaneous punishment in this world, due to others around us. But, when we turn to the hereafter, we do not see any similar social effect. A transgressor will face judgment for their deeds in the hereafter and will have to face punishment without the interference of any other creature.

---

[22] The Holy Quran, 11:117.
[23] Al-Kulayni, *al-Kafi*, 2:276.

Similarly, the virtuous will face judgment and will be rewarded with Paradise without the interference of any other creature. The hereafter is the world of separation between good and evil. On that day, a caller will call,

$$\text{وَامْتَازُوا الْيَوْمَ أَيُّهَا الْمُجْرِمُونَ}$$

Stand apart today, you guilty ones![24]

In the hereafter, there will be a clear separation between people. God describes this as follows:

$$\text{فَأَمَّا إِن كَانَ مِنَ الْمُقَرَّبِينَ ﴿٨٨﴾ فَرَوْحٌ وَرَيْحَانٌ وَجَنَّتُ نَعِيمٍ ﴿٨٩﴾ وَأَمَّا إِن كَانَ مِنْ أَصْحَابِ الْيَمِينِ ﴿٩٠﴾ فَسَلَامٌ لَكَ مِنْ أَصْحَابِ الْيَمِينِ ﴿٩١﴾ وَأَمَّا إِن كَانَ مِنَ الْمُكَذِّبِينَ الضَّالِّينَ ﴿٩٢﴾ فَنُزُلٌ مِّنْ حَمِيمٍ ﴿٩٣﴾ وَتَصْلِيَةُ جَحِيمٍ ﴿٩٤﴾ إِنَّ هَذَا لَهُوَ حَقُّ الْيَقِينِ ﴿٩٥﴾ فَسَبِّحْ بِاسْمِ رَبِّكَ الْعَظِيمِ ﴿٩٦﴾}$$

If he be of those brought near, then [his reward shall be] ease, abundance, and a garden of bliss. if he be of the People of the Right Hand, then [he will be told,] 'Peace be on you, from the People of the Right Hand!' But if he be of the impugners, the astray ones, then [his reward shall be] a treat of boiling water and entry into Hell. Indeed, this is certain truth. So, celebrate the Name of your Lord, the All-Supreme![25]

---

[24] The Holy Quran, 36:59.
[25] The Holy Quran, 56:88-96.

In another verse, God describes the process by which people will be separated, so that no one has any effect on others:

$$يَوْمَ تَرَى الْمُؤْمِنِينَ وَالْمُؤْمِنَاتِ يَسْعَىٰ نُورُهُم بَيْنَ أَيْدِيهِمْ وَبِأَيْمَانِهِم بُشْرَاكُمُ الْيَوْمَ جَنَّاتٌ تَجْرِي مِن تَحْتِهَا الْأَنْهَارُ خَالِدِينَ فِيهَا ۚ ذَٰلِكَ هُوَ الْفَوْزُ الْعَظِيمُ$$

[On that] day, you will see the faithful, men and women, with their light moving swiftly in front of them and on their right, [and they are greeted with the words:] 'There is good news for you today! Gardens with streams running in them, to remain in them [forever]. That is the great success.' [26]

If we wish to achieve everlasting happiness and success in the hereafter, we must study and learn about the nature of that world. To treat the hereafter the same way that we treat this world will only cause us to miss our mark. We ask God Almighty to illuminate our hearts with the light of knowledge and guide us towards what is best for us in this world and next.

Notes:
- How we view this world will determine what we make of it.

---

[26] The Holy Quran, 57:12.

WHY DO WE LACK IN WORSHIP?

In the Name of God, the Most Beneficent, the Most Merciful

فَأَمَّا مَنْ أَعْطَىٰ وَاتَّقَىٰ ﴿٥﴾ وَصَدَّقَ بِالْحُسْنَىٰ ﴿٦﴾ فَسَنُيَسِّرُهُ لِلْيُسْرَىٰ ﴿٧﴾ وَأَمَّا مَن بَخِلَ وَاسْتَغْنَىٰ ﴿٨﴾ وَكَذَّبَ بِالْحُسْنَىٰ ﴿٩﴾ فَسَنُيَسِّرُهُ لِلْعُسْرَىٰ ﴿١٠﴾

As for he who gives and is Godwary and confirms the best promise, We will surely ease him toward facility. But as for he who is stingy and self-complacent, and denies the best promise, We will surely ease him toward hardship...[1]

وَالَّذِينَ جَاهَدُوا فِينَا لَنَهْدِيَنَّهُمْ سُبُلَنَا ۚ وَإِنَّ اللَّهَ لَمَعَ الْمُحْسِنِينَ

As for those who strive in Us, We shall surely guide them in Our ways, and God is indeed with the virtuous.[2]

Everything in life is at its best when it is fulfilling its true role and purpose. Tools, for example, are at their best when they are used for the purpose for which they were manufactured. A car will not

---

[1] The Holy Quran, 92:5-10.
[2] The Holy Quran, 29:69.

do well if it is driven into the water and used as a boat – in fact, such misuse will ruin the car. When something is not serving its purpose, it is not in its best state and could even be approaching its own ruin.

Mankind, the noblest of God's creations, is the same way. We were created for the greatest and most honorable purpose. God created us so that we can worship Him and draw closer to him through knowledge and service. He says in the Holy Quran,

وَمَا خَلَقْتُ الْجِنَّ وَالْإِنسَ إِلَّا لِيَعْبُدُونِ

I did not create the jinn and the humans except that they may worship Me.[3]

We were created by God Almighty to seek excellence and perfection through knowledge and worship of Him. This high purpose courses through our veins and flows through our bodies. Fulfilling our purpose comes only through worship. Without worship, we are simply walking down the path of degradation and ruin. This is what God Almighty describes in the verse:

وَمَنْ أَعْرَضَ عَن ذِكْرِي فَإِنَّ لَهُ مَعِيشَةً ضَنكًا وَنَحْشُرُهُ يَوْمَ الْقِيَامَةِ أَعْمَىٰ

But whoever disregards My remembrance, his shall be a wretched life, and We shall raise him blind on the Day of Resurrection.[4]

God also says:

---

[3] The Holy Quran, 51:56.
[4] The Holy Quran, 20:124.

> فَمَن يُرِدِ اللَّهُ أَن يَهْدِيَهُ يَشْرَحْ صَدْرَهُ لِلْإِسْلَامِ ۖ وَمَن يُرِدْ أَن يُضِلَّهُ يَجْعَلْ صَدْرَهُ ضَيِّقًا حَرَجًا كَأَنَّمَا يَصَّعَّدُ فِي السَّمَاءِ ۚ كَذَٰلِكَ يَجْعَلُ اللَّهُ الرِّجْسَ عَلَى الَّذِينَ لَا يُؤْمِنُونَ

> *Whomever God desires to guide, He opens his breast to Islam, and whomever He desires to lead astray, He makes his breast narrow and straightened, as if he were climbing to a height. Thus, does God lay [spiritual] defilement on those who do not have faith.*[5]

We can come to two conclusions based on the verses mentioned above. First, that mankind was created to seek closeness to God through worship. Second, that mankind cannot fulfill its purpose and find true happiness and harmony without worship.

However, many of us seem to be heedless of these facts. We do not read these verses of the Quran and work in accordance with their guidance. Many times, people cannot find the will to worship or are easily distracted when they do. Why do we keep on ignoring our grand purpose?

We must look for the causes behind our neglect, so that we can solve the problem at the root. Once we identify the cause, we can find practical solutions that will allow us to engage in our worship, fulfill our purpose, and reach the excellence that God Almighty created us for.

The reasons behind this phenomenon are many, but we will focus in this chapter on five of the main causes of the problem.

---

[5] The Holy Quran, 6:125.

IGNORANCE

The first and greatest problem facing mankind is the problem of ignorance. It is ignorance that takes an individual down from an honorable position that is superior to all other creations, to a position that is inferior to many other beings. Ignorance is what drives us into losing the blessing of being able to engage in worship and taste the sweetness of drawing closer to God through worship.

To find practical solutions to this issue, we must first identify the types of ignorance that can cause this problem. In general, we can say that ignorance of God, ignorance of oneself, and ignorance of the nature of worship are the roots behind the issue. Let us discuss these one by one.

Firstly, ignorance of God is a major cause of our lack of worship. Knowledge is a primary pillar of worship – an individual with greater knowledge has a better understanding, not only of the process of worship, but of the One he is worshipping. An individual with greater knowledge of the divine will find in that knowledge the necessary encouragement to drive him toward worship. That is why we see the Divine Legislator placing great emphasis on knowledge and learning.

Why is knowledge so important? An individual cannot worship something that they do not know and understand. Without knowledge of God's majesty and grandeur, how can someone bring themselves to obey and worship Him? Furthermore, worship without knowledge will not allow us to reap the full benefits of worship. That is why the Commander of the Faithful says:

سكّنوا في أنفسكم معرفة ما تعبدون، حتى ينفعكم ما تحركون من الجوارح بعبادة من تعرفون

> *Secure in yourselves knowledge of what you worship, so that you may reap the benefits of the movements of your limbs through worship of the One whom you know.*[6]

Knowledge is intertwined even with the smallest details of worship. Worship cannot be a simple movement of the limbs in a particular fashion. To reach beyond that point and reap the true benefits of worship, the individual needs to know who he is worshipping. That is why knowledge itself is described as a great form of worship. Imam al-Rida (a) once said in a sermon,

أول عبادة الله معرفته وأصل معرفة الله توحيده

> *The first step in worshipping God is to know Him. The pillar of knowing God is believing in His Oneness.*[7]

Secondly, one of the greatest reasons for people to lack in worship is their ignorance of themselves. We do not understand who we are and why we were created. It is not enough to have a theoretical understanding of our purpose. Our understanding must be real and practical.

We need to understand that we were created to know and worship God Almighty, and that knowledge must be practically

---

[6] Al-Majlisi, *Bihar al-Anwar*, 75:63.
[7] Al-Sadouq, *'Oyoun Akhbar al-Rida (a)*, 2:135.

translated into action. It is not enough to read and pay lip service to this verse –

$$\text{وَمَا خَلَقْتُ الْجِنَّ وَالْإِنسَ إِلَّا لِيَعْبُدُونِ}$$

> *I did not create the jinn and the humans except that they may worship Me.*[8]

A true reading of the verse must render this reality a driving force of our thoughts, emotions, and behaviors. We must translate this verse into the fuel we need to act in accordance with our purpose.

If we cannot translate this understanding into action, then there is a problem in our understanding of the verse. What is the meaning of an individual neglecting the true purpose that will lead him toward eternal happiness, while pursuing other trivialities that earn him fleeting happiness in this transitory world? It simply means that such an individual does not understand their true purpose. They do not understand the true meaning and value of their creation.

In the story of creation relayed in the Holy Quran, we are told that God Almighty commanded Satan and the angels to prostrate themselves to Adam. The angels did as God commanded, but Satan refused out of his arrogance. This arrogance was the reason for him being driven out of the true happiness he had attained, and into the epitome of disgrace.

---

[8] The Holy Quran, 51:56.

Now we see mankind, who God commanded Satan to prostrate to, prostrating to Satan and following him into deviance and disgrace. Does this not mean that mankind does not understand what the reward truly is and the value it holds?

Thirdly, mankind does not understand the true meaning and method of worshipping God Almighty. This lack of understanding of worship results in a lack of will to worship. When most people think of worship, they only think of the physical aspects of prayer, fasting, Hajj, and the other forms of worship. They do not think of their deep meanings and consequences, and so they do not engage with these acts of worship as they should.

People think that worship is an issue of quantity – the more you pray, the better. But, the narrations of our Imams point out that a little worship with knowledge and understanding is better than much worship in ignorance. The Commander of the Faithful (a) said:

المتعبد على غير فقه كحمار الطاحونة يدور ولا يبرح، وركعتان من عالم خير من سبعين ركعة من جاهل لان العالم تأتيه الفتنة فيخرج منها بعلمه، وتأتي الجاهل فتنسفه نسفا ، وقليل العمل مع كثير العلم خير من كثير العمل مع قليل العلم والشك والشبهة

A worshipper without an understanding [of the religion] is like a mule in a mill, going around but not going anywhere. Two raka'at from a knowledgeable individual are better than seventy raka'at from an ignorant individual. That is because a knowledgeable individual is faced with sedition and is able to evade it by his

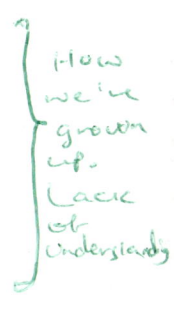

knowledge, whereas sedition comes over the ignorant and destroys him thoroughly. Little action with much knowledge is better than much action with little knowledge, doubt, and misconceptions.[9]

In addition, too much worship can result in boredom and disinterest. Prophet Muhammad (s) once said to Imam Ali (a):

يا علي إن هذا الدين متين، فأوغل فيه برفق ولا تبغض إلى نفسك عبادة ربك، فإن المنبت يعني المفرط لا ظهرا أبقى ولا أرضا قطع، فاعمل عمل من يرجو أن يموت هرما واحذر حذر من يتخوف أن يموت غدا

O' Ali, this religion is comprehensive, so delve in it gently. Do not let yourself resent the worship of your Lord – surely the exuberant [who does not take a rest on his journey] neither preserves [himself from fatigue] nor covers a great distance. So, work with the hope that you will die at an elderly age, and be wary in fear that you might die tomorrow.[10]

Therefore, we see some people going on sprints of worship then going back to their old ways. Something drives them to worship God and seek closeness to Him, but they go about it the wrong way. They start to worship more and more – praying and fasting much more than they are used to. Then they get bored and disinterested in these acts of worship and they go back to their old ways.

---

[9] Al-Mufeed, *al-Ikhtisas*, 245.
[10] Al-Kulayni, *al-Kafi*, 2:87.

Why do we Lack in Worship?

This is all a result of a lack of knowledge and understanding of what worship is and what it truly means. It is a result of not going back to the guides who were appointed for us by God Almighty to instruct us on the correct means of growing closer to Him. It is a result of not listening to and heeding the words of the Holy Prophet (s) and his blessed Progeny (a).

People are also mistaken in thinking that worship is encompassed in prayer, fasting, Hajj, and the other prescribed forms of worship. Yes, prayer and fasting may be the greatest *forms* of worship, but true worship is tied to something greater than these physical forms. True worship is realized in a state of remembering, mentioning, and glorifying God Almighty. God says in the Holy Quran:

$$\text{اتْلُ مَا أُوحِيَ إِلَيْكَ مِنَ الْكِتَابِ وَأَقِمِ الصَّلَاةَ إِنَّ الصَّلَاةَ تَنْهَىٰ عَنِ الْفَحْشَاءِ وَالْمُنكَرِ ۗ وَلَذِكْرُ اللَّهِ أَكْبَرُ ۗ وَاللَّهُ يَعْلَمُ مَا تَصْنَعُونَ}$$

Recite what has been revealed to you of the Book, and maintain the prayer. Indeed, the prayer restrains from indecent and wrongful conduct, and the remembrance of God is surely greater. And God knows whatever [deeds] you do.[11]

"The remembrance of God is surely greater." True worship involves an individual living in the state of remembrance. We can change every action that we take into a form of worship, by having God at the forefront of our minds and only acting in ways that bring us closer to Him. Thus, our food, drink, work, and

---

[11] The Holy Quran, 29:45.

sleep could become forms of worship, if God Almighty is always the end goal.

Of course, all this is not possible without the requisite knowledge of God, of ourselves, and of worship. This knowledge cannot be attained without going back to God's appointed guides. Only through going back to the narrations of the Holy Prophet (s) and the Immaculate Imams (a) can we attain true worship and turn our lives into a constant journey of closeness toward God Almighty.

Sin and Disobedience

Sin is one of the greatest things that corrupts an individual and impedes his ability to worship and gain closeness to God. So long as a person refrains from sin, they can find inner peace and tranquility and will be constantly drawn towards remembering and worshipping God. A person's pure and unaltered innate nature will continue to be active, calling them to seek refuge in God's infinite perfection. However, when sin and disobedience get in the way and corrupt the individual's preexisting pure nature, they will become further and further inclined towards deviance. With each sin and act of disobedience, more and more filth and rust will gather around the heart and undermine the individual's judgment and foresight. As the heart grows darker, the individual will grow further away from worship until their heart becomes sealed and they will no longer be willing to change. God says in the Holy Quran:

Why do we Lack in Worship?

أَفَرَأَيْتَ مَنِ اتَّخَذَ إِلَهَهُ هَوَاهُ وَأَضَلَّهُ اللَّهُ عَلَى عِلْمٍ وَخَتَمَ عَلَى سَمْعِهِ وَقَلْبِهِ وَجَعَلَ عَلَى بَصَرِهِ غِشَاوَةً فَمَن يَهْدِيهِ مِن بَعْدِ اللَّهِ ۚ أَفَلَا تَذَكَّرُونَ

> Have you seen him who has taken his desire to be his own god and whom God has led astray knowingly, set a seal upon his hearing and heart, and put a blindfold on his sight? So, who will guide him after God [has consigned him to error]? Will you not then take admonition?[12]

There are many other verses and narrations that speak of this 'sealing' of the heart. As the heart is the tool of guidance and the compass that leads toward God Almighty, an individual with a sealed heart is bound to go astray.

The blessed traditions and narrations have focused on this issue, and on the question of how to purify a heart from the darkness of sin and disobedience. Imam al-Sadiq (a) says:

ما من شيء أفسد للقلب من الخطيئة، إن القلب ليواقع الخطيئة فما تزال به حتى تغلب عليه، فيصير أعلاه أسفله

> *There is nothing more corrupting of the heart than sin. Surely, when the heart tastes a sin, the sin shall reside inside until it overtakes it, turning it upside down.*[13]

There are dozens of narrations that refer to this reality. Sin and disobedience are the primary factor that causes an individual to wander astray from the path of God. They create a malfunction

---

[12] The Holy Quran, 45:23.
[13] Al-Kulayni, *al-Kafi*, 2:267.

in the heart that stops it from drawing them closer to God. All of this means that the individual is not able to understand worship and engage their heart in it, thus rendering them unable to reap its vast benefits.

LOVE OF THIS WORLD

Mankind is not created for this world. Our true home has always been in the hereafter. The more an individual is attached to the true life of the hereafter, the more he is drawn closer toward achieving the higher virtues that have a practical impact on that everlasting life. This is not possible by any means other than worship and constant remembrance of God Almighty, always seeking His contentment and pleasure. Indeed, whoever chooses for themselves a great goal like this, will have the path toward that goal prepared for them and they will taste the sweetness in taking every step toward that goal.

However, when an individual grows too attached to this worldly life, their love of this world and their lust for it will destroy any bridge they might have taken towards that higher goal. Whenever an individual takes this world as a goal, it begins to draw them away from their true and most noble goal. It will distract them from the path to true eternal happiness in the pleasure of God Almighty and under his unceasing grace.

The Holy Prophet (s) and his family would always warn their companions about this treacherous path. There are hundreds of narrations that warn us of this world, just as the Holy Quran warned us of taking the world as a goal. Indeed, this world is the best lure away from worship of and obedience to God Almighty. That is why the Commander of the Faithful (a) said:

إِنَّ الدُّنْيَا لَمَفْسَدَةٌ لِلدِّينِ وَمَسْلَبَةُ الْيَقِينِ، وَإِنَّهَا لَرَأْسُ الْفِتَنِ وَأَصْلُ الْمِحَنِ

Surely, this world corrupts an individual's faith and dispossesses him of his certainty. It is the head of sedition and the root of tribulation.[14]

Imam Ali (a) also explained to us the differences between the road towards the hereafter and the road towards the pleasures of this world. He said:

إِنَّ الدُّنْيَا وَ الْآخِرَةَ عَدُوَّانِ مُتَفَاوِتَانِ وَ سَبِيلَانِ مُخْتَلِفَانِ فَمَنْ أَحَبَّ الدُّنْيَا وَ تَوَلَّاهَا أَبْغَضَ الْآخِرَةَ وَ عَادَاهَا وَ هُمَا بِمَنْزِلَةِ الْمَشْرِقِ وَ الْمَغْرِبِ وَ مَاشٍ بَيْنَهُمَا كُلَّمَا قَرُبَ مِنْ وَاحِدٍ بَعُدَ مِنَ الْآخَرِ

This world and the hereafter are hostile enemies and divergent roads. Whoever loves this world and seeks it, hates the hereafter and is averse to it. They are like the east and west: if the walker between them gets near to one, he gets farther from the other.[15]

Attachment to this world and its pleasures creates a constant distraction away from the remembrance of God. Since remembrance is the fuel that lights our passion and ignites our energies to head towards God Almighty and seek His pleasure, the distractions of this world are nothing but hindrances and impediments on our path towards true, eternal happiness. When our

---

[14] Al-Wasiti, *'Oyoun al-Hikam*, 152.
[15] Al-Radi, *Nahj al-Balagha*, 4:23, Saying 103.

whims are in control and not our minds, we cannot come to understand and engage with our worship and reap its true benefits. We draw further away from worship and fall into constant forgetfulness and heedlessness of God Almighty. As the Commander of the Faithful (a) said,

$$كيف يجد لذة العبادة من لا يصوم عن الهوى$$

> *How can a person who does not fast from [obeying his] desire taste the beauty of worship?*[16]

It is also narrated that the Holy Prophet (s) said,

$$من كان أكثر همه نيل الشهوات نزع من قلبه حلاوة الإيمان$$

> *A person preoccupied with satisfying his desires will have the sweetness of faith uprooted from his heart.*[17]

Imam al-Sadiq (a) said,

$$حرام على قلوبكم أن تعرف حلاوة الإيمان حتى تزهد في الدنيا$$

> *Your hearts are forbidden from tasting the sweetness of faith until they become [austere] in this world.*[18]

Piety is a consequence of devoted worship and an individual cannot attain it and the true pleasure of God's contentment if he is constantly occupied with this transient world. How can we achieve piety if we are constantly distracted by the world of entertainment? How are we to achieve piety if the sole goal we set

---

[16] Al-Wasiti, *'Oyoun al-Hikam*, 384.
[17] Al-Rayshahri, *Mizan al-Hikma*, 1:201.
[18] Al-Kulayni, *al-Kafi*, 2:128.

for ourselves is to make money and live a comfortable life? We are easily distracted like this, because we do not understand the realities of this world and the hereafter. We do not understand the words of God when He declares:

$$\text{وَمَا هَٰذِهِ الْحَيَاةُ الدُّنْيَا إِلَّا لَهْوٌ وَلَعِبٌ ۚ وَإِنَّ الدَّارَ الْآخِرَةَ لَهِيَ الْحَيَوَانُ ۚ لَوْ كَانُوا يَعْلَمُونَ}$$

The life of this world is nothing but diversion and play, but the abode of the Hereafter is indeed Life (itself), had they known![19]

The Holy Quran also says:

$$\text{اعْلَمُوا أَنَّمَا الْحَيَاةُ الدُّنْيَا لَعِبٌ وَلَهْوٌ وَزِينَةٌ وَتَفَاخُرٌ بَيْنَكُمْ وَتَكَاثُرٌ فِي الْأَمْوَالِ وَالْأَوْلَادِ ۖ كَمَثَلِ غَيْثٍ أَعْجَبَ الْكُفَّارَ نَبَاتُهُ ثُمَّ يَهِيجُ فَتَرَاهُ مُصْفَرًّا ثُمَّ يَكُونُ حُطَامًا ۖ وَفِي الْآخِرَةِ عَذَابٌ شَدِيدٌ وَمَغْفِرَةٌ مِّنَ اللَّهِ وَرِضْوَانٌ ۚ وَمَا الْحَيَاةُ الدُّنْيَا إِلَّا مَتَاعُ الْغُرُورِ}$$

Know that the life of this world is mere diversion and play, glamour and mutual vainglory among you and rivalry for wealth and children – like rain, whose growth impresses the farmer. Then, it withers and you see it turn yellow, then it becomes chaff. Whereas, in the Hereafter, there is forgiveness from God and His approval and a severe punishment. The life of this world is nothing but the wares of delusion.[20]

---

[19] The Holy Quran, 29:64.
[20] The Holy Quran, 57:20.

God Almighty also says:

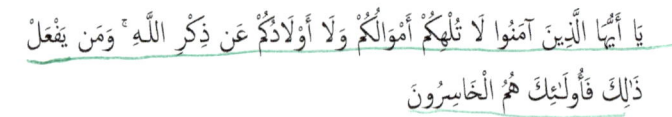

$$\text{يَا أَيُّهَا الَّذِينَ آمَنُوا لَا تُلْهِكُمْ أَمْوَالُكُمْ وَلَا أَوْلَادُكُمْ عَن ذِكْرِ اللَّهِ ۚ وَمَن يَفْعَلْ ذَٰلِكَ فَأُولَٰئِكَ هُمُ الْخَاسِرُونَ}$$

O you who have faith! Do not let your possessions and children distract you from the remembrance of God, and whoever does that – it is they who are the losers.[21]

In all this, we should make the point that tending to this world is not entirely and absolutely a bad thing. It is only when it distracts us from the remembrance of God that it can have these severe consequences for us. When we take this world as a gift from God and a means to achieve His contentment, then we can see it as a boundless grace and great mercy. The narrations and verses mentioned above are all about this world when it is taken as a goal in itself, and not when it is taken as a means to the hereafter.

Not Trusting in God

One of the reasons why an individual may be stripped of the blessings of worship is due to their ignorant self-reliance and lack of trust in God Almighty. This is in fact a dangerous path and can lead to *shirk* (ascribing a partner to God). A person should always know they are always dependent – in every way – on God Almighty and His graces. We should always keep in mind that we need our Creator, whereas He is the independent

---

[21] The Holy Quran, 63:9.

being who is in need of no one. We must always look toward God and ask Him to support us in our path towards Him.

That is, in fact, what we do in our daily prayers. In every prayer, we read the first chapter of the Holy Quran, *al-Fatiha*. We recite the verse and ask God Almighty,

$$اهْدِنَا الصِّرَاطَ الْمُسْتَقِيمَ$$

Guide us on the straight path.[22]

We cannot simply rely on ourselves to reach and continue the straight path. Guidance is something that requires our conscious reliance on God Almighty. For this reason, we must constantly ask God in our prayers to bless us with the strength and will to worship and obey him. This is what the Holy Household of the Prophet (s) taught us to do through their prayers and supplications. In one supplication, taught by our Holy Twelfth Imam (a), we say,

$$اللهم ارزقنا توفيق الطاعة، وبعد المعصية، وصدق النية، وعرفان الحرمة، وأكرمنا بالهدى والاستقامة، وسدد ألسنتنا بالصواب والحكمة$$

Our Lord! Grant us the blessings of obedience, distance from disobedience, sincerity in intention, and an understanding of sanctity. Honor us with guidance and rectitude. Support our tongues with precision and wisdom.[23]

---

[22] The Holy Quran, 1:6.
[23] Al-Qayyoumi, *Sahifat al-Mahdi (a)*, 18.

God will surely answer such a prayer recited in sincere devotion to Him. As He declared in the Holy Quran,

$$\text{وَالَّذِينَ جَاهَدُوا فِينَا لَنَهْدِيَنَّهُمْ سُبُلَنَا ۚ وَإِنَّ اللَّهَ لَمَعَ الْمُحْسِنِينَ}$$

As for those who strive in Us, We shall surely guide them in Our ways, and God is indeed with the virtuous.[24]

Indulgence in the Forbidden

One of the material causes behind an individual's lack of worship is the indulgence in what is *Haram*, or forbidden. God created mankind out of a body and a soul, both of which must be in harmony on the path toward the hereafter. So, much like there are spiritual factors that influence an individual's ability to seek closeness to God and taste the sweetness of worshipping Him, there are also material, physical factors that can have their affect.

Eating haram is one of those physical causes that can influence our ability to move closer towards God Almighty. We must keep our bodies pure so that what we take in does not influence our hearts and our innate nature. That is why the Holy Household of the Prophet (s) warned against eating what is forbidden and the harm that it could do to us on our journey towards our eternal home in the hereafter. The Holy Prophet (s) is narrated to have said,

$$\text{لعبادة مع أكل الحرام كالبناء على الرمل}$$

---

[24] The Holy Quran, 29:69.

Worship while eating Haram is like building on sand.[25]

He is also narrated to have said:

من اكتسب مالا حراما لم يقبل الله منه صدقة و لا عتقا و لا حجا و لا اعتمارا و كتب الله عز و جل له بعدد ذلك أجر أوزارا و ما بقي بعد موته كان زاده إلى النار و من قدر عليها فتركها مخافة الله عز و جل دخل في محبته و رحمته و يؤمر به إلى الجنة

Whoever acquires Haram wealth, God will not accept from him any charity, emancipation [of a slave], Hajj, or 'Umra. God will write for him instead of rewards, an increase in guilt. What remains of his [ill-earned] wealth will be his provision in Hellfire. Whoever is able to [acquire such Haram wealth] but forgoes it for fear of God Almighty, he will enter under His love and mercy, and he shall be commanded to enter Paradise.[26]

---

[25] Al-Majlisi, *Bihar al-Anwar*, 100:16.
[26] Al-Majlisi, *Bihar al-Anwar*, 100:17.

LOVE OF THE WORLD

In the Name of God, the Most Beneficent, the Most Merciful

يَا أَيُّهَا الَّذِينَ آمَنُوا مَا لَكُمْ إِذَا قِيلَ لَكُمُ انفِرُوا فِي سَبِيلِ اللَّهِ اثَّاقَلْتُمْ إِلَى الْأَرْضِ ۚ أَرَضِيتُم بِالْحَيَاةِ الدُّنْيَا مِنَ الْآخِرَةِ ۚ فَمَا مَتَاعُ الْحَيَاةِ الدُّنْيَا فِي الْآخِرَةِ إِلَّا قَلِيلٌ

O you who have faith! What is the matter with you that when you are told: 'Go forth in the way of God,' you sink heavily to the ground? Are you pleased with the life of this world instead of the Hereafter? But the wares of the life of this world compared with the Hereafter are but insignificant.[1]

In the previous chapter, we discussed love of this world as a reason why many of us lack in our worship and devotion to God Almighty. It is a doubtless fact that this world is a transient and short one, to be left behind by everyone at the moment of death. Every individual knows with absolute certainty that they are not immune to death. So, in the grand scheme of creation, this world

---

[1] The Holy Quran, 9:38.

is a short stage to be followed by a long journey – at the end of which a person will either find "ease, abundance, and a garden of bliss"[2] or "a treat of boiling water and entry into Hell."[3]

Moreover, it seems to be an evident truth that every individual on this Earth carries problems and burdens that they imagine are unique and greater than the burdens of any other individual. Every individual – young or old, rich or poor, devout or sinful – will always complain about this world and all its troubles. There is no one on Earth who is living in complete comfort and tranquility without complaint.

In addition, the faithful know – through the realities explained by God in the Holy Quran and through His prophets – that the pleasures of this material world are transient. We know that the hereafter is the home of eternal happiness and bliss, whereas any pleasure that we may attain in this world is fleeting. Besides, we know that anything we take in this world will be accounted for in the hereafter.

Despite all this, we find that people – and even us believers – have a strong love and attachment to this world. We work tirelessly for its pleasures and seek its rewards. Each one of us wishes to remain indefinitely on this Earth. That is why God addresses us believers in the Quran and asks, "O you who have faith! What

---

[2] The Holy Quran, 56:89.
[3] The Holy Quran, 56:93-94.

is the matter with you that when you are told: 'Go forth in the way of God,' you sink heavily to the ground?"[4]

Why are we so attached to this transient world? How can we shake off this deeply entrenched attachment?

Our attachment to this world and practical preference for it over the hereafter has several causes, which are deeply rooted in our minds. Every individual may have a set of factors for this attachment that differ from the factors driving any other individual. We will mention here a few of the most common, shared causes.

NURTURE

An individual's attachment and love for any matter can certainly be traced back to their upbringing. Thus, the nurturing of an individual doubtlessly has an impact on their attachment and love for this world.

Most people are fed with attachment to this world from a young age. A child is taught from a young age to tend to everything that would help them thrive in this world. Right and wrong is taught in terms of worldly consequences. Learning is made out to be a means toward achieving a career as a doctor, engineer, or the like. Accordingly, learning and education is, at a young age, tied to the issue of money and the idea of generating wealth and living a comfortable life on this Earth.

---

[4] The Holy Quran, 9:38.

Of course, all of this can be taught to a child without creating this deep materialistic link. Instead, a link can be created with the hereafter. For example, learning and education can be stressed to a child because it is something that our religion teaches us. We must learn because God loves the learned and educated. The Holy Quran says,

$$\text{يَرْفَعِ اللَّهُ الَّذِينَ آمَنُوا مِنكُمْ وَالَّذِينَ أُوتُوا الْعِلْمَ دَرَجَاتٍ}$$

God will raise in rank those of you who have faith and those who have been given knowledge.[5]

We can teach our children the importance of work ethics and of earning a living, but without the emphasis on material wealth. We must teach them that this world is not a goal but a means, while the true goal lies in the hereafter. The Holy Prophet (s) says:

$$\text{فليتزود العبد من دنياه لآخرته ومن حياته لموته ومن شبابه لهرمه، فإن الدنيا خلقت لكم وأنتم خلقتم للآخرة}$$

Let a servant take his provisions from this world for his hereafter, from his life for his death, and from his youth for his old age. Surely, this world was created for you and you were created for the hereafter.[6]

As such, we can nurture our children to have an attachment to the hereafter and to minimize their attachment to this world to

---

[5] The Holy Quran, 58:11.

[6] Al-Rayshahri, *Mizan al-Hikma*, 2:891.

the extent that they can use it as a means toward the hereafter. However, this method can be rare in society today.

Some people claim that we need to teach our children in such a way as to open the horizons of their future for them and that it is not helpful to complicate their minds and their personalities by tying everything to the hereafter. It is as if they are assuming that having an attachment to the hereafter is a gateway towards depression and death. One of the great causes of our struggle and unhappiness is that we do not realize the truth of our world. If a person truly understands this world and its relation to the hereafter, they will live in complete tranquility and mental stability.

A person who grows too attached to this world, on the other hand, will in time lose it and lose their hereafter as well. The Holy Prophet (s) once said,

إن الله عز وجل أوحى إلى لدنيا أن أتعبي من خدمك وأخدمي من رفضك

> God Almighty commanded this world, 'Be tiresome to whoever serves you, and serve whoever rejects you.'[7]

Imam al-Sadiq (a) also said:

مَنْ أَصْبَحَ وَأَمْسى وَالدُّنْيَا أَكْبَرُ هَمَّهُ، جَعَلَ اللهُ الفَقْرَ بَيْنَ عَيْنَيْهِ وَشَتَّتَ أَمْرَهُ وَلَمْ يَنَلْ مِنَ الدُّنْيَا إِلاَّ مَا قُسِمَ لَهُ وَمَنْ أَصْبَحَ وَأَمْسَى وَالآخِرَةُ أَكْبَرُ هَمَّهُ، جَعَلَ اللهُ الغِنَى فِي قَلْبِهِ وَجَمَعَ لَهُ أَمْرَهُ

---

[7] Al-Sadouq, *al-Amali*, 354.

Whoever goes on in his days and nights having this world as his biggest worry, God will [strike him with poverty] and scatter his efforts. He will not reap of this world anything more than what God had preordained for him. Whoever goes on in his days and nights having the hereafter as his biggest worry, God will plant contentment in his heart and gather for him his affairs.[8]

So, our love for our children should drive us to plant in them a love for the hereafter, rather than an attachment to this world. It is enough to recall the tradition of the Holy Prophet (s) who said:

من أصبح والدنيا أكبر همه فليس من الله في شيء وألزم قلبه أربع خصالٍ هماً لا ينقطع عنه أبداً وشغلاً لا ينفرج منه أبداً وفقراً لا يبلغ غناه أبداً وأملاً لا يبلغ منتهاه أبداً

Whoever awakens while the world is his biggest worry, God will have nothing to do with him. His heart will be bound by four characteristics: worry that will never leave him, obligations from which he will never be released, poverty which he will never be content with, and aspirations that he will never fulfill.[9]

Why is it that we teach our children to lead a life of worry and unhappiness by planting in them the seeds of love and attachment to this world? Our love for them should lead us to plant in them a love for the hereafter.

---

[8] Al-Kulayni, *al-Kafi*, 2:319.
[9] Al-Hindi, *Kanz al-'Ommal*, 3:226.

After all, what a great distance there is between a person who aspires for the pleasures of a fleeting world, and the one who aspires for the infinite happiness of an eternal world.

CRAVING IMMORTALITY

Every individual craves immortality and hopes to live eternally on this world. No one wishes to die and pass on to the next world. This stems from the love of this world and the lack of understanding of its true nature. God gives us this parable:

$$\text{وَاتْلُ عَلَيْهِمْ نَبَأَ الَّذِي آتَيْنَاهُ آيَاتِنَا فَانْسَلَخَ مِنْهَا فَأَتْبَعَهُ الشَّيْطَانُ فَكَانَ مِنَ الْغَاوِينَ ﴿١٧٥﴾ وَلَوْ شِئْنَا لَرَفَعْنَاهُ بِهَا وَلَكِنَّهُ أَخْلَدَ إِلَى الْأَرْضِ وَاتَّبَعَ هَوَاهُ ۚ فَمَثَلُهُ كَمَثَلِ الْكَلْبِ إِنْ تَحْمِلْ عَلَيْهِ يَلْهَثْ أَوْ تَتْرُكْهُ يَلْهَثْ ۚ ذَٰلِكَ مَثَلُ الْقَوْمِ الَّذِينَ كَذَّبُوا بِآيَاتِنَا ۚ فَاقْصُصِ الْقَصَصَ لَعَلَّهُمْ يَتَفَكَّرُونَ ﴿١٧٦﴾}$$

Relate to them an account of him to whom We gave Our signs, but he cast them off. Thereupon Satan pursued him, and he became one of the perverse. Had We wished, We would have surely raised him by their means, but he clung to the Earth and followed his [base] desires. So, his parable is that of a dog: if you make for it, it lolls out its tongue, and if you let it alone, it lolls out its tongue. Such is the parable of the people who deny Our signs. So, recount these narratives, so that they may reflect.[10]

---

[10] The Holy Quran, 7:175-76.

An individual who was given the signs of God deviated and cast those signs away. Why? Because he "clung to the Earth." He grew too attached to this world, as if he is going to live forever.

This desire in us should be addressed like any other desire. It is a blessing like all the other desires that God endowed us with, but it must be tamed like all other desires. We must have it work within the framework of our reason, rather than allowing it to overtake our reason. Thus, we must take this desire for eternal life and direct it away from this world and towards the hereafter, where true happiness and immortality can be attained. That is why Luqman the Wise said to his son,

يا بني بع دنياك بآخرتك تربحها جميعا، ولا تبع آخرتك بدنياك تخسرهما جميعا

My son, trade this world for the hereafter and you shall win them both. Do not trade your hereafter for this world and lose them both.[11]

WORLDLY DECEPTION

One of the reasons why mankind grows so attached to this world is due to the wondrous nature of its adornments and pleasures. We become enamored with the fleeting pleasures of the world. That is why God describes this world as one of deception in multiple verses of the Holy Quran. God says,

---

[11] Al-Majlisi, *Bihar al-Anwar*, 13:422.

$$\text{وَمَا الْحَيَاةُ الدُّنْيَا إِلَّا مَتَاعُ الْغُرُورِ}$$

The life of this world is nothing but the wares of delusion.[12]

He also warns,

$$\text{فَلَا تَغُرَّنَّكُمُ الْحَيَاةُ الدُّنْيَا وَلَا يَغُرَّنَّكُم بِاللَّهِ الْغَرُورُ}$$

Do not let the life of the world deceive you, nor let the Deceiver deceive you concerning God.[13]

In another verse He says,

$$\text{ذَٰلِكُم بِأَنَّكُمُ اتَّخَذْتُمْ آيَاتِ اللَّهِ هُزُوًا وَغَرَّتْكُمُ الْحَيَاةُ الدُّنْيَا ۚ فَالْيَوْمَ لَا يُخْرَجُونَ مِنْهَا وَلَا هُمْ يُسْتَعْتَبُونَ}$$

That is because you took the signs of God in derision, and the life of the world had deceived you. So today, they will not be brought out of it, nor will they be asked to propitiate [God].[14]

This is in addition to all the verses where God draws the distinction between the pleasures of this world and those of the hereafter. For example, God Almighty says:

$$\text{زُيِّنَ لِلنَّاسِ حُبُّ الشَّهَوَاتِ مِنَ النِّسَاءِ وَالْبَنِينَ وَالْقَنَاطِيرِ الْمُقَنطَرَةِ مِنَ الذَّهَبِ وَالْفِضَّةِ وَالْخَيْلِ الْمُسَوَّمَةِ وَالْأَنْعَامِ وَالْحَرْثِ ۗ ذَٰلِكَ مَتَاعُ الْحَيَاةِ الدُّنْيَا ۖ وَاللَّهُ عِندَهُ حُسْنُ الْمَآبِ}$$

---

[12] The Holy Quran, 3:185.

[13] The Holy Quran, 31:33.

[14] The Holy Quran, 45:35.

The love of [worldly] allures, including women and children, accumulated piles of gold and silver, horses of mark, livestock, and farms has been made to seem decorous to mankind. Those are the wares of the life of this world, but the goodness of one's ultimate destination lies near God.[15]

God also says,

الْمَالُ وَالْبَنُونَ زِينَةُ الْحَيَاةِ الدُّنْيَا ۖ وَالْبَاقِيَاتُ الصَّالِحَاتُ خَيْرٌ عِندَ رَبِّكَ ثَوَابًا وَخَيْرٌ أَمَلًا

Wealth and children are an adornment of the life of the world, but lasting righteous deeds are better with your Lord in reward and better in hope.[16]

God continues to remind us that true eternal life and happiness lies in the hereafter and that everything in this world is merely a mirage when compared to the hereafter. Everything that has been put at our disposal in this world must be used to draw us closer to God's contentedness and pleasure.

The noble traditions also warn us from being deceived by this world and its pleasures. We must seek to understand its reality and engage with it on that basis. We must seek to be like the Commander of the Faithful (a), who knew the reality of this world and acted accordingly. Imam Ali (a) was not an individual who did not understand the pleasures of this world. He was a

---

[15] The Holy Quran, 3:14.
[16] The Holy Quran, 18:46.

living human being, experiencing the pains and pleasures that we all experience. Yet, he did not approach things in the way that we do. He understood the deepest aspects of reality and acted in accordance with the truth that he saw. That is why he saw the things that others fought over to be vile and disgusting. He once spoke of the world and said,

لدنياكم أهون عندي من ورقة في فيّ جرادة تقضمها ، وأقذر عندي من عراقة خنزير ...

This transient world of yours is less valuable to me than a mouthful of leaves in the mouth of a locust, and more repugnant to me than a meatless pig bone....[17]

For us to rid ourselves of attachment to this world, we need to tread carefully on it and not let our desires shackle us. We must have the foresight to see the reality of things and their true outcomes, just like our immaculate role model Imam Ali (a).

---

[17] Al-Majlisi, *Bihar al-Anwar*, 40:348.

WHIM

In the Name of God, the Most Beneficent, the Most Merciful

يَا دَاوُودُ إِنَّا جَعَلْنَاكَ خَلِيفَةً فِي الْأَرْضِ فَاحْكُم بَيْنَ النَّاسِ بِالْحَقِّ وَلَا تَتَّبِعِ الْهَوَىٰ فَيُضِلَّكَ عَن سَبِيلِ اللَّهِ ۚ إِنَّ الَّذِينَ يَضِلُّونَ عَن سَبِيلِ اللَّهِ لَهُمْ عَذَابٌ شَدِيدٌ بِمَا نَسُوا يَوْمَ الْحِسَابِ

O David! Indeed, We have made you a vicegerent on the Earth. So, judge between people with justice, and do not follow your desires, or they will lead you astray from the way of God. Indeed, there is a severe punishment for those who stray from the way of God, because of their forgetting the Day of Reckoning.[1]

WHAT IS WHIM?

We have been speaking of whim and desires and how an individual should deal with them. But what exactly do we mean by these terms? What are the desires that need to be put in check? What is the whim and how can we control it?

---

[1] The Holy Quran, 38:26.

On our constant journey toward God, we find that some of us do not completely utilize all the faculties that God has granted us. Instead, we may misdirect these energies toward things outside of what God has prescribed for us.

Mankind is the greatest of God's creations and is endowed with faculties beyond anything granted to any other creature. An individual may also rise in rank above the angels if he properly utilizes the abilities that he was given. Chief amongst these talents is the faculty of the intellect, which plays a key role in our journey.

When someone utilizes these faculties in ways other than those prescribed by God, we say that they are simply following their whims. In other words, to follow the whim is to seek the fulfillment of any desire without regard to the boundaries set by God Almighty. Following the whim is one of the things that makes an individual lose control over them and their faculties.

But is everything that we desire a vice? Is everything that we do not desire a virtue?

There are those who believe that virtue lies in going against the self in everything that it desires, and that true happiness does not come except through complete rejection of worldly pleasures. Others believe that the intellect with which we were endowed condones the desires that are innate to our nature, and that we should do everything in our ability to satisfy these desires.

We cannot consider everything that we desire to be a vice and that virtue lies in complete rejection of all desires. Neither can we take the second approach and consider fulfillment of all desires to be the rational course.

The true standard in this regard lies in acting in accordance with what pleases God Almighty. Take, for example, food and drink. If an individual gluttonously devours everything in reach, they cannot be said to be acting rationally. Neither should an individual refrain from all food and drink simply because they desire it.

The correct course lies in approaching our desires with God as the focus of our intention. We should engage our desire for food and drink only in so much as it satisfies our desire within God's prescribed rules and that it gives us the energy to continue our journey toward God. Thus, engaging our desire for food and drink becomes a method by which we seek closeness to God.

The same analysis holds true when we refrain from indulging in our desires. Take again the example of food and drink. Simply not indulging in the pleasures of a good meal does not equate to being a virtuous individual. In fact, if an individual is doing so simply to be recognized as a religious and austere individual, they are practicing duplicity and engaging in vice. But if an individual limits their indulgence out of a desire for God's pleasure, then their intention dictates the admirable nature of his actions.

Therefore, the true standard by which we judge whether indulging in a desire is sinful or not, is the intention behind our actions and behaviors.

Types of Whim

Of course, whim is not limited to the sinful fulfillment of our base desires. In fact, we can categorize whim into the following types.

Behavioral Whim. When an individual seeks to fulfill their base desires without regard to God's commands, they are following their whim. This type of whim can be clearly seen in the sins of greed, gluttony, and the like. God describes this in the Holy Quran when He says:

زُيِّنَ لِلنَّاسِ حُبُّ الشَّهَوَاتِ مِنَ النِّسَاءِ وَالْبَنِينَ وَالْقَنَاطِيرِ الْمُقَنطَرَةِ مِنَ الذَّهَبِ وَالْفِضَّةِ وَالْخَيْلِ الْمُسَوَّمَةِ وَالْأَنْعَامِ وَالْحَرْثِ ۗ ذَٰلِكَ مَتَاعُ الْحَيَاةِ الدُّنْيَا ۖ وَاللَّهُ عِندَهُ حُسْنُ الْمَآبِ

The love of [worldly] allures, including women and children, accumulated piles of gold and silver, horses of mark, livestock, and farms has been made to seem decorous to mankind. Those are the wares of the life of this world, but the goodness of one's ultimate destination lies near God.[2]

Social Whim. Another type of whim is apparent in people's interactions with one another. The most evident examples of this can be seen when we judge one another without any proof or evidence. How often do we judge people, for good or bad, with-

---

[2] The Holy Quran, 3:14.

out care or regard for proof? In those circumstances, our passions gain control of our intellect and we start to make decisions based on impressions and emotions.

When it comes to someone we dislike, we quickly judge them as the worst of people without giving them any excuse or justification. On the other hand, when it comes to a person who we love and care for, we turn a blind eye to their shortcomings and try to find any justification for their actions. This subjugation of reason to emotion is a vice that God forbade us from. This is clear in the verse of the Holy Quran mentioned at the beginning of this chapter.

Doctrinal Whim. People may also follow their whims when it comes to their beliefs and worldview. A person may blindly follow the beliefs of their family without proof. Others may adopt a different doctrine simply to be rebellious and without proof. Others still follow their whim in choosing their worldview because they find the truth to be inconvenient or even damaging to them. God addressed this kind of whim in the Holy Quran and said:

وَإِذَا قِيلَ لَهُمُ اتَّبِعُوا مَا أَنزَلَ اللَّهُ قَالُوا بَلْ نَتَّبِعُ مَا أَلْفَيْنَا عَلَيْهِ آبَاءَنَا ۚ أَوَلَوْ كَانَ آبَاؤُهُمْ لَا يَعْقِلُونَ شَيْئًا وَلَا يَهْتَدُونَ

When they are told, 'Follow what God has sent down,' they say, 'No, we will follow what we have found our fathers following.' What, even if their fathers neither exercised their reason nor were guided?![3]

---

[3] The Holy Quran, 2:170.

In another verse, the Holy Quran relays to us the words of the people of hellfire:

وَقَالُوا رَبَّنَا إِنَّا أَطَعْنَا سَادَتَنَا وَكُبَرَاءَنَا فَأَضَلُّونَا السَّبِيلَا

They will say, 'Our Lord! We obeyed our leaders and elders, and they led us astray from the way.'[4]

This is the most dangerous type of whim, as it will clearly steer an individual away from the path of truth and make their life based entirely on desire. That is why we pray in the supplication taught to us by Imam al-Sadiq (a):

اللهم صل على محمد وآل محمد، و أرني الحق حقا حتى أتبعه، وأرني الباطل باطلا حتى أجتنبه، ولا تجعلها علي متشابهين، فأتبع هواي بغير هدى منك

O' God! Send peace and blessings upon Muhammad (s) and the Household of Muhammad (a)! And let me see the truth for what it is so that I may follow it! And let me see falsity for what it is so that I may avoid it! And do not make them seem similar to me so that I follow my whim without any guidance from You!

واجعل هواي تبعا لرضاك وطاعتك، وخذ لنفسك رضاها من نفسي، واهدني لما اختلف فيه من الحق بإذنك، إنك تهدي من تشاء إلى صراط مستقيم

---

[4] The Holy Quran, 33:67.

Make my whim fall in obedience to You! Take for Yourself from me whatever contents You! Guide me to what has been disputed of the truth by Your decree! Surely, You guide whomever You wish to a straight path![5]

A person may become lost because of the confusion between what is true and what is false. As a result, they may follow their whims in forming a worldview or adopting a doctrine and will deviate from the path set for them by God. However, an individual must be steadfast in following God's commands, as that is the true distinction between virtue and vice.

Why do People Follow Whim?

The reasons for following whim differ across the multiple types discussed above. However, the following reasons can generally be the causes of following whim.

Social Factors. One of the important factors for why people may follow their whim without exercising their reason is that they are influenced by their environments and communities. Some people may adopt a certain behavior, attitude, or worldview simply because it gives them a unique social connection or a higher social status. Some people are influenced by peers and friends to conform without rational justification but simply to 'fit-in.' This peer pressure does not stop at the behavioral level, but can also rise to the level of changing a worldview. God says in the Holy Quran:

---

[5] Al-Majlisi, *Bihar al-Anwar*, 83:120.

وَاللَّهُ يُرِيدُ أَن يَتُوبَ عَلَيْكُمْ وَيُرِيدُ الَّذِينَ يَتَّبِعُونَ الشَّهَوَاتِ أَن تَمِيلُوا مَيْلًا عَظِيمًا

> *God desires to turn toward you clemently, but those who pursue their [base] appetites desire that you fall into gross waywardness.*[6]

God also says:

وَاصْبِرْ نَفْسَكَ مَعَ الَّذِينَ يَدْعُونَ رَبَّهُم بِالْغَدَاةِ وَالْعَشِيِّ يُرِيدُونَ وَجْهَهُ ۖ وَلَا تَعْدُ عَيْنَاكَ عَنْهُمْ تُرِيدُ زِينَةَ الْحَيَاةِ الدُّنْيَا ۖ وَلَا تُطِعْ مَنْ أَغْفَلْنَا قَلْبَهُ عَن ذِكْرِنَا وَاتَّبَعَ هَوَاهُ وَكَانَ أَمْرُهُ فُرُطًا

> *Content yourself with the company of those who supplicate their Lord morning and evening, desiring His Face, and do not lose sight of them, desiring the glitter of the life of this world. And do not obey him whose heart We have made oblivious to Our remembrance, and who follows his own desires, and whose conduct is [mere] profligacy.*[7]

God warns against following these deviants who wish to misguide others. God warns against following anyone without exercising our reason and thinking through our actions.

We should also realize that it is not an excuse for a follower that they were misguided by someone else. The Holy Quran gives us many parables about individuals and societies that went astray

---

[6] The Holy Quran, 4:27.
[7] The Holy Quran, 18:28.

because they followed a misguided leader. Yet, this does not excuse these followers of fault – they are still blameworthy for following a misguided leader into deviance.

In fact, such blind following is an affront to faith and reason. In our worldly lives, we look at all alternatives and spend time and effort on finding the best of them. How can we – when something is related to our hereafter – follow blindly without exercising an ounce of reason? God Almighty describes the wretched outcome for both the leaders and followers in such a situation. He says in the blessed verse:

﴿إِذْ تَبَرَّأَ الَّذِينَ اتُّبِعُوا مِنَ الَّذِينَ اتَّبَعُوا وَرَأَوُا الْعَذَابَ وَتَقَطَّعَتْ بِهِمُ الْأَسْبَابُ ١٦٦﴾ ﴿وَقَالَ الَّذِينَ اتَّبَعُوا لَوْ أَنَّ لَنَا كَرَّةً فَنَتَبَرَّأَ مِنْهُمْ كَمَا تَبَرَّءُوا مِنَّا ۗ كَذَٰلِكَ يُرِيهِمُ اللَّهُ أَعْمَالَهُمْ حَسَرَاتٍ عَلَيْهِمْ ۖ وَمَا هُم بِخَارِجِينَ مِنَ النَّارِ ١٦٧﴾

When those who were followed will disown the followers, and they will sight the punishment while all their means of recourse will be cut off, and when the followers will say, 'Had there been another turn for us, we would disown them as they disown us [now]', thus shall God show them their deeds as regrets for themselves, and they shall not leave the Fire.[8]

Moreover, we see those followers asking God to multiply the punishment of those who were the cause of their misguidance. The Holy Quran describes this scene:

---

[8] The Holy Quran, 2:166-67.

قَالَ ادْخُلُوا فِي أُمَمٍ قَدْ خَلَتْ مِن قَبْلِكُم مِّنَ الْجِنِّ وَالْإِنسِ فِي النَّارِ ۖ كُلَّمَا دَخَلَتْ أُمَّةٌ لَّعَنَتْ أُخْتَهَا ۖ حَتَّىٰ إِذَا ادَّارَكُوا فِيهَا جَمِيعًا قَالَتْ أُخْرَاهُمْ لِأُولَاهُمْ رَبَّنَا هَٰؤُلَاءِ أَضَلُّونَا فَآتِهِمْ عَذَابًا ضِعْفًا مِّنَ النَّارِ ۖ قَالَ لِكُلٍّ ضِعْفٌ وَلَٰكِن لَّا تَعْلَمُونَ

He will say, 'Enter the Fire, along with the nations of jinn and humans who passed before you!' Every time that a nation enters [Hell], it will curse its sister [nation]. When they all rejoin in it, the last of them will say about the first of them, 'Our Lord, it was they who led us astray, so give them a double punishment of the Fire.' He will say, 'It is double for each [of you], but you do not know.'[9]

Internal Factors. Another reason why many individuals follow their whim is because they are not able to resist their temptations and to persevere against their base desires. So, despite knowing the negative effects of the sin and how it could lead to terrible consequences in this world and next, they proceed to commit it because of their weakness and intemperance. The Holy Quran speaks to us regarding such individuals and the consequences that they will face. At the same time, it tells us of the great rewards that one can expect once they pass the trial of their temptations. The Holy Quran says:

---

[9] The Holy Quran, 7:38.

فَأَمَّا مَن طَغَىٰ ﴿٣٧﴾ وَآثَرَ الْحَيَاةَ الدُّنْيَا ﴿٣٨﴾ فَإِنَّ الْجَحِيمَ هِيَ الْمَأْوَىٰ ﴿٣٩﴾ وَأَمَّا مَنْ خَافَ مَقَامَ رَبِّهِ وَنَهَى النَّفْسَ عَنِ الْهَوَىٰ ﴿٤٠﴾ فَإِنَّ الْجَنَّةَ هِيَ الْمَأْوَىٰ ﴿٤١﴾

As for him who has been rebellious and preferred the life of this world, his refuge will indeed be Hell. But as for him who is awed to stand before his Lord and restrains his soul from [following] desires, his refuge will indeed be Paradise.[10]

The Holy Prophet (s) and his Household (a) also reiterated this in many of their narrations. The Commander of the Faithful (a) said:

إِنَّ رَسُولَ اللهِ (صلى الله عليه وآله) كَانَ يَقُولُ: إِنَّ الْجَنَّةَ حُفَّتْ بِالْمَكَارِهِ، وَإِنَّ النَّارَ حُفَّتْ بِالشَّهَوَاتِ. وَاعْلَمُوا أَنَّهُ مَا مِنْ طَاعَةِ اللهِ شَيْءٌ إِلَّا يَأْتِي فِي كُرْهٍ، وَمَا مِنْ مَعْصِيَةِ اللهِ شَيْءٌ إِلَّا يَأْتِي فِي شَهْوَةٍ

The Messenger of God (s) used to say, '[The path to] Paradise is filled with troubles and [the path to] Hellfire is filled with [satisfaction of] desires.' You should know that every obedience to God is unpleasant in appearance while every disobedience to God has the appearance of satisfaction.

فَرَحِمَ اللهُ رَجُلًا نَزَعَ عَنْ شَهْوَتِهِ، وَقَمَعَ هَوَى نَفْسِهِ، فَإِنَّ هَذِهِ النَّفْسَ أَبْعَدُ شَيْءٍ مَنْزِعاً، وَإِنَّهَا لَا تَزَالُ تَنْزِعُ إِلَى مَعْصِيَةٍ فِي هَوًى

---

[10] The Holy Quran, 79:37-41.

> *May God have mercy on the person who avoided his whims and uprooted the appetite of his heart. Surely, the heart is difficult to safeguard as it continuously pursues disobedience through whim.*[11]

An individual who can succeed in their struggle against their whim and desires is surely successful. Indeed, the Commander of the Faithful (a) said,

$$\text{أشجع الناس من غلب هواه}$$

> *The bravest of people is the one who conquers his whims.*[12]

As for the individual who is not able to be patient and persevere against their base desires, their whim will surely overpower them and draw them into the deviance and despair.

Combatting Whim

After discussing whim, its different types, and its causes, we must now turn to the practical means by which we can restrain it. This is where many people think to themselves that they are fighting a losing battle. Many think it is too hard an endeavor to combat and restrain the desires that are innate to our creation. They are right in some respect, as this struggle is truly a difficult one and should not be taken lightly. The Holy Prophet (s) would constantly refer to this battle against the whim as 'the Great

---

[11] Al-Radi, *Nahj al-Balagha*, 2:90, Sermon 176.
[12] Al-Majlisi, *Bihar al-Anwar*, 67:76.

Struggle.' Therefore, we must seek the practical means by which we can ensure our success in this challenge.

The following is a brief discussion of four practical mechanisms we have at our disposal.

Realizing the Consequences. Many think that people who have embraced their desires and willfully threw off the 'shackles' of religion are living happy and successful lives. They are satisfying their every desire and indulging in every pleasure. So, at first glance, it might seem that they are leading happy and luxurious lives.

However, we cannot content ourselves to this shallow approach. We must turn to our reason and look carefully at our own lives and the lives of those who have chosen deviance. Only then can we see the reality of this deceptive world.

We will not delve here into a discussion of the reality of deviants' lives – whether they are genuinely happy or not. Instead, we will simply relay a narration from Imam al-Baqir (a) in this regard. He narrates that the Holy Prophet (s) once told his companions that God Almighty said:

يقول الله عزوجل: وعزتي وجلالي وعظمتي وكبريائي ونوري وعلوي وارتفاع مكاني لا يؤثر عبد هواه على هواي إلا شتت أمره، ولبست عليه دنياه وشغلت قلبه بها ولم اوته منها إلا ما قدرت له

By My might, majesty, grandeur, glory, light, highness, and elevated position, no servant shall favor his whim over My will, or I shall scatter his efforts and disguise

the world against him! I shall make his heart preoccupied with this world and not give him of it except what I have previously ordained for him!

وعزتي وجلالي وعظمتي وكبريائي ونوري وعلوي وارتفاع مكاني لا يؤثر عبد هواي على هواه إلا استحفظته ملائكتي وكفلت السماوات والارض رزقه، وكنت له من وراء تجارة كل تاجر، وأتته الدنيا وهي راغمة

By My might, majesty, grandeur, glory, light, highness, and elevated position, no servant shall favor My will over his whim, except that I shall safeguard him with my angels and grant the heavens and the Earth the blessings to confer upon him. I shall be behind his trade with any merchant [supporting him], and the world shall come to him whether it likes it or not![13]

The reader should not take lightly the unique oath and assertion that God is making here. God could have simply sworn by His name. But instead, he listed seven of His glorified attributes. Aside from the meaning of each, this is a clear indication of the importance of the statement being made.

God swears by His glorified names that anyone who follows their whims will be blinded so that they do not know what is good for them and what is bad. Such an individual will live in constant confusion and deviance, attaining nothing more than what God in His grace decides to endow them with.

---

[13] Al-Majlisi, *Bihar al-Anwar*, 67:78.

For us to practically combat our whim, we must realize the futile end that they will lead us to. Instead, we must realize the great promise that God makes to those who are able to endure this challenge and keep their base desires in check.

Remembering Death. The discussion of remembering death and the positive effects it can have is a broad and lengthy one. In general, we must remember death and contemplate on the temporary nature of this world, while at the same time remembering those who have passed away. This has a great impact on the individual, strengthening their will to combat their desires and conquer their whim. The Commander of the Faithful (a) says:

أكثروا ذكر الموت عندما تنازعكم إليه أنفسكم من الشهوات فإنه كفى بالموت واعظاً، وكان رسول الله (ص) يوصي أصحابه بذكر الموت فيقول:
أكثروا ذكر الموت، فإنّه هادم اللّذات

Remember death whenever you are urged by your hearts towards satisfaction of your desires [through impermissible means]. Surely, death is the best instructor. The Messenger of God (s) used to advise his companions to remember death. He used to say, 'Remember death, for it is the destroyer of desires....'[14]

Choosing Friends. The most influential relationship in any individual's life is their friends. A great individual may mix with the wrong crowd and begin to deviate towards their whim. On the other hand, an individual can benefit greatly from keeping

---

[14] Al-'Amili, *Wasa'el al-Shia*, 2:65.

good company. Accordingly, we must be thoughtful in choosing who we spend our time with, as they can be either a gateway to deviance or a supporter in rectitude.

The Commander of the Faithful (a) said,

خير إخوانك من عنفك في طاعة الله سبحانه

The best of your brothers is the one who chastises you towards the obedience of God Almighty.[15]

He also said,

خَيْرُ إِخْوانِكَ مَنْ سارَعَ إِلَى الْخَيْرِ وَ جَذَبَكَ إِلَيْهِ وَ أَمَرَكَ بِالْبِرِّ وَ أَعانَكَ عَلَيْهِ

The best of your brothers is the one who rushes toward good works and draws you toward it, and advises you to do good and supports you in that regard.[16]

In another narration he said,

خَيْرُ إِخْوانِكَ مَنْ دَعاكَ إِلَى صِدْقِ الْمَقالِ بِصِدْقِ مَقالِهِ وَ نَدَبَكَ إِلَى أَفْضَلِ الْأَعْمالِ بِحُسْنِ أَعْمالِهِ

The best of your brothers is the one who calls you to truthfulness in your words by the truthfulness in his words, and encourages you to the best of deeds by the goodness of his deeds.[17]

---

[15] Al-Wasiti, *'Oyoun al-Hikam*, 238.
[16] Ibid, 239.
[17] Ibid.

It is also relayed that the Holy Prophet (s) said,

خيرُ إخوانِك مَن أعانَك على طاعةِ اللهِ وصَدَّك عن مَعاصيهِ وأمرَك برِضاه

The best of your brothers is the one who supports you in obedience to God, deters you from disobeying Him, and advises you to [seek] His contentment.[18]

Creating the Right Environment. Just as an individual is influenced by their friends and company, the environment around them can also have a great influence on them. That is why we find religious admonishments against moving to a community where religion does not have a strong presence. In the formative years of Islam, that normally meant a return to nomadism as opposed to remaining in the city, where a society and support system existed. Thus, we see that Imam al-Rida (a) once wrote to one of his companions:

وَحَرَّمَ اللهُ التَّعَرُّبَ بَعْدَ الْهِجْرَةِ لِلرُّجُوعِ عَنِ الدِّينِ وَتَرْكِ الْمُؤَازَرَةِ لِلْأَنْبِيَاءِ وَالْحُجَجِ... وَلِذَلِكَ لَوْ عَرَفَ الرَّجُلُ الدِّينَ كَامِلاً لَمْ يَجُزْ لَهُ مُسَاكَنَةُ أَهْلِ الْجَهْلِ وَالْخَوْفِ عَلَيْهِ، لِأَنَّهُ لَا يُؤْمَنُ أَنْ يَقَعَ مِنْهُ تَرْكُ الْعِلْمِ وَالدُّخُولُ مَعَ أَهْلِ الْجَهْلِ وَالتَّمَادِي فِي ذَلِكَ.

God forbade [the return to nomadism] after migration, as it would mean abandoning the faith and neglecting to support the prophets and [viceroys of God]... That is why a man who may have a comprehensive understanding of the religion is not permitted to associate

---

[18] Al-Rayshahri, *Mizan al-Hikma*, 1:46.

with the people of ignorance. One should be uncertain of his matter, as he is not safe from the possibility of leaving the people of knowledge and [fully assimilating] with the people of ignorance.[19]

The Imam gave a practical historical example for this concept. He said that a learned individual should not go out and live alongside the nomads, who were largely illiterate and uneducated. A person who does so will incrementally begin to forget their knowledge. They will become like those around them, who have little knowledge of the faith. Soon, they will begin to forget about their creed and begin to indulge their whim.

A person who wishes to succeed in their struggle against their base desires needs to make sure they live in an environment of faith and spiritual uplifting. They should stay away from environments of materialism and deviance. They should make it a habit to go to the mosque and religious centers, where God, His prophets, and His chosen servants are constantly remembered. This remembrance will serve as a safeguard and support for him in this great struggle.

---

[19] Al-'Amili, *Wasa'el al-Shia*, 11:75-76.

Austerity

In the Name of God, the Most Beneficent, the Most Merciful

وَلَا تَمُدَّنَّ عَيْنَيْكَ إِلَىٰ مَا مَتَّعْنَا بِهِ أَزْوَاجًا مِّنْهُمْ زَهْرَةَ الْحَيَاةِ الدُّنْيَا لِنَفْتِنَهُمْ فِيهِ ۚ وَرِزْقُ رَبِّكَ خَيْرٌ وَأَبْقَىٰ

Do not extend your glance toward what We have provided certain groups of them as a glitter of the life of this world, so that We may test them thereby. The provision of your Lord is better and more lasting.[1]

Austerity is one of the key concepts that Islam focuses on. Austerity is the best method to train oneself and achieve the greatest virtue. This makes it a central theme in the religion; virtue is a major purpose for which God sent us prophets and messengers. The Holy Prophet (s) famously said,

إنما بعثت لأتمم مكارم الأخلاق

Indeed, I have been sent to complete the best of morals.[2]

---

[1] The Holy Quran, 20:131.

[2] Al-Majlisi, *Bihar al-Anwar*, 16:210.

Perhaps many people willfully neglect this issue, because they perceive it to be a gateway to poverty, neediness, and destitution. There are also many people who recognize the value of austerity, but do not seek it because they are not obliged to do so, and they do not think that they can achieve it. While it is true that God did not oblige us to be austere, this does not mean that austerity is not a priority and of high value within the religion of Islam.

In fact, we can see the priority given to this concept in the words of our Holy Prophet (s). He said,

ما تعبدوا لله بشيء مثل الزهد في الدنيا

They [i.e. mankind] did not worship God with anything comparable to austerity in this world.[3]

In another narration he said,

ما عبد الله بشيء أفضل من الزهد في الدنيا

God was never worshiped with anything better than austerity in this world.[4]

Indeed, austerity is not of any less importance than the other worships prescribed by God. In fact, it is one of the best forms of worship.

We talk about austerity, due to its importance, but it is a mysterious and often misunderstood topic. It is also important to discuss austerity, because of the growing strength of materialism and its control over many aspects of our lives. That is why we

---

[3] Al-Majlisi, *Bihar al-Anwar*, 67:322.
[4] Al-Nuri, *Mustadrak al-Wasa'el*, 12:50.

must discuss the spiritual topics that can have a practical effect on our lives.

Materialism has become an overwhelming trend and that has left a great gap in society's spiritual attainment. This has been a cause for great confusion and anxiety, as individuals are not able to find tranquility within themselves. In turn, this has caused a great deal of deviant movements to emerge. Each of these movements presents itself as if it has the solutions to all of humanity's problems. However, they are all mirages that cannot satisfy mankind's needs.

God Almighty says:

وَالَّذِينَ كَفَرُوا أَعْمَالُهُمْ كَسَرَابٍ بِقِيعَةٍ يَحْسَبُهُ الظَّمْآنُ مَاءً حَتَّى إِذَا جَاءَهُ لَمْ يَجِدْهُ شَيْئًا وَوَجَدَ اللَّهَ عِندَهُ فَوَفَّاهُ حِسَابَهُ ۗ وَاللَّهُ سَرِيعُ الْحِسَابِ ﴿٣٩﴾ أَوْ كَظُلُمَاتٍ فِي بَحْرٍ لُّجِّيٍّ يَغْشَاهُ مَوْجٌ مِّن فَوْقِهِ مَوْجٌ مِّن فَوْقِهِ سَحَابٌ ۚ ظُلُمَاتٌ بَعْضُهَا فَوْقَ بَعْضٍ إِذَا أَخْرَجَ يَدَهُ لَمْ يَكَدْ يَرَاهَا ۗ وَمَن لَّمْ يَجْعَلِ اللَّهُ لَهُ نُورًا فَمَا لَهُ مِن نُّورٍ ﴿٤٠﴾

As for the faithless, their works are like a mirage in a plain, which the thirsty man supposes to be water. When he comes to it, he finds it to be nothing; but there he finds God, who will pay him his full account, and God is swift at reckoning. Or like the manifold darkness in a deep sea, covered by billow upon billow, overcast by clouds; manifold [layers of] darkness, one on top of another: when he brings out his hand, he can hardly see it. One whom God has not granted any light has no light.[5]

How Important is this World?

Austerity should not be understood as a call to leave all means of comfort or to neglect our future in this world. Austerity does not mean that we should work for the hereafter by neglecting ourselves and our families in this world. This is a common misunderstanding of austerity that has led many to neglect this important topic.

Austerity in the Islamic worldview does not mean neglecting our lives in this world. Rather, it means that we should understand the true value of this world, and the purpose for which it was created. It means that we should seek to understand our purpose in this world. Through careful reading of the Holy Quran and the noble traditions, we can identify several important aspects of austerity that Islam calls for.

One of these aspects is not being unduly attentive to and concerned with this world. However, this inattentiveness must be built on a true understanding of reality. It must be built on a true measure of the value of this world and its purpose – and not based on mere laziness or irresponsibility. That would be in complete contradiction to what God Almighty wants of us.

---

[5] The Holy Quran, 24:39-40.

The austere individual must always be fully aware of their responsibilities and must strive to meet them. After all, everyone is responsible for themselves, their family, their kin, and their community. Everyone has a responsibility to contribute to the development of this world. These are all responsibilities that God placed on our shoulders.

The indifference that God demands of us is rather based on understanding the reality and value of this world. It is based on the realization that this life is short and transient – that it is only a prelude to an eternal life to come. God describes this in the Holy Quran and says,

لِّكَيْلَا تَأْسَوْا عَلَىٰ مَا فَاتَكُمْ وَلَا تَفْرَحُوا بِمَا آتَاكُمْ ۗ وَاللَّهُ لَا يُحِبُّ كُلَّ مُخْتَالٍ فَخُورٍ

So, that you may not grieve for what escapes you, nor boast for what comes your way, and God does not like any swaggering braggart.[6]

Imam al-Sadiq (a) is reported to have explained this verse as follows:

الزهد كله في كلمتين (لكيلا تأسوا على ما فاتكم ...) من لم ييأس على الماضي ولم يفرح بالآتي، فهو الزاهد.

---

[6] The Holy Quran, 57:23.

Austerity is encompassed in two words. [God says,] 'So that you may not grieve for what escapes you...' Whoever does not grieve for what is lost or boasts for what is to come is [truly] austere.[7]

The real drive behind austerity must be an understanding of this world and the individual's purpose in it. We should not grieve for what we miss in this world, because we need to be fully aware that this is a fleeting world, and that time will inevitably create ups and downs for every individual. Neither should we boast about what we have been given in this world. We need to be fully aware that anything we gain is a trial, with which God is testing us.

An austere individual must fully comprehend the transient nature of this world. They should know that they cannot hold on to anything forever – that everything in this world is fleeting. Thus, the fleeting pleasures of this world will not affect their movement towards the eternal life.

An individual who does not deal with the world in this matter will find only difficulty and failure. They will not be able to fulfill all of their desires and ambitions. They were not created for this limited life, but for an infinite and eternal one. The world and all that is in it cannot satisfy our ambitions. That is why even the richest of people still feel needy – this world cannot satisfy them. Yet, they continue to spend all their energies on gathering more wealth in an attempt to satisfy their feeling of neediness. Little

---

[7] Al-Majlisi, *Bihar al-Anwar*, 75:70.

do they know that only the world of the hereafter will satisfy them.

Yet, austerity does not mean that we should live a poor and miserable life. It is only a lens through which we view the world. It means we should concern ourselves with the greater and eternal life, rather than this transient world. It means that a person should live contently, without feeling any need for amassing the wares and wealth of this world.

A wealthy individual lives poor if they cannot find contentedness in austerity. A poor individual lives content and happy if their austerity shows them that they do not need the excesses of this world.

We should also point out that austerity has nothing to do with an individual seeking to build a career and earn a living. Austerity and wealth can coexist in the same individual. Again, the issue is one of worldview – it is about how everyone examines this world and its value. As the Commander of the Faithful (a) said,

ليس الزهد ألا تملك شيئا، إنما الزهد ألا يملكك شيء

> *Austerity is not that you do not own anything. It is that nothing owns you.*[8]

Preparing for the Hereafter

Austerity also means that the individual prepares for the hereafter. The root of austerity is a rejection of this material world and

---

[8] Al-Rayshahri, *Mizan al-Hikma*, 4:2990.

an outlook toward the infinite treasures of the hereafter. In this sense, the austere person is always looking for the greatest reward and will go through any hardship to achieve this.

The narrations of the Holy Household (a) describe to us the characteristics of the austere. They tell us about how an austere individual will tirelessly seek the greatest of eternal pleasures. They tell us of their complete comfort in knowing that the rewards of the hereafter are eternal, and that they will live eternally in bliss if they are successful in reaching that goal. It is relayed that Imam al-Sadiq (a) once said:

والزاهد الذي يختار الآخرة على الدنيا ، والذل على العز ، والجهد على الراحة والجوع على الشبع ، وعاقبة الآجل على محبة العاجل ، والذكر على الغفلة ويكون نفسه في الدنيا وقلبه في الآخرة.

The austere is the one who chooses the hereafter over the [transitory] world, humility over honor, strife over leisure, hunger over satisfaction, a delayed reward over immediate gratification and remembrance over heedlessness. He would be in this [transitory] world while his heart is in the hereafter.[9]

The austere will endure humility, strife, and hunger so that they can achieve his goal. They know that anything that they may miss in this world, they will be more than adequately compensated for in the hereafter. They endure all of this in hopes of everlasting bliss and happiness. It is not because they does not

---

[9] Al-Majlisi, *Bihar al-Anwar*, 67:315.

value or seek honor, luxury, and satisfaction. They understand, value, and seek all of these, but their reason drives them to choose between the two – between this world and the hereafter. It leads them to choose God's pleasure over their own pleasure and desire, as they seek the rewards that God promised. That is why our Immaculate Imams (a) draw a link between austerity and reason. As Imam al-Kadhim (a) said:

إن العقلاء زهدوا في الدنيا ورغبوا في الآخرة، لأنهم علموا أن الدنيا طالبة مطلوبة والآخرة طالبة ومطلوبة، فمن طلب الآخرة طلبته الدنيا حتى يستوفي منها رزقه ومن طلب الدنيا طلبته الآخرة فيأتيه الموت فيفسد عليه دنياه وآخرته.

The intellectuals are austere in this world and seek the hereafter. They know that the world both seeks and is sought after, and that the hereafter both seeks and is sought after. Whoever seeks the hereafter, this world will seek him, so that he will suffice himself of its bounties. Whoever seeks this world, the hereafter will seek him, so that death will befall him and he will have lost both this world and the hereafter.[10]

Imam Ali (a) also said,

احزمكم ازهدكم

The most disciplined amongst you is the most austere.[11]

---

[10] Al-Harrani, *Tuhaf al-'Oqool*, 387.
[11] Al-Wasiti, *'Oyoun al-Hikam*, 113.

Avoiding Distractions

Throughout our lives, we face constant distractions that divert us away from remembering God Almighty. We are too busy indulging in this world and thinking about our present and future on this Earth. Sometimes we forget about ourselves and our families when we get too preoccupied with worldly attainment. The irony is that the more engaged we become with this world, the more we feel an urge to continue to seek its treasures and luxuries.

This is where austerity finds its purpose. It triggers our reason and allows us to accurately assess our circumstances and prioritize among our options. A reasonable individual will thus keep God in mind, not allowing their present occupations to prevent them from remembering the Almighty. A reasonable individual knows that if they forget God, God will also forget them. God says,

$$\text{نَسُوا اللَّهَ فَنَسِيَهُمْ}$$

They have forgotten God, so He has forgotten them.[12]

Moreover, when an individual forgets God, God will allow them to proceed in their indulgences and forget themselves and their reality. God says in the Holy Quran:

$$\text{وَلَا تَكُونُوا كَالَّذِينَ نَسُوا اللَّهَ فَأَنسَاهُمْ أَنفُسَهُمْ ۚ أُولَٰئِكَ هُمُ الْفَاسِقُونَ}$$

---

[12] The Holy Quran, 9:67.

Do not be like those who forget God, so He makes them forget their own souls. It is they who are the transgressors.[13]

Austerity therefore lies in making God's pleasure the top priority in our lives. It means that we should not allow anything to distract us from remembering Him. The Imams (a) have clearly explained this to us. As Imam al-Sadiq (a) said

الزهد مفتاح باب الآخرة ، والبراءة من النار ، وهو تركك كل شئ يشغلك عن الله ، عن غير تأسف على فوتها ، ولا إعجاب في تركها ، ولا انتظار فرج منها ، ولا طلب محمدة عليها ، ولا عوض منها ، بل ترى فوتها راحة ، وكونها آفة

Austerity is the key to the hereafter and the gate of freedom from Hellfire. It is to abstain from everything that distracts you from God, while not grieving over, being vain about, aspiring relief from, or seeking praise or reward for such abstinence. Rather, it is to take comfort in escaping these things and seeing them as a scourge.[14]

This noble tradition provides several specific implications of austerity. As discussed before, the true meaning of austerity comes in understanding the reality of this world and our purpose in it. This world is transient and fleeting – it is only a test that precedes the true and eternal life of the hereafter.

---

[13] The Holy Quran, 59:19.
[14] Al-Majlisi, *Bihar al-Anwar*, 67:315.

True austerity lies in remembering God. If we seek to be austere, we must consider anything that distracts us from remembering God as a scourge in our lives. Again, we must emphasize that remembering God does not mean forgetting about our lives and families in this world. Instead, we should engage ourselves in this world, because it is – as the noble traditions emphasize – the "farmland of the hereafter."[15] So long as we approach our world as a means for attaining God's pleasure, we will continue to be engaged in remembering God and practicing austerity in our lives.

TRUST IN GOD

There is an important distinction that must be made between practical faith and theoretical faith. We all believe in the importance of worship and charity, and that God Almighty will shower the charitable and the worshipper with His infinite blessings and mercy. We all know about the Holy Prophet (s) and his Household (a), and all their virtue. We all know, for example, about Imam Hassan (a) and how he split his wealth multiple times during his life, giving half of it or more for the sake of God. We have full faith that the Imam's (a) actions were good, and that God will reward him generously.

Yet how many of us can bring ourselves to act like the Imam (a)? We cannot because we have a fear of the future. We think to ourselves, 'How can I continue to live my life and feed my family if

---

[15] Al-Ihsa'ei, *'Awali al-La'ali*, 1:267.

I do this?' We grow attached to this world and give only within limited circumstances.

All of this is because we do not have practical faith and trust in God Almighty. This is the exact opposite of what we consider to be austerity in Islam. Again, austerity is not about forbidding ourselves the pleasures that God has permitted for us. God explicitly says:

$$\text{قُلْ مَنْ حَرَّمَ زِينَةَ اللَّهِ الَّتِي أَخْرَجَ لِعِبَادِهِ وَالطَّيِّبَاتِ مِنَ الرِّزْقِ ۚ قُلْ هِيَ لِلَّذِينَ آمَنُوا فِي الْحَيَاةِ الدُّنْيَا خَالِصَةً يَوْمَ الْقِيَامَةِ ۗ كَذَٰلِكَ نُفَصِّلُ الْآيَاتِ لِقَوْمٍ يَعْلَمُونَ}$$

Say, 'Who has forbidden the adornment of God, which He has brought forth for His servants, and the good things of [His] provision?' Say, 'These are for the faithful in the life of this world, and exclusively for them on the Day of Resurrection.' Thus do We elaborate the signs for a people who have knowledge.[16]

Austerity is not about forgoing luxury, wealth, and pleasure. Real austerity lies in what the Holy Prophet (s) described when he said:

$$\text{الزهادة في الدنيا ليست بتحريم الحلال ولا إضاعة المال ولكن الزهادة في الدنيا أن لا تكون بما في يديك أوثق مما في يد الله وأن تكون في ثواب المصيبة إذا أنت أصبت بها أرغب فيها لو أنها أبقيت لك}$$

---

[16] The Holy Quran, 7:32.

Austerity in this world is not [achieved] through forbidding what is permissible or forsaking wealth. Rather, Austerity lies in not placing more trust in what is in your hand than the trust you give to what is in the hands of God. It is in being more content with [God's] rewards for a loss that may strike you, than your contentment had [your wealth] been kept for you.[17]

---

[17] Al-Hindi, *Kanz al-'Ommal*, 3:181.

PIETY

In the Name of God, the Most Beneficent, the Most Merciful

يَا أَيُّهَا الَّذِينَ آمَنُوا اتَّقُوا اللَّهَ وَلْتَنظُرْ نَفْسٌ مَّا قَدَّمَتْ لِغَدٍ ۖ وَاتَّقُوا اللَّهَ ۚ إِنَّ اللَّهَ خَبِيرٌ بِمَا تَعْمَلُونَ

O you who have faith! Be wary of God, and let every soul consider what it sends ahead for Tomorrow, and be wary of God. God is indeed well aware of what you do.[1]

Piety is a broad and multifaceted subject and speaking of it can become lengthy and complex. We cannot address every aspect of the topic in this short book. We will thus keep the discussion brief and address the most important aspects.

WHAT IS PIETY?

Piety is "the quality of being religious or reverent."[2] Piety is thus a feeling of connection to God through deep respect for God, awe of His majesty, hope in His rewards, and wariness of His

---

[1] The Holy Quran, 59:18.
[2] *Oxford Dictionaries*, s.v. "Piety."

punishment. In the context of this book, we use the word piety as a translation for the Arabic word *Taqwa* – the state of being conscious of God's presence and wary of His judgment.

Thus, our scholars say that piety lies in avoiding what God has forbidden and maintaining what He has obligated. Additionally, a pious individual avoids actions that may not be forbidden per se, but that may be problematic. Thus, piety comes with precaution in terms of obeying God's commands. That is why it is narrated that:

الحلال بيّن والحرام بيّن ، ومن وقع حول الحمى فحقيق أن يقع فيه

> *What is permissible is clear and what is impermissible is clear. Yet whoever treads at the edge will likely fall [into sin].*[3]

We also find that our Immaculate Imams (a) identified piety into categories as a means of illustrating this concept. As Imam al-Sadiq (a) said:

التقوى على ثلاثة أوجه: تقوى الله في الله وهو ترك الحلال فضلا عن الشبهة وهو تقوى خاص الخاص، وتقوى من الله وهو ترك الشبهات فضلا عن حرام، وهو تقوى الخاص، وتقوى من خوف النار والعقاب وهو ترك الحرام وهو تقوى العام

> *Piety is of three types. [The first is] fear of God for God's sake [by which the pious] refrain from what is permissible [but might detriment their faith]. That is the piety of*

---

[3] Al-Asfahani, *al-Mufradat*, 530.

> *the most select of the select. [The second is the simple] fear of God [by which the pious] refrain from what is doubtful [in its permissibility] let alone what is impermissible. That is the piety of the select. [The third is] a fear of hellfire and punishment [by which the pious] refrain from what is impermissible. That is the piety of the masses.*[4]

Thus, we can see that piety is a broad concept with many aspects and levels. The Imams outline three broad layers of piety. The first is seeking to avoid eternal punishment through applying the simplest outlines of the faith. The second lies in avoiding any sin, which is broader than simply fulfilling obligations and avoiding what is forbidden. The third is having the patience and fortitude to forsake anything that might distract the individual from remembering God. This third level of piety "is the piety of the most select of the select."

The Importance of Piety

We can see the importance of piety in several ways.

First, we see that piety is constantly mentioned in the Holy Quran. Tens of verses command us to be pious and promise us God's grand rewards if we practice piety. If piety were not this important, it would not be so constantly mentioned in God's words. Moreover, if we read these noble verses, we find that God

---

[4] Al-Majlisi, *Bihar al-Anwar*, 67:295.

Almighty attaches ultimate happiness and proximity to Him to piety and being wary and reverent of Him.

Second, we find that piety was the call of the messengers and prophets that God sent to us. When we read the verses of the Holy Quran, we find in the narratives of all the prophets that their first call was a call to piety. For example, when Moses was sent to the people of Egypt, he was commanded to call them toward piety. We read in the noble verse,

وَإِذْ نَادَىٰ رَبُّكَ مُوسَىٰ أَنِ ائْتِ الْقَوْمَ الظَّالِمِينَ ﴿١٠﴾ قَوْمَ فِرْعَوْنَ ۚ أَلَا يَتَّقُونَ ﴿١١﴾

When your Lord called out to Moses: [saying,] 'Go to those wrongdoing people, the people of Pharaoh, will they not be pious?'[5]

The same issue was repeated with the people of Prophet Noah "when their brother Noah said to them, 'Will you not be pious?'" It was again repeated with the people of 'Ad "when their brother Hud said to them, 'Will you not be pious?'" And again, with the people of Thamud "when their brother Salih said to them, 'Will you not be pious?'" And with the people of Sodom "when their brother Lot said to them, 'Will you not be pious?'" And the people of Aykah "when Shu'ayb said to them, 'Will you not be pious?'"[6]

---

[5] The Holy Quran, 26:10-11.
[6] The Holy Quran, 26:106, 124, 142, 161, and 177.

Thus, we see through the Holy Quran that the call to piety was a priority among God's messengers.

In addition, we should also mention that these noble verses draw our attention to an important concept. Each of these prophets and messengers came at a different time in the history of mankind. Each of their nations were being impious in a different way. Each of them called to piety in a distinct realm of human behavior and interaction, and they all called for piety in all aspects of their lives.

We see that Prophet Moses called his people to be pious when it came to government. Noah called his people to be pious and shed their arrogance in their worship. Salih called his people to be pious and not to obey the deviants. Hud called his people to be pious in their pursuits of worldly wealth and pleasures. Shu'ayb called his people to be pious when it came to trade and earning a livelihood.

Piety is a concept that should be present in all aspects of our lives. We cannot implement it in one facet of our dealings, but not apply it elsewhere. That would contradict the concept of piety, which applies to all our actions, behaviors, and habits. To be pious is to avoid falling into sin and disobedience of God, no matter where and no matter which aspect of our lives is involved.

Third, we must realize that piety is the true standard of comparison between mankind. At times, we may compare ourselves to others and judge others based on some standards that we have in our minds. These standards may be valuable norms, such as the different virtues, or they may be false standards that people have created amongst themselves.

There are some people who set wealth, social status, or political influence as the standard by which they categorize people. Others may look at an individual's family, bloodline, and ethnicity.

All these are false standards, as they are fleeting measures placed and valued by mankind. On the other hand, the Divine Legislator set a standard for us to live by. God says in the Holy Quran:

يَا أَيُّهَا النَّاسُ إِنَّا خَلَقْنَاكُم مِّن ذَكَرٍ وَأُنثَىٰ وَجَعَلْنَاكُمْ شُعُوبًا وَقَبَائِلَ لِتَعَارَفُوا ۚ إِنَّ أَكْرَمَكُمْ عِندَ اللَّهِ أَتْقَاكُمْ ۚ إِنَّ اللَّهَ عَلِيمٌ خَبِيرٌ

> O mankind! Indeed, We created you from a male and a female, and made you nations and tribes that you may identify yourselves with one another. Indeed, the noblest of you in the sight of God is the most pious among you. Indeed God is all-knowing, all-aware.[7]

Piety is doubtlessly the only true standard to be sought. It is the only one set by God, rather than by His creatures. Even the virtues – like knowledge and humility – are false standards if they are applied in anything but faithful devotion to God Almighty. Indeed, no virtue can deliver true happiness to an individual if it is not coupled with piety.

Piety is the trait that we must hold dear to our hearts. We must understand that it is the true standard by which we are all judged. In piety lies true honor and wealth. As Imam al-Sadiq (a) said:

---

[7] The Holy Quran, 49:13.

> ما نقل الله عز وجل عبدا من ذل المعاصي إلى عز التقوى إلا أغناه من غير مال، وأعزه من غير عشيرة، وآنسه من غير بشر

> *God Almighty has never taken a servant out of the shame of sin and into the honor of piety, except that He enriched him without need for wealth, honored him without need for a tribe, and gave him comfort without need for mankind.*[8]

We see that God rejected the idea that there may be a multitude of standards by which we are judged when He placed piety as the sole standard. In fact, if we look at all other possible standards – bloodline, wealth, morals, knowledge – they are worldly standards that either end with the death of the individual, or continue in this fleeting world shortly thereafter. Yet, all of these possible standards become eternal and everlasting if they are coupled with the true standard of piety in devotion to God.

How to Attain Piety

Many of us experience great difficulty in achieving piety through refraining from our natural instincts and desires. Indeed, this is by no means an easy task. However, God did not create any individual without endowing him with the ability and the means to obey His commands and attain His pleasure.

> لَا يُكَلِّفُ اللَّهُ نَفْسًا إِلَّا وُسْعَهَا لَهَا مَا كَسَبَتْ وَعَلَيْهَا مَا اكْتَسَبَتْ

---

[8] Al-Majlisi, Bihar al-Anwar, 67:282.

God does not task any soul beyond its capacity. Whatever [good] it earns is to its own benefit, and whatever [evil] it incurs is to its own harm.[9]

Despite having the ability to attain piety and overcome our desires, many still find it to be a difficult task. Why? Many of us do not put the time and energy needed into finding the means needed to attain it. God, in his boundless mercy, provided us with everything we needed and guided us to it through His Holy Book and appointed Immaculate guides. Through looking at the verses of the Holy Quran and the noble traditions, we can list the following means to attain piety:

Knowledge and Understanding

An individual must first seek to know God before he can attain piety. The more we know about God, the more we grow in awe of Him and fear of His punishment. This in turn leads us to piety in devoting ourselves to Him. That is why God says,

إِنَّمَا يَخْشَى اللَّهَ مِنْ عِبَادِهِ الْعُلَمَاءُ

Only those of God's servants having knowledge fear Him.[10]

An individual should also know what pleases God and what does not, and what He wants and abhors. That way, we can live in accordance with what He has commanded and refrain from what He forbade. Piety cannot be attained without knowledge.

---

[9] The Holy Quran, 2:286.
[10] The Holy Quran, 35:28.

We must learn the rules that God has legislated, in order to comply with His commands and devote ourselves in piety to Him.

We must also realize that there is a relationship between knowledge and behavior, just as there is a relationship between knowledge and piety. The more knowledge a person gains, the more pious he will become. At the same time, the more pious an individual becomes, the more knowledge he will gain. God says,

$$وَاتَّقُوا اللَّهَ وَيُعَلِّمُكُمُ اللَّهُ وَاللَّهُ بِكُلِّ شَيْءٍ عَلِيمٌ$$

Be wary of God and God will teach you, and God has knowledge of all things.[11]

We see a similar relationship between knowledge and behavior. Our Holy Prophet (s) tells us that the more we act in obedience of God, the more He will increase us in knowledge. The Holy Prophet (s) said,

$$من عمل بما علم ورثه الله علم ما لم يعلم$$

Whoever acts in accordance with what he knows, God will grant him knowledge of what he does not know.[12]

From this, we can clearly see the relationship between piety and our behavior. It is those actions that are undertaken piously that grant the actor greater knowledge. It is those actions that are undertaken piously that are deemed worthy by God. That is why Imam Ali (a) would say:

---

[11] The Holy Quran, 2:282.

[12] Al-Majlisi, *Bihar al-Anwar*, 40:128.

لا يقل عمل مع تقوى وكيف يقل ما يتقبل

An act conducted in piety cannot be undervalued. How can one undervalue an act that is accepted [by God]?[13]

Indeed, the Holy Prophet (s) described the relationship between behavior, knowledge, and piety when he said,

إن تمام التقوى أن تتعلم ما جهلت وأن تعمل بما علمت

The pinnacle of piety is to learn what you do not know and to act by what you do know.[14]

Worship

Worship plays a large role in our ability to attain piety. Attaining piety is the ultimate goal of worship. An individual cannot reach their goal of excellence except through piety. Piety is reached only through worship and good deeds. The Holy Quran has many verses that address this concept. For example, God says in one verse,

أَيُّهَا النَّاسُ اعْبُدُوا رَبَّكُمُ الَّذِي خَلَقَكُمْ وَالَّذِينَ مِن قَبْلِكُمْ لَعَلَّكُمْ تَتَّقُونَ

O mankind! Worship your Lord, who created you and those who were before you, so that you may be pious.[15]

We were commanded to worship, because that is the route towards a greater goal – the goal of attaining excellence through piety. Worship prepares us to reach that goal. Some verses even

---

[13] Al-Kulayni, *al-Kafi*, 2:75.//
[14] Al-Rayshahri, *Mizan al-Hikma*, 4:3638.//
[15] The Holy Quran, 2:21.

PIETY

address specific acts of worship and how they help in building piety. God says in one verse:

$$\text{يَا أَيُّهَا الَّذِينَ آمَنُوا كُتِبَ عَلَيْكُمُ الصِّيَامُ كَمَا كُتِبَ عَلَى الَّذِينَ مِن قَبْلِكُمْ لَعَلَّكُمْ تَتَّقُونَ}$$

O you who have faith! Prescribed for you is fasting as it was prescribed for those who were before you, so that you may be pious.[16]

God also says:

$$\text{لَيْسَ الْبِرَّ أَن تُوَلُّوا وُجُوهَكُمْ قِبَلَ الْمَشْرِقِ وَالْمَغْرِبِ وَلَٰكِنَّ الْبِرَّ مَنْ آمَنَ بِاللَّهِ وَالْيَوْمِ الْآخِرِ وَالْمَلَائِكَةِ وَالْكِتَابِ وَالنَّبِيِّينَ وَآتَى الْمَالَ عَلَىٰ حُبِّهِ ذَوِي الْقُرْبَىٰ وَالْيَتَامَىٰ وَالْمَسَاكِينَ وَابْنَ السَّبِيلِ وَالسَّائِلِينَ وَفِي الرِّقَابِ وَأَقَامَ الصَّلَاةَ وَآتَى الزَّكَاةَ وَالْمُوفُونَ بِعَهْدِهِمْ إِذَا عَاهَدُوا ۖ وَالصَّابِرِينَ فِي الْبَأْسَاءِ وَالضَّرَّاءِ وَحِينَ الْبَأْسِ ۗ أُولَٰئِكَ الَّذِينَ صَدَقُوا ۖ وَأُولَٰئِكَ هُمُ الْمُتَّقُونَ}$$

Piety is not to turn your faces to the east or the west; rather, piety is [personified by] those who have faith in God and the Last Day, the angels, the Book, and the prophets, and who give their wealth, for the love of Him, to relatives, orphans, the needy, the traveller and the beggar, and for [the freeing of] the slaves, and maintain the prayer and give the zakat, and those who fulfill their covenants, when they pledge themselves, and those who

---

[16] The Holy Quran, 2:183.

113

are patient in stress and distress, and in the heat of battle. They are the ones who are true [to their covenant], and it is they who are the pious.[17]

We see that the pious are foremost in undertaking these righteous acts, while at the same time it is these acts that build piety for an individual. As we read in the Holy Quran:

اتْلُ مَا أُوحِيَ إِلَيْكَ مِنَ الْكِتَابِ وَأَقِمِ الصَّلَاةَ ۖ إِنَّ الصَّلَاةَ تَنْهَىٰ عَنِ الْفَحْشَاءِ وَالْمُنكَرِ ۗ وَلَذِكْرُ اللَّهِ أَكْبَرُ ۗ وَاللَّهُ يَعْلَمُ مَا تَصْنَعُونَ

Recite what has been revealed to you of the Book, and maintain the prayer. Indeed, the prayer restrains from indecent and wrongful conduct, and the remembrance of God is surely greater. And God knows whichever [deeds] you do.[18]

A person who wishes to attain the central goal of worship – who wishes to attain piety – must dedicate their time and attention to worship. The more an individual engages in service to God, reflecting on their worships, and maintaining their proper etiquettes, the closer they are to attaining piety. Piety will be their safeguard against all temptation and the key to their happiness in this world and the next.

Austerity

This world and the next are like opposite directions. If one seeks one of the two, the other will doubtlessly be neglected. Whoever

---

[17] The Holy Quran, 2:177.
[18] The Holy Quran, 29:45.

seeks this world will fall short in preparing for the hereafter. Whoever seeks the afterlife will live an austere life in this world and dedicate their efforts to the hereafter.

When we look at the narrations of the Holy Household (a), we find that they always emphasize that whoever seeks this world will not share in the bounties of the hereafter. On the other hand, whoever seeks the hereafter will share in the best of the blessings of this world. The Commander of the Faithful (a) said:

وَاعْلَمُوا عِبَادَ اللهِ، أَنَّ الْمُتَّقِينَ ذَهَبُوا بِعَاجِلِ الدُّنْيَا وَآجِلِ الْآخِرَةِ، فَشَارَكُوا أَهْلَ الدُّنْيَا فِي دُنْيَاهُمْ، وَلَمْ يُشَارِكْهُم أَهْلُ الدُّنْيَا فِي آخِرَتِهِمْ

Know, O' servants of God, that the God-fearing have shared the joys of this transient world as well as the next coming world, for they shared with the people of this world in their worldly matters while their people did not share with them in the matters of the next world.[19]

An individual who sees and seeks only the bounties of this transient world will dedicate all of their efforts and time to it. This is a state of mind that is irreconcilable to the state of piety that we are trying to achieve. Piety requires an individual to constantly be aware of God's commands and seek as much of His pleasure as they can, while avoiding anything that would displease Him. The divergence between this and the state of mind of the worldly is quite clear. Moreover, the narrations of our Immaculate

---

[19] Al-Radi, *Nahj al-Balagha*, 3:27, Letter 27.

Imams (a) emphasize for us that these two approaches are irreconcilable. Imam Ali (a) says,

حرام على كل قلب متوله بالدنيا أن تسكنه التقوى

> It has been forbidden for piety to reside in any heart that is infatuated with this transient world.[20]

Indeed, a pious individual lives austerely in his life. He does not seek the pleasures of this world as if it was his end goal. Imam Ali (a), in a famous sermon about the characteristics of the pious, mentioned this trait. He said:

أَرَادَتْهُمُ الدُّنْيَا وَلَمْ يُرِيدُوهَا، وَأَسَرَتْهُمْ فَفَدَوْا أَنْفُسَهُمْ مِنْهَا

> The world aimed at them, but they did not aim at it. It captured them, but they freed themselves from it by a ransom.[21]

The Holy Prophet (s) as a Role Model

The best path to attaining piety comes through following the example of the Holy Prophet (s). This is because of two specific traits granted to our beloved Prophet (s).

First, our Holy Prophet Muhammad (s) is the only means to God. The religion which our beloved Prophet (s) delivered to us is the one that God made as a route to Him. Working in accordance with its teachings is the true path to God. The Holy Quran is clear in stating that the path to God is one, and that path is the

---

[20] Al-Wasiti, 'Oyoun al-Hikam, 233.
[21] Al-Radi, *Nahj al-Balagha*, 2:161, Sermon 193.

straight path drawn by the Almighty Himself. God says in the holy verse:

$$\text{وَأَنَّ هَٰذَا صِرَاطِي مُسْتَقِيمًا فَاتَّبِعُوهُ ۖ وَلَا تَتَّبِعُوا السُّبُلَ فَتَفَرَّقَ بِكُمْ عَن سَبِيلِهِ ۚ ذَٰلِكُمْ وَصَّاكُم بِهِ لَعَلَّكُمْ تَتَّقُونَ}$$

This indeed is my straight path, so follow it, and do not follow [other] ways, for they will separate you from His way. This is what He enjoins upon you so that you may be pious.[22]

Thus, the path to God is the one drawn for us by God, who sent us Prophet Muhammad (s) as a guide on that path. That path is a path of piety, as God says in the foregoing verse, "This indeed is my straight path, so follow it… so that you may be pious."

Second, following the Holy Prophet (s) as a role model is our prime means of manifesting our love for God. This is something that our scholars have pointed out to us in their exegesis of the Holy Quran. To understand the point, we must first discuss a couple of premises.

The best way to achieve piety is through loving God. When an individual worships God with true devotion and comes to know more and more of Him, this generates a true love for Him within the individual's heart. Indeed, our hearts are automatically drawn to God – the source of all majesty and beauty. The more our knowledge of Him increases, the more we grow in love, until He becomes our one true love. When our heart melts completely

---

[22] The Holy Quran, 6:153.

into Him, we will see nothing in this world but Him, as everything is a sign to Him.

However, all of this is speaking of our love for God. But what about His love for us? There is no other way to gain more and more of His divine love than following the path of the Holy Prophet (s). God says in the Holy Book:

قُلْ إِن كُنتُمْ تُحِبُّونَ اللَّهَ فَاتَّبِعُونِي يُحْبِبْكُمُ اللَّهُ وَيَغْفِرْ لَكُمْ ذُنُوبَكُمْ ۗ وَاللَّهُ غَفُورٌ رَّحِيمٌ

> *Say [O' Prophet Muhammad (s)], 'If you love God, then follow me; God will love you and forgive you your sins, and God is all-forgiving, all-merciful.'*[23]

The Holy Prophet (s) in turn showed us the path towards God Almighty – the path of true and devoted monotheistic belief. As we read in the Holy Quran:

قُلْ هَٰذِهِ سَبِيلِي أَدْعُو إِلَى اللَّهِ ۚ عَلَىٰ بَصِيرَةٍ أَنَا وَمَنِ اتَّبَعَنِي ۖ وَسُبْحَانَ اللَّهِ وَمَا أَنَا مِنَ الْمُشْرِكِينَ

> *Say, 'This is my way. I summon to God with insight – I and he who follows me. Immaculate is God, and I am not one of the polytheists.'*[24]

Of course, the only true representation of this path is found in the teachings of the Holy Prophet (s) – his sayings, morals, and conduct. Following the path of the Holy Prophet (s) necessitates

---

[23] The Holy Quran, 3:31.
[24] The Holy Quran, 12:108.

that we follow his true successors, who God chose for him – namely the Immaculate Imams from his Holy Household (a).

Thus, God is telling us in these blessed verses that if you wish to devote yourself to love for Him and service of Him, then follow this path that He has given you. Follow this religion of love that takes you through the straight path of devotion and submission. Follow the Holy Prophet (s) who is the guide for us on our path towards the Almighty. If you do all this, then you will prepare yourself to receive the greatest of gifts – the gift of divine love.

Piety is ultimately our path towards attaining that love. It clears the heart of anything but Him and draws us closer and closer towards following His path and the path of His chosen servants.

These are a few methods for attaining piety – a state that drives the individual towards excellence, perfection, and the pleasure of God Almighty. And as God promises us in the Holy Quran:

إِنَّ الْمُتَّقِينَ فِي جَنَّاتٍ وَنَهَرٍ ﴿٥٤﴾ فِي مَقْعَدِ صِدْقٍ عِندَ مَلِيكٍ مُّقْتَدِرٍ ﴿٥٥﴾

Indeed the pious will be amid gardens and streams, in the abode of truthfulness with an omnipotent King.[25]

---

[25] The Holy Quran, 54:54-55.

Rectitude

In the Name of God, the Most Beneficent, the Most Merciful

فَٱسْتَقِمْ كَمَا أُمِرْتَ وَمَن تَابَ مَعَكَ وَلَا تَطْغَوْا ۚ إِنَّهُ بِمَا تَعْمَلُونَ بَصِيرٌ

So be upright, just as you have been commanded – [you] and whoever has turned [to God] with you – and do not overstep the bounds. Indeed, He watches what you do.[1]

The above verse speaks of a particularly important issue when it comes to an individual's worship, as well as attaining piety and the advanced levels of belief and certainty. Ultimately, the verse addresses an issue at the heart of seeking the pleasure of God.

At first glance, this short verse from Surat Hud might seem simple and straightforward. However, we see the true significance of the verse when we see how our Holy Prophet (s) reacted to its revelation. The narrations tell us of the deep personal reaction Prophet Muhammad (s) had to the verse when it was revealed and thereafter. In the books of exegesis, our scholars narrate that Ibn Abbas said:

> *There was no verse revealed to the Messenger of God that took a heavier toll on him than this one. That is*

---

[1] The Holy Quran, 11:112.

why he said, when his companions commented that his hair turned grey too soon,

شيبتني هود والواقعة

'I've been turned grey by [the Quranic chapters of] Hud and al-Waqi'a.'[2]

How can we explain this reaction to the verse from the greatest of God's creations? Our Holy Prophet (s) was not only Immaculate and free of any sin or defect, but was also reassured in the Holy Quran that he was of a flawless nature. God told Prophet Muhammad (s),

إِنَّا فَتَحْنَا لَكَ فَتْحًا مُبِينًا ﴿١﴾ لِيَغْفِرَ لَكَ اللَّهُ مَا تَقَدَّمَ مِن ذَنبِكَ وَمَا تَأَخَّرَ وَيُتِمَّ نِعْمَتَهُ عَلَيْكَ وَيَهْدِيَكَ صِرَاطًا مُّسْتَقِيمًا ﴿٢﴾

Indeed, We have inaugurated for you a clear victory, that God may forgive you what is past of your sin and what is to come, and that He may perfect His blessing upon you and guide you on a straight path.[3]

Why would the Holy Prophet (s) have such a reaction to a verse that commands us to be upright – so much so, that it is narrated that he was not seen laughing after the revelation of this verse? If this is the state of the Holy Prophet (s), how should we be, as his followers, who hope to be among those mentioned in the verse? We should know that the blessed verses do not only apply

---

[2] Al-Tabrasi, *Majma' al-Bayan*, 5:342.
[3] The Holy Quran, 48:1-2.

to those they speak directly to, but to anyone who receives the message across the span of time and geography.

We must take a serious look at this divine command and attempt to understand and apply it. To better understand the blessed verse, we will discuss several issues.

What is Rectitude?

Having rectitude – or being upright – is "the quality or state of being straight."[4] In the translation of the verse, it is used as a substitute for *istiqama* – a word of similar meaning. Linguistically speaking, an individual is upright or has rectitude if he is standing up straight, as opposed to sitting, sleeping, lounging, or any other physical state. It connotes being fully alert, ready, and able to manoeuver the body.

The quality of being upright means that the individual lives and acts in a way that is free from any vice or shortcoming. The Holy Prophet (s) and the believers are commanded to be steadfast in their religion and give it its due. It is a command to fulfill all obligations in the best way possible and avoid everything that God forbade. The command to be upright is a command to excel in following God's commands. Indeed, this is an issue of great significance.

Let us reflect on how naïve we are when we think that we are 'religious' individuals who have fulfilled the commands of God.

---

[4] *Merriam-Webster, s.v.* "Rectitude."

Should we ponder, we will find that our shortcomings are countless. Our past is filled with faults and failures. If the Holy Prophet (s) was not seen laughing after he was commanded to be upright, then the rest of us should not cease weeping for falling short of God's command. We must realize that everything God grants us is not due to us deserving any of it. It is only out of his boundless mercy and generosity that He continues to give and sustain.

Achieving Rectitude

Achieving this level of rectitude requires us to follow God Almighty's prescriptions and commands so that we can reach the level of excellence that He wants of us. We can elucidate five general tools by which we can achieve this state:

Knowledge

There is little doubt that knowledge plays a significant role in this process, especially when it comes to knowledge of God's divine commands. But is knowledge limited to theoretical information and frameworks, or is it something greater?

The type of knowledge we seek in this regard is the type described in the narrations of our Imams (a) as

نور يقذفه الله في قلب من يشاء

> *A light planted by God in the heart of whomever He wishes.*[5]

---

[5] Al-'Amili, *Munyat al-Mureed*, 167.

When we usually speak of knowledge, we are referring to the mental images that we gain from observation and study. But this alone does not allow us to achieve true knowledge and understanding. Rather, the type of knowledge that we must seek to attain rectitude is the knowledge which God blesses his servants with, because of their servitude to Him. The more devoted an individual is to the service and worship of God, the more God will bless them with knowledge and understanding.

The knowledge we seek comes as a result of worship and servitude. In turn, this knowledge is sought to achieve greater levels of servitude and devotion to God. This process is explained by Imam al-Sadiq (a) in a long narration, part of which reads:

لَيْسَ العِلْمُ بِالتَّعَلُّمِ ، إِنَّمَا هُوَ نُورٌ يَقَعُ فِي قَلْبِ مَنْ يُرِيدُ اللَّهُ تَبَارَكَ وتَعَالى أَنْ يَهْدِيَهُ ، فَإِنْ أَرَدْتَ العِلْمَ فَاطْلُبْ أَوَّلاً فِي نَفْسِكَ حَقِيقَةَ العُبُودِيَّةِ ، وَاطْلُبِ العِلْمَ بِاسْتِعْمَالِهِ ، وَاسْتَفْهِمِ اللَّهَ يُفْهِمْكَ

Knowledge does not come through excessive study. Rather, it is a light that shines into the heart of whomever God wishes to guide. If you seek knowledge, then first seek in yourself true servitude [of God]. Seek knowledge by using it [in the service of God]. Ask God and He will grant you understanding.[6]

An individual whose knowledge does not give them foresight and an understanding of the world and the divine, does not have true knowledge, no matter how much information he retains.

---

[6] Al-'Amili, *Munyat al-Mureed*, 149.

True knowledge is that light which God implants in the heart of whomever He wishes. It is a lamp that lights for us the path of excellence and is thus a means to attain rectitude. It is the light that opens the foresight and allows us to know what pleases and what displeases God.

Patience

Patience is another characteristic that is needed to attain rectitude. After all, the path to rectitude is not easy. God says in the Holy Quran:

يَا أَيُّهَا الَّذِينَ آمَنُوا لَا تَخُونُوا اللَّهَ وَالرَّسُولَ وَتَخُونُوا أَمَانَاتِكُمْ وَأَنْتُمْ تَعْلَمُونَ

O you who have faith! Do not betray God and the Apostle, and do not betray your trusts knowingly.[7]

The Holy Prophet (s) is also narrated to have said,

حفت الجنة بالمكاره وحفت النار بالشهوات

[The path to] Paradise is filled with troubles and [the path to] Hellfire is filled with [satisfaction of] desires.[8]

The path to God is filled with trials and tribulations that distinguish the good from the bad and test the devotion of God's believing servants. It is only with patience that an individual can advance further down the road towards God's pleasure.

Some of us may think that it is sufficient to be patient in fulfilling some of God's commands, such as having patience in prayer,

---

[7] The Holy Quran, 8:27.
[8] Al-Radi, *al-Majazat al-Nabawiyya*, 387.

fasting, and almsgiving. These actions might seem hard to some, but they are easy for others. Some of us have even established these actions as habits that we undertake without much thought to the time or effort that they require.

While all this is well and good, patience must encompass much more. There are many who may find patience in undertaking these worships, but cannot find the patience in the face of social norms, thus falling into the same vices as those of peers and family. Others may not have the patience to connect with their kin or keep good relations with their neighbors.

We must look up to our Holy Prophet (s) and our Immaculate Imams (a) and learn from them. We must look at Imam al-Sajjad (a), for example, and his patience in the aftermath of the tragedy of Karbala. It is narrated that during the uprising that took place in the city of Medina after the tragedy of Karbala, the Umayyads began to search for a safe refuge for their women so that no one would transgress against them. No one in the city accepted to take them, except for our Imam al-Sajjad (a). This is even though these were people who had played a significant role in the massacre of his father, Imam Hussein (a), his family, and his companions. Imam al-Sajjad (a) had the patience to take in the families of those who massacred his family so that he could showcase for us the true ideals of the message of Islam. The Imam would provide so much for his guests that one of the Umayyad women would say that she did not see the same respect and care in her own home. This is true patience that allows an individual to overcome any vendetta to apply the sublime ideals and teachings of our faith.

Patience is a tool by which we can advance along the path towards God and attain greater levels of service and rectitude.

Trust in God

There are many hardships and difficulties we face in our lives that may push us away from the path of rectitude. These hardships shake an individual's confidence in their ability to continue this path. Therefore, placing our trust in God is important. We must always feel the presence of this force which continues to surround us and sustain us in our lives, and which supports us on our path of righteousness and rectitude. This is a promise made to us by God in the Holy Quran when He says,

$$\text{وَمَن يَتَوَكَّلْ عَلَى اللَّهِ فَهُوَ حَسْبُهُ}$$

And whoever puts his trust in God, He will suffice him.[9]

God promises us that He will provide for us if we rely on Him and put our trust in Him. We also see in the words of our Immaculate Imams (a) numerous warnings about relying on ourselves and being heedless of the support God provides. We are taught to recite in some supplications,

$$\text{رب لا تكلني الى نفسي طرفة عين أبدا}$$

---

[9] The Holy Quran, 65:3.

> *My Lord, do not ever leave me to [rely on] myself [alone] – not even for a twinkling of an eye.*[10]

This is because an individual who relies solely and completely on their own abilities will surely veer astray from the path of guidance and rectitude. Indeed, rectitude cannot be attained without reliance on God, as He is the only force that can sustain and support an individual on this path.

Austerity

We spoke about austerity in some detail in a previous chapter. Here, we want to point out the important role it plays in helping an individual to attain and maintain rectitude on the path towards God. The root cause of many people's failures and shortcomings is an undue attachment to this world. As Imam al-Sadiq (a) said,

$$\text{حب الدنيا رأس كل خطيئة}$$

> *Love of this world is at the helm of every misdeed.*[11]

An individual who grows too fond of this world will not be able to continue the arduous path of spiritual advancement. When we realize that this material world is transient and fleeting, and that the true abode is in the eternal hereafter, we will find it much easier to persevere on the path of rectitude. An austere individual who does not seek anything but God's endless bounties and

---

[10] Al-Kulayni, *al-Kafi*, 2:581.
[11] Al-Sadouq, *al-Khisal*, 25.

strives for nothing but God's eternal pleasure will surely be able to achieve rectitude on his path towards the Almighty.

Watchfulness

Sometimes an individual may think that they are continuing on their path towards God, but they are actually heedless of the fact that they have been veering astray and falling into greater failures and shortcomings. This can be the result of accumulated misconceptions and misunderstandings in their mind. They may take many actions and stances, thinking that they will bring them closer to God, but they are in fact only distancing them further and further. Such an individual is an example of the blessed verse,

$$\text{الَّذِينَ ضَلَّ سَعْيُهُمْ فِي الْحَيَاةِ الدُّنْيَا وَهُمْ يَحْسَبُونَ أَنَّهُمْ يُحْسِنُونَ صُنْعًا}$$

Those whose efforts are misguided in the life of the world, while they suppose they are doing good.[12]

Therefore, we must always be watchful of ourselves and have a daily accounting with ourselves to make sure we are not misguiding ourselves so. An upright individual will always weigh their actions and judge themself – always putting themself in the position of the accused wrongdoer – to make sure that they have not veered astray. If we learn how to hold ourselves accountable and be watchful of our actions, habits, and behaviors, we will be much less susceptible to veering off the straight path.

---

[12] The Holy Quran, 18:104.

Perseverance in Self Struggle

In the Name of God, the Most Beneficent, the Most Merciful

يَا أَيُّهَا الَّذِينَ آمَنُوا اصْبِرُوا وَصَابِرُوا وَرَابِطُوا وَاتَّقُوا اللَّهَ لَعَلَّكُمْ تُفْلِحُونَ

O you who have faith! Be patient, stand firm, and persevere, and be wary of God so that you may be felicitous.[1]

The struggle between virtue and vice has been ongoing and will continue so long as humanity inhabits this Earth. Growing closer to God and garnering his pleasure only comes through patience, sacrifice, and perseverance. At the outset of humanity's existence, Satan refused to bow to Adam as he was commanded, then promised God that he would attempt to draw mankind towards deviance and corruption. This struggle continues, despite the fact that God and his servants will inevitably be victorious. God says in the Holy Quran:

إِنَّ الَّذِينَ يُحَادُّونَ اللَّهَ وَرَسُولَهُ أُولَٰئِكَ فِي الْأَذَلِّينَ ﴿٢٠﴾ كَتَبَ اللَّهُ لَأَغْلِبَنَّ أَنَا وَرُسُلِي ۚ إِنَّ اللَّهَ قَوِيٌّ عَزِيزٌ ﴿٢١﴾

Indeed, those who oppose God and His Apostle – they will be among the most abased. God has ordained: 'I

---

[1] The Holy Quran, 3:196-200.

shall surely prevail, I and My apostles.' Indeed God is all-strong, all-mighty.[2]

God willed that everything flows through the course and system of cause and effect. He willed that there be a divine test in which His servants are subjected to trials and tribulations, which they must overcome to garner His pleasure. Within this system, vice might overcome and come to reign, albeit for a limited time in the grand scheme of things. The reason for vice's victory stems from human choices, who were created with moral agency and given a choice between virtue and vice.

If we study this divine equation, we see that just as vice might overcome, due to humanity's wrong choices, so will virtue overcome when humanity makes the right choices. A victory for virtue comes when the believers of God devote themselves to Him and obey His commands, seeking His pleasure in all things. It is our sincerity in God's service and devotion to seeking His pleasure that will allow virtue to reign in ourselves, our homes, and our communities.

Therefore, self-struggle is given great importance in Islamic discourse – so much so that the Holy Prophet (s) would call it the "greater struggle." So long as vice continues to exist within us and our communities, we must continue to persevere in this struggle and attempt to overcome vice in all its forms.

---

[2] The Holy Quran, 58:20-21.

What is Perseverance?

Perseverance is a word often used in Islamic discourse, including in the Holy Quran and the noble traditions. It refers to the need for believers to be always ready for the continuous face-off with Satan and the forces of vice. We see this meaning in many of the traditions. For example, the Holy Prophet (s) referred to this idea in his last advice to his companion, Abu Thar. The Holy Prophet (s) said:

يا أبا ذر : إن الله يعطيك ـ ما دمت جالساً في المسجد ـ بكل نَفَس تنفست فيه درجة في الجنة وتصلي عليك الملائكة . ويُكتب لك بكل نفس تنفست فيه عشر حسنات ، ويمحى عنك عشر سيئات

O' Abu Thar! For every breath that you take, as long as you sit in the mosque, God will give you a level in Paradise, along with praise from the angels. For each breath you take, He will write for you ten good deeds and erase ten misdeeds.

يا أبا ذر : أتعلم في أي شيء أُنزلت هذه الآية : إصبروا وصابروا ورَبِطوا واتقوا الله لعلكم تفلحون؟ في ... كثرة (الإختلاف الى المساجد) انتظار الصلاة بعد الصلاة ، فذلكم الرباط.

O' Abu Thar, do you know why this verse was revealed – 'Be patient, stand firm, and persevere, and be wary of God so that you may be felicitous'? [It was revealed in regards to] continuous attendance in the mosques and waiting for prayer after completing an earlier one. That is perseverance.

يا أبا ذر : كلّ جلوس في المسجد لغو إلا ثلاثة ، قراءة مُصلّ ، أو ذكر
الله ، أو سائل عن علم .

> *O' Abu Thar, staying in a mosque is frivolous if it is not in one of the following three: the reading of prayers, remembrance of God, or seeking knowledge.*[3]

This is a description of perseverance as a state of readiness in the face of the greater struggle against humanity's two great enemies – Satan and our base desires. We also see that some noble traditions describe the scholars as perseverant, because they are the ones who stand at the front lines of our struggle against Satan and against the forces of deviance and misguidance. The scholars' duty requires them to stand against any idea that aims to spread deviance, misguidance, and disbelief in this world. It is narrated that Imam al-Sadiq (a) said:

علماء شيعتنا مرابطون في الثغر الذي يلي إبليس وعفاريته ، يمنعوهم عن الخروج على ضعفاء شيعتنا وعن أن يتسلط عليهم إبليس وشيعته والنواصب . ألا فمن انتصب لذلك من شيعتنا كان أفضل ممن جاهد الروم والترك والخزر ألف ألف مرة لأنه يدفع عن أديان محبينا وذلك يدفع عن أبدانهم

> *The scholars amongst our Shia are perseverant [at the battlefront with] Satan and his ifrits. They fend off their attacks against the weak amongst our Shia. They safe-*

---

[3] Al-'Amili, *Wasa'el al-Shia*, 3:86.

guard [the weak amongst our Shia] from being controlled by Satan, his followers, and the Nawasib.[4] *Surely, whoever of our Shia dedicates himself to this, he will be better [rewarded] than those who fight against the Romans, Turks, and the Khazars a thousand thousand fold. That is because they defend the faith of our devotees, while the others defend their lives.*[5]

The scholars are the guardians of the faith who were tasked with preserving its teachings against any misconceptions, fabrications, and misguided ideas. This is a crucial role in our collective struggle on the path towards eternal happiness.

Perseverance in the Great Struggle

Our scholars have given perseverance great attention in their books of ethics. Perseverance in the great struggle against deviance is a crucial factor in our ability to garner God's pleasure. The scholars of ethics have studied the subject in detail and outlined its stages and levels, all of which we will address briefly in this chapter.

Perseverance is no easy task, and we must muster all our strength and gather all of our efforts to gain and maintain such a status. The Holy Quran emphasizes that before we persevere, we must

---

[4] *Nasibi* – plural, *Nawasib* – is a term to refer to those who outwardly show hatred towards the Holy Prophet (s), his Holy Household (a), and their followers.

[5] Al-Tabrasi, *al-Ihtijaj*, 1:8.

"be patient and stand firm." Patience plays a key role in our ability to gain eternal bliss and is an important aspect of faith. The Commander of the Faithful (a) said:

عَلَيْكُمْ بِالصَّبْرِ فَإِنَّ الصَّبْرَ مِنَ الْإِيمَانِ كَالرَّأْسِ مِنَ الْجَسَدِ وَ لَا خَيْرَ فِي جَسَدٍ لَا رَأْسَ مَعَهُ وَ لَا فِي إِيمَانٍ لَا صَبْرَ مَعَهُ.

> *Practice patience! Surely, patience is to belief as the head is to the body. Just as there is no good in a body without a head, there is no good in belief without patience.*[6]

We must also "stand firm" – practicing patience and rectitude in the face of this world's many trials. This struggle is continuous and ongoing and there is no time for rest and no end to the struggle.

Successfully reaching the desired goal – the pleasure of God and eternal happiness – can only come through perseverance, patience, and standing firm in the great struggle against temptation and desires.

STAGES OF PERSEVERANCE

The scholars of ethics divided perseverance in the great struggle into four stages. By implementing these four stages, an individual can train himself to persevere and gain the highest levels of eternal happiness in the hereafter. The four stages are as follows:

---

[6] Al-Radi, *Nahj al-Balagha*, 4:18, Saying 82.

Self-Stipulation

The first stage comes with making the decision and stipulating to ourselves that we will not engage in anything that goes against God's commands. Because we are all at divergent levels of obedience and disobedience, individual stipulations will vary. A person who commits a particular sin needs to make the decision and commit to themself to not go back to this sin. A person who does not fulfill all of their obligations must stipulate to themself that they will start doing so. An individual who can reach the level where they do not engage in anything that is forbidden and do not forsake any of their obligations should go a step further. The stipulation for them will be that they will engage in more recommended actions and refrain from more abhorred actions. Finally, anyone who is blessed to cross this stage should stipulate to themself that they will not engage in any action unless it draws them closer to God. So, as an individual transcends in their servitude to God, the stipulation they will make to themself will be different than the stipulations of others.

Now each one of us needs to look at ourselves and determine where we are at in terms of servitude to God Almighty. Based on my level, I set a commitment to myself. When I am successful in following through with it, I can set a higher commitment and continue on my path of self-advancement.

An individual who has a problem with a certain sin should stipulate to themself that they will disengage from it for a day. Once they do that, their new stipulation will be to refrain from that sin for two days. Then a week. Then a month. A person should continue like this, improving their faults deliberately and gradually. This approach simplifies the process, especially with God's promise to support us in this path. God says,

$$\text{وَالَّذِينَ جَاهَدُوا فِينَا لَنَهْدِيَنَّهُمْ سُبُلَنَا ۚ وَإِنَّ اللَّهَ لَمَعَ الْمُحْسِنِينَ}$$

> As for those who strive in Us, We shall surely guide them in Our ways, and God is indeed with the virtuous.[7]

God also says,

$$\text{فَأَمَّا مَنْ أَعْطَىٰ وَاتَّقَىٰ ﴿٥﴾ وَصَدَّقَ بِالْحُسْنَىٰ ﴿٦﴾ فَسَنُيَسِّرُهُ لِلْيُسْرَىٰ ﴿٧﴾}$$

> As for him who gives and is pious and confirms the best promise, We will surely ease him toward facility.[8]

A person should realize that every moment of their life and every breath that they take is an irreplaceable treasure that they can use to earn greater rewards and eternal happiness. An individual who makes and acts upon this realization has surely made a great stride on their path towards God.

Time is our capital in this world. We can either invest it to gain the pleasure of God or squander it on the pleasures of this world. A person who makes the right investment will reap the returns of eternal bliss and happiness in the proximity of God Almighty.

---

[7] The Holy Quran, 29:69.
[8] The Holy Quran, 92:5-7.

A person who makes the wrong investment will find nothing but disappointment and regret. God says:

$$\text{حَتَّىٰٓ إِذَا جَآءَ أَحَدَهُمُ ٱلْمَوْتُ قَالَ رَبِّ ٱرْجِعُونِ ﴿٩٩﴾ لَعَلِّىٓ أَعْمَلُ صَٰلِحًا فِيمَا تَرَكْتُ ۚ كَلَّآ ۚ إِنَّهَا كَلِمَةٌ هُوَ قَآئِلُهَا ۖ وَمِن وَرَآئِهِم بَرْزَخٌ إِلَىٰ يَوْمِ يُبْعَثُونَ ﴿١٠٠﴾}$$

When death comes to one of them, he says, 'My Lord! Take me back, that I may act righteously in what I have left behind.' 'By no means! These are mere words that he says.' And before them is a barrier until the day they will be resurrected.[9]

Self-Watchfulness

Each of us must realize that we have an uncooperative and combative partner within ourselves. Often, it is not enough to make promises and stipulations, despite the positive effects these may have. We are often persuaded to act in accordance with our desires and temptations, despite the promises we might make. Therefore, we must be watchful of ourselves to make sure that we comply with all of the stipulations we make to ourselves.

We must live in a constant state of vigilance and awareness of how we comply with our own expectations and stipulations. Whenever we start to veer away from the path, we must be aware, so that we can remind ourselves of our stipulations and attempt to bring ourselves back.

---

[9] The Holy Quran, 23:99-100.

We must also be cognizant that when we start on this path of self-struggle, Satan will always be ready to influence us. He will make us forget and break our promises. We must always remember that although he can whisper and attempt to persuade, he has no further power over us. As we read in the Holy Quran:

$$إِنَّ كَيْدَ الشَّيْطَانِ كَانَ ضَعِيفًا ... إِنَّهُ لَيْسَ لَهُ سُلْطَانٌ عَلَى الَّذِينَ آمَنُوا وَعَلَىٰ رَبِّهِمْ يَتَوَكَّلُونَ ... إِنَّ عِبَادِي لَيْسَ لَكَ عَلَيْهِمْ سُلْطَانٌ ۚ وَكَفَىٰ بِرَبِّكَ وَكِيلًا$$

Indeed, the stratagems of Satan are always flimsy...[10] *Indeed, he does not have any authority over those who have faith and put their trust in their Lord...*[11] *[God says to Satan,] 'As for My servants, you shall have no authority over them.' And your Lord suffices as trustee.*[12]

Moreover, Satan himself acknowledges that his power is limited in tempting mankind. In one of the verses of the Holy Quran, Satan is described as saying:

$$وَمَا كَانَ لِيَ عَلَيْكُم مِّن سُلْطَانٍ إِلَّا أَن دَعَوْتُكُمْ فَاسْتَجَبْتُمْ لِي ۖ فَلَا تَلُومُونِي وَلُومُوا أَنفُسَكُم$$

---

[10] The Holy Quran, 4:76.
[11] The Holy Quran, 16:99.
[12] The Holy Quran, 17:65.

I had no authority over you, except that I called you and you responded to me. So do not blame me, but blame yourselves.[13]

An individual may go against the commitments they set for themself, perhaps due to forgetfulness, weakness, or some other reason. Each of us must be watchful of ourselves, so we can remind ourselves that God is witness to our stipulations. We must remember our promises and remember the countless blessings of God upon us. We must remember the many rights God holds over us and how we are unable to fulfill one of His rights, let alone all of them. We must remind ourselves that it is inappropriate to break our promises and stipulations when God is our witness.

Some people might think that this is too arduous a task, taking time away from an individual's obligations of study and work. But these traits, and any virtue for that matter, if exercised enough, can be turned into a habit that is implemented by the individual without much need of their conscious attention. There may be some difficulty at the beginning, but if we understand the importance of these issues and implement them continuously, they will eventually become habits. The same goes for self-watchfulness – once it becomes a habit, it can be applied continuously and with ease.

---

[13] The Holy Quran, 14:22.

Self-Assessment

To reap the fruits of self-stipulation and self-watchfulness, a person needs to advance to the next stage of self-assessment. This is the stage of assessing how many of our stipulations we are truly applying and of managing our progress in the sphere of self-advancement.

In this great struggle, our enemies – ourselves – are deceptive and conniving. We must be constantly aware of our progress on this journey, and if we are moving forward, remaining at a standstill, or regressing. This is the process of self-assessment, a process often mentioned in the narrations of the Holy Prophet (s) and his Holy Household (a). We will mention only a few of those many narrations here. The Holy Prophet (s) is narrated to have said:

لا يكون الرجل من المتقين حتى يحاسب نفسه أشد من محاسبة الشريك شريكه، فيعلم من أين مطعمه ومن أين مشربه ومن أين ملبسه أمن حل ذلك أم من حرام

> *A person is not amongst the pious unless he holds himself accountable with a more stringent accounting than what one partner may hold the other. He should know where he acquires his food, drink, and clothing, and whether they are earned lawfully or not.*[14]

---

[14] Al-Majlisi, *Bihar al-Anwar*, 74:86.

For a person to be pious – and to be perseverant and steadfast in piety – they must continuously assess themselves. This assessment allows us to avoid the traps laid for us by our own daemons and desires. Imam al-Kadhim (a) said:

ليس منا من لم يحاسب نفسه في كل يوم، فإن عمل حسنا إستزاد الله، وإن عمل سيئا استغفر الله منه وتاب اليه

> *A person who does not hold himself accountable every night is not of us. [He should look back at the actions of his days], so that if he did good he should ask God for more, and if he did ill he should seek forgiveness from God and repent to Him.* [15]

The narrations are clear in pointing out that self-assessment is an important process that allows us to rectify our error as soon as possible. A person who falls into sin, but is constantly assessing their own actions and behaviors, can assess themself, realize their shortcomings, and rectify their behaviors before it is too late. An individual who does not practice self-assessment may slowly fall into corruption and deviance, without realizing where they are heading. This is what the Holy Quran referred to the in this blessed verse:

قُلْ هَلْ نُنَبِّئُكُم بِالْأَخْسَرِينَ أَعْمَالًا ﴿١٠٣﴾ الَّذِينَ ضَلَّ سَعْيُهُمْ فِي الْحَيَاةِ الدُّنْيَا وَهُمْ يَحْسَبُونَ أَنَّهُمْ يُحْسِنُونَ صُنْعًا ﴿١٠٤﴾

> *Say, 'Shall we inform you who are the biggest losers in their works? Those whose efforts are misguided in the*

---

[15] Al-Kulayni, *al-Kafi*, 2:453.

life of the world, while they suppose they are doing good.'[16]

An individual who wants to attain eternal happiness must continuously assess themself, as that will allow them to discover and recognize their own failings and shortcomings. This allows for the person to rectify their behavior and repent, paving their path to eternal happiness. The Commander of the Faithful (a) said,

من حاسب نفسه سعد

Whoever holds himself accountable is truly felicitous.[17]

He also said:

من حاسب نفسه وقف على عيوبه وأحاط بذنوبه واستقال الذنوب وأصلح العيوب

Whoever holds himself accountable will see his flaws and realize his misdeeds. He will renounce his misdeeds and fix his flaws.[18]

Self-Chastisement

After the individual is done stipulating to themself, being watchful of themself, and thoroughly assessing themself, they will come to know full well their shortcomings in their relationship with his Lord. At this stage, the individual must deter themself from falling into the same shortcomings, by sternly chastising

---

[16] The Holy Quran, 18:103-04.

[17] Al-Nouri, *Mustadrak al-Wasa'el*, 12:154.

[18] Ibid.

themself. Each of us must set for ourselves a progressive system of penalties if we fail to meet the standards that God set for us.

At this stage, we begin to discipline ourselves. Just as a parent disciplines their child through chastisement and punishment, each one of us must treat ourselves as a disobedient child. If there is no means of discipline, we will surely commit that same mistake again. Just as a mother may be harsh and stern with her child because she loves him and wants only the best for him, we must use that same 'tough love' with ourselves. We must keep our long-term best interest in mind and discipline ourselves so that we become the best individuals we can be.

One scholar of ethics mentions the deterrent that our scholars would set for themselves in this regard. He says:

> *Some of our scholars would stipulate and promise God that they would undertake a particular action or refrain from a particular action, and make an oath to fast two years – as an example – if they fail to fulfill their promise.*[19]

The weight of such a consequence deters the individual from breaking the promise. The important thing is that this deterrent factor is not neglected. Neglecting to discipline the self will allow it to continue in its wayward behavior. Everyone should come up with a schedule of disciplinary actions that suits them and

---

[19] Al-Haydari, *al-Tarbiya al-Roohiya*, 246.

their needs. For example, a person who eats what is impermissible (*Haram*) should discipline themself by going hungry through fasting.

Of course, any disciplinary action should still fall within the realm of God's commands. God does not allow us to inflict undue harm on ourselves or to completely prohibit ourselves from what He has allowed for us. The deterrents we choose for ourselves must themselves fall within what God wants of us. Otherwise, what good is a deterrent if it is itself a sin?

Finally, we must realize that the process of perseverance will always be easier if it is approached earlier on in life. This is true for much of what we do in our lives; learning a skill or a habit earlier in life is always easier and longer lasting. The older an individual becomes, the more entrenched they become in their ways, making change harder to achieve. The process may seem difficult, but it is achievable with enough patience and persistence.

Fasting and Strengthening the Will

In the Name of God, the Most Beneficent, the Most Merciful

يَا أَيُّهَا الَّذِينَ آمَنُوا كُتِبَ عَلَيْكُمُ الصِّيَامُ كَمَا كُتِبَ عَلَى الَّذِينَ مِن قَبْلِكُمْ لَعَلَّكُمْ تَتَّقُونَ

O you who have faith! Prescribed for you is fasting, as it was prescribed for those who were before you, so that you may be Godwary.[1]

Mankind, having been granted the greatest of abilities and faculties, is the dearest creation to God. That is why God has blessed us more abundantly than any other creature. God continued to nurture and educate us through sending prophets and messengers who guided us to what is best for us. God has always held our hands in our path toward Him.

However, we did not meet God's great blessings with the proper thankfulness and appreciation. Instead, we disbelieve, oppress, and distance ourselves from Him. Surely,

---

[1] The Holy Quran, 2:183.

وَإِن تَعُدُّوا نِعْمَتَ اللَّهِ لَا تُحْصُوهَا ۗ إِنَّ الْإِنسَانَ لَظَلُومٌ كَفَّارٌ

> *If you enumerate God's blessings, you will not be able to count them. Indeed man is most unfair and ungrateful!*[2]

Many times, we can recognize our shortcomings in the face of God's abundant blessings. However, we find ourselves unable to change ourselves as we simply continue to fall deeper and deeper into sin. We realize that we are growing farther and farther from God and His straight path, but we do nothing to stop it. As God says,

بَلِ الْإِنسَانُ عَلَىٰ نَفْسِهِ بَصِيرَةٌ ﴿١٤﴾ وَلَوْ أَلْقَىٰ مَعَاذِيرَهُ ﴿١٥﴾

> *Indeed, man is a witness to himself, though he offers excuses [to justify his failings].*[3]

An individual may realize that they continue to sin in the face of God's continued sustenance and blessings, yet they offer excuses for their actions. Yet, such an individual's soul is the greatest witness against them. We live a continued internal conflict between following the guidance of God, which we know to be true, and following our whims and base desires.

The result of this conflict is decided by an aspect of our selves which we call the will. We can define this faculty as the aspect of ourselves that seeks to balance our reason and our desire. This faculty is a divine blessing, which we must strengthen and utilize so that it can support us on the straight path.

---

[2] The Holy Quran, 14:34.
[3] The Holy Quran, 75:14-15.

The Reality of Blessing

Throughout our lives, we are met with successes and failures, all of which we relate back to divine blessings. We see that whenever an individual fails in some way or commits a sin, they say that God did not bless them to do what is better. If a person succeeds, then God has blessed them so.

But are blessings an unknowable, metaphysical force? Or can they be traced back to our own actions and behaviors?

A blessing is not an unknowable force that decides the outcome of life events without relation to our actions. God does not simply give some people more than others. We cannot say one person was blessed and another was not because God wanted to give to one individual and not the other. Assuming as such would lead us to doubt God's divine justice – surely, He is sublime above any form of oppression, injustice, and unfairness. God says in the Holy Quran,

ذَٰلِكَ بِمَا قَدَّمَتْ أَيْدِيكُمْ وَأَنَّ اللَّهَ لَيْسَ بِظَلَّامٍ لِّلْعَبِيدِ

That is because of what your hands have sent ahead, and because God is not tyrannical to His servants.[4]

God also says,

مَا يُبَدَّلُ الْقَوْلُ لَدَيَّ وَمَا أَنَا بِظَلَّامٍ لِّلْعَبِيدِ

---

[4] The Holy Quran, 3:182.

> *The word [of judgement] is unalterable with Me, and I am not tyrannical to My servants.*[5]

An individual's blessings are ultimately in their own hands. Blessings are nothing but the natural outcome of an individual's actions and efforts towards certain ends. This is a reality we see around us every day. We can see that an individual who remains hesitant and does not act will not reach their desired goal. On the other hand, an individual who has the will and puts forth the effort to reach a goal will likely reach it.

Everything goes back to the individual's willpower and the effort put forth toward a goal. Whenever an individual utilizes their willpower, they will see that their goal is not out of reach and can be realized with enough effort.

Blessings can be summed up in an individual's utilization of their willpower. We see this issue being addressed in some of the narrations of the Holy Household. For example, we see that Imam Sajjad (a) would supplicate on the 27th day of the month of Rajab and say:

اللَّهُمَّ إِنِّي أَجِدُ سُبُلَ الْمَطَالِبِ إِلَيْكَ مُشْرَعَةً، وَمَنَاهِلَ الرَّجَاءِ لَدَيْكَ مُتْرَعَةً، وَأَبْوَابَ الدُّعَاءِ لِمَنْ دَعَاكَ مُفَتَّحَةً، وَالِاسْتِعَانَةَ لِمَنِ اسْتَعَانَ بِكَ مُبَاحَةً، وَأَعْلَمُ أَنَّكَ لِدَاعِيكَ بِمَوْضِعِ إِجَابَةٍ، وَلِلصَّارِخِ إِلَيْكَ بِمَرْصَدِ إِغَاثَةٍ

> *O' God, I find the paths to requesting from You wide open and the springs of hope in You quenching! I find the doors of supplication unlocked for him who implores*

---

[5] The Holy Quran, 50:29.

You, and Your aid available for those who seek You! And I know that You are in the position of response for him who beseeches You, and in the position of relief for him who resorts to You.

وَأَنَّ فِي اللَّهْفِ إِلَى جُودِكَ وَالضَّمَانِ بِعِدَتِكَ عِوَضاً مِنْ مَنْعِ الْبَاخِلِينَ وَمَنْدُوحَةً عَمَّا فِي أَيْدِي الْمُسْتَأْثِرِينَ، وَأَنَّكَ لَا تَحْتَجِبُ عَنْ خَلْقِكَ إِلاَّ أَنْ تَحْجُبَهُمُ الأَعْمَالُ دُونَكَ، وَقَدْ عَلِمْتُ أَنَّ أَفْضَلَ زَادِ الرَّاحِلِ إِلَيْكَ عَزْمُ إِرَادَةٍ يَخْتَارُكَ بِهَا

[And I know] that hastening to Your magnanimity and reliance upon Your promise compensate for the stinginess of the miserly and suffice from that which is grasped by the mean. [And I know] that You never veil Yourself against Your creations, but it is their ill-deeds that hinder them from [reaching closer to] You. I have also known that the best provisions of whoever intends to travel to You is a true will by which He chooses You![6]

In this supplication, the Imam teaches us that everything we need to reach closer to God is readily available to us. The best tool available to us on our journey is a strength of will, which we can utilize in seeking God's pleasure.

Strengthening our willpower becomes a high priority.

---

[6] Al-Tousi, *Misbah al-Mutahajjid*, 815.

Strengthening Willpower

God, who creates and sustains all things, continues to bless and teach us how to strengthen our willpower through the system of worships He drew for us. Indeed, one of the greatest methods God gave us by which we can strengthen our will is the worship of fasting during the Holy Month of Ramadan.

Indeed, fasting the Holy Month of Ramadan is a great blessing and honor given to Muslims and not to any other people. A companion of Imam al-Sadiq (a) relays that the Imam said,

إن شهر رمضان لم يفرض الله صيامه على أحد من الأمم قبلنا

The fasting of the month of Ramadan was not imposed on any nation before us.

The companion asked about the verse of the Holy Quran,

يَا أَيُّهَا الَّذِينَ آمَنُوا كُتِبَ عَلَيْكُمُ الصِّيَامُ كَمَا كُتِبَ عَلَى الَّذِينَ مِن قَبْلِكُمْ لَعَلَّكُمْ تَتَّقُونَ

O you who have faith! Prescribed for you is fasting, as it was prescribed for those who were before you, so that you may be Godwary.[7]

The Imam (a) replied,

إنما فرض الله صيام شهر رمضان على الأنبياء دون الأمم ففضل الله به هذه الأمة وجعل صيامه فرضا على رسول الله (ص) وعلى أمته

---

[7] The Holy Quran, 2:183.

> *Indeed, God obligated the fasting of the month of Ramadan upon the prophets and not their nations. He favored this nation with [this special responsibility and honor]. He made the fasting of the month an obligation upon the Messenger of God (s) and his nation.*[8]

The prescription of fasting the Holy Month of Ramadan is a great mercy with which the nation of Prophet Muhammad (s) has been blessed.

If we take a closer look at fasting and the Holy Month of Ramadan, we can see the important role the two play in removing any restraint and strengthening the power of the will. How can we benefit from this great worship in this great month? We can list several ways:

Refraining from Engagement in Desires

To fast is to refrain from a few acts – such as eating, drinking, and sexual activity – for a specified period. If we analyze the things we were commanded to stay away from during fasting, we find that they are essential to human survival, but are also the cause of many evils.

When an individual refrains from all these activities, as a form of submission to God, they will gradually become better equipped to resist the other desires and temptations of the body. It is a training process that we are commanded to undertake for at least one month of the year. It is a chance for us to prove to ourselves that we can stand in the face of temptation and worldly

---
[8] Al-Rayshahri, *Mizan al-Hikma*, 2:1684.

desires. By this training, we strengthen our willpower and our ability to use this faculty to develop ourselves.

This is what Imam al-Rida (a) taught us in one narration when he said:

فإن قال فلم أمروا بالصوم قيل لكي يعرفوا ألم الجوع و العطش فيستدلوا على فقر الآخرة و ليكون الصائم خاشعا ذليلا مستكينا مأجورا محتسبا عارفا صابرا لما أصابه من الجوع و العطش فيستوجب الثواب مع ما فيه من الانكسار عن الشهوات و ليكون ذلك واعظا لهم في العاجل و رائضا لهم على أداء ما كلفهم و دليلا في الآجل

If it was asked, 'why were they commanded to fast?' then the answer would be 'so that they come to know the pain of hunger and thirst and infer from that [the severity of] the poverty of the hereafter. And so the person who is fasting becomes reverent, humble, servile, rewarded, saving [his reward to come from God for his sacrifice], realizing [of God's majesty], and patient over what has struck him of hunger and thirst so that he can deserve a reward [from God] for what he has undergone of refraining from desires. And so that [fasting] can become an admonishment for them in the short-term, a training for them to fulfil what God has obligated upon them, and a guide for them in the long-term.'[9]

---

[9] Al-Sadouq, *'Ilal Al-Sharai'*, 1:270. See also: Al-Majlisi, *Bihar Al-Anwar*, 93:370.

Fasting and Strengthening the Will

Fasting is an opportunity for us to train ourselves to fulfill God's commands.

In the world of athletics, an athlete cannot play a sport and excel in it without the proper training. An individual who did not go through the proper training would not be able to earn an Olympic gold medal in gymnastics or weightlifting. Just as an athlete needs practice and training to hone their skills and strengthen their faculties to excel in sports, we too need practice and training to strengthen our willpower.

An individual who can refrain from permissible (*Halal*) food and drink can easily refrain from impermisslbe (*Haram*) food and drink. A person who cannot control hunger for a short while will continue to live weak-willed and helpless.

Hunger Strengthens the Will

There are many narrations that speak of overeating and the role it plays in corrupting an individual and weakening their willpower. There are also a great number of narrations that emphasize the positive effects of hunger. Overeating influences an individual's ability to reason and make the right choices. It is narrated that the Holy Prophet (s) said,

من تعود كثرة الطعام الشراب قسا قلبه

> *Whoever grows used to plentiful food and drink, his heart will become hard.*[10]

---

[10] Al-Rayshahri, *Mizan al-Hikma*, 1:90.

The hardening of the heart means that an individual will not be able to identify what is truly in their own best interest and will not have the willpower to make the right choices.

In another narration the Holy Prophet (s) says,

لا تشبعوا فيطفأ نور المعرفة من قلوبكم

> *Do not fully satisfy your hunger, as the light of knowledge will escape your hearts.*[11]

If the light of knowledge escapes an individual's heart, they will not be able to tell right from wrong. In other words, they will remain the prisoner of their own desires and will not find anything to guide them towards anything contrary to their base desires.

It is also narrated that the Commander of the Faithful (a) said,

الشبع يفسد الورع

> *Full satisfaction of hunger corrupts piety.*[12]

There are many narrations that speak in the same vein. Fasting plays a great role in opening an individual's mind and allowing them to realize right from wrong. This creates a greater benefit for the individual, allowing them to make the right choices in all aspects of his life. Thus, we can see that hunger is a great spiritual exercise that God commanded us to partake in through worship.

---

[11] Al-Rayshahri, *Mizan al-Hikma*, 3:1873.
[12] Al-Rayshahri, *Mizan al-Hikma*, 1:90.

Indeed, Imam al-Sajjad (a) encouraged hunger as a means of spiritual training when he said,

إن العاقل عن الله الخائف منه العامل له ليمرن نفسه ويعودها الجوع حتى تشتاق الى الشبع وكذلك تضمر الخيل لسباق الرهان

An individual who is cognizant of God, fearful of Him, and working for Him will train himself to become used to hunger, so that he does not long for full satisfaction – just as a horse is trained for a betting race.[13]

We must utilize hunger as part of a diet that will allow us to strengthen our will and be able to bear the long journey towards God

Worship and Certainty

Many of us give special attention to our faith during the Holy Month of Ramadan. We put more time into worship and reflection. Worship, in turn, plays a role in strengthening an individual's willpower. The closer an individual gets to God through worship and piety, the more they will achieve in terms of certainty, which in turn strengthens the will. This is because an individual can more easily make decisions when it comes to issues where they have certainty, as opposed to issues of probability, where the will grows weaker as a probability dwindles.

We see this equation in all aspects of our lives. A businessman will enter a deal without hesitation if making a profit is certain.

---

[13] Al-Rayshahri, *Mizan al-Hikma*, 1:90.

But the more doubtful the profit is, the more he will hesitate to take the plunge.

Worship is a means to certainty, which in turn strengthens the will. God says,

وَاعْبُدْ رَبَّكَ حَتَّىٰ يَأْتِيَكَ الْيَقِينُ

Worship your Lord until certainty comes to you.[14]

The Holy Month of Ramadan comes with its own set of worships that distinguishes it from all other months. Fasting plays a large role in solidifying an individual's certainty. It is narrated that the Holy Prophet (s) had the following conversation with God Almighty:

قال يا رب وما ميراث الصوم؟ قال: الصوم يورث الحكمة، والحكمة تورث المعرفة، والمعرفة تورث اليقين، فإذا استيقن العبد لا يبالي كيف أصبح بعسر أم بيسر

He said, 'My Lord, what does fasting endow?' God said, 'Fasting endows wisdom. Wisdom endows knowledge. Knowledge endows certainty. Surely, if a servant reaches certainty, he shall not care whether he is at hardship or at ease.'[15]

A person who reaches certainty will not care they are in hardship or at ease. Their circumstances will not stand to weaken their will or influence them to make the wrong decisions.

---

[14] The Holy Quran, 15:99.
[15] Al-Rayshahri, *Mizan al-Hikma*, 2:1689.

As for the other worships during the Holy Month, we find that the Immaculate Imams (a) taught us some form of prayer or supplication to occupy any time during the days and nights of the month. There are also prayers and supplications taught specifically for certain nights of the month, including *Laylat al-Qadr* – the most important night of the year. An individual should prepare themselves throughout the year for this occasion.

All these worships play an important role in strengthening an individual's willpower and attaining divine blessings. God says,

$$وَالَّذِينَ جَاهَدُوا فِينَا لَنَهْدِيَنَّهُمْ سُبُلَنَا ۚ وَإِنَّ اللَّهَ لَمَعَ الْمُحْسِنِينَ$$

As for those who strive in Us, We shall surely guide them in Our ways, and God is indeed with the virtuous.[16]

God also says,

$$فَأَمَّا مَنْ أَعْطَىٰ وَاتَّقَىٰ ﴿٥﴾ وَصَدَّقَ بِالْحُسْنَىٰ ﴿٦﴾ فَسَنُيَسِّرُهُ لِلْيُسْرَىٰ ﴿٧﴾$$

As for him who gives and is Godwary and confirms the best promise, We will surely ease him toward facility.[17]

We can see that blessings are attained by our own choices and actions. The process begins by us making the right decisions in seeking closeness to God. We must live within the bounds that God Almighty drew for us, so that we can attain true happiness in this life and the next.

---

[16] The Holy Quran, 29:69.
[17] The Holy Quran, 92:5-7.

WORSHIP AND HAPPINESS

In the Name of God, the Most Beneficent, the Most Merciful

وَمَا خَلَقْتُ الْجِنَّ وَالْإِنسَ إِلَّا لِيَعْبُدُونِ ﴿٥٦﴾ مَا أُرِيدُ مِنْهُم مِّن رِّزْقٍ وَمَا أُرِيدُ أَن يُطْعِمُونِ ﴿٥٧﴾ إِنَّ اللَّهَ هُوَ الرَّزَّاقُ ذُو الْقُوَّةِ الْمَتِينُ ﴿٥٨﴾

I did not create the jinn and the humans except that they may worship Me. I desire no provision from them, nor do I desire that they should feed Me. Indeed it is God who is the All-provider, Powerful and All-strong.[1]

THE PURPOSE OF CREATION

God created mankind and honored us above all other creatures. He prepared for us a life of happiness and luxury without any hardship or displeasure. He created that world for us to be free to worship Him and ascend in our knowledge of Him until we reach the greatest heights of knowledge. We find the link between knowledge and worship that is mentioned in many of our narrations.

---

[1] The Holy Quran, 51:56-58.

In any case, God did not create mankind to endure hardship and constantly toil in pursuit of their sustenance. Mankind is much dearer to God, and a brief look at the verses of the Holy Quran will show us this reality. It was mankind's own choices that brought about this world of hardship and toil, and away from that world of ease and luxury.

God Almighty relays to us the story of that world He created for us and how we grew distant from that world. He says:

وَإِذْ قُلْنَا لِلْمَلَائِكَةِ اسْجُدُوا لِآدَمَ فَسَجَدُوا إِلَّا إِبْلِيسَ أَبَىٰ ﴿١١٦﴾ فَقُلْنَا يَا آدَمُ إِنَّ هَٰذَا عَدُوٌّ لَكَ وَلِزَوْجِكَ فَلَا يُخْرِجَنَّكُمَا مِنَ الْجَنَّةِ فَتَشْقَىٰ ﴿١١٧﴾ إِنَّ لَكَ أَلَّا تَجُوعَ فِيهَا وَلَا تَعْرَىٰ ﴿١١٨﴾ وَأَنَّكَ لَا تَظْمَأُ فِيهَا وَلَا تَضْحَىٰ ﴿١١٩﴾

When We said to the angels, 'Prostrate before Adam,' they prostrated, but not Iblis: he refused. We said, 'O Adam! This is indeed an enemy of yours and your mate's. So do not let him expel you from Paradise, or you will be miserable. You will neither be hungry in it nor naked. You will neither be thirsty in it, nor suffer from [the heat of] the sun.' [2]

But then Satan's conspiracy got between us and staying in that world of ease, where we could worship freely without hardship or toil:

---

[2] The Holy Quran, 20:116-19.

WORSHIP AND HAPPINESS

فَوَسْوَسَ إِلَيْهِ الشَّيْطَانُ قَالَ يَا آدَمُ هَلْ أَدُلُّكَ عَلَىٰ شَجَرَةِ الْخُلْدِ وَمُلْكٍ لَّا يَبْلَىٰ ﴿١٢٠﴾ فَأَكَلَا مِنْهَا فَبَدَتْ لَهُمَا سَوْآتُهُمَا وَطَفِقَا يَخْصِفَانِ عَلَيْهِمَا مِن وَرَقِ الْجَنَّةِ ۚ وَعَصَىٰ آدَمُ رَبَّهُ فَغَوَىٰ ﴿١٢١﴾ ثُمَّ اجْتَبَاهُ رَبُّهُ فَتَابَ عَلَيْهِ وَهَدَىٰ ﴿١٢٢﴾ قَالَ اهْبِطَا مِنْهَا جَمِيعًا ۖ بَعْضُكُمْ لِبَعْضٍ عَدُوٌّ ۖ فَإِمَّا يَأْتِيَنَّكُم مِّنِّي هُدًى فَمَنِ اتَّبَعَ هُدَايَ فَلَا يَضِلُّ وَلَا يَشْقَىٰ ﴿١٢٣﴾

Then Satan tempted him. He said, 'O Adam! Shall I show you the tree of immortality, and an imperishable kingdom?' So they both ate of it, and their nakedness became evident to them, and they began to stitch over themselves with the leaves of Paradise. Adam disobeyed his Lord, and went amiss. Then his Lord chose him, and turned to him clemently, and guided him. He said, 'Get down both of you from it, all together, being enemies of one another! Yet, should any guidance come to you from Me, those who follow My guidance will not go astray, nor will they be miserable....'[3]

God's divine promise was that He would place us in a paradise where there is no hardship or toil, and we would not even feel hunger, thirst, heat, or cold. This world was created for us to dedicate ourselves to the worship of God. However, mankind fell victim to the whispers of Satan and disobeyed the commands God issued for mankind's best interest. This became the reason for us to face constant tests and tribulations so that we can prove our connection with and servitude to God.

---

[3] The Holy Quran, 20:120-23.

Despite descending to this world and being stripped of all those luxuries, God's boundless mercy never parted with us. God's blessings and sustenance continue to rain down upon us, most importantly of which are the prophets and messengers that God continued to send to guide us back to Him. As we read in the Holy Quran,

$$\text{وَمَنْ أَعْرَضَ عَن ذِكْرِي فَإِنَّ لَهُ مَعِيشَةً ضَنكًا وَنَحْشُرُهُ يَوْمَ الْقِيَامَةِ أَعْمَىٰ}$$

But whoever disregards My remembrance, his shall be a wretched life, and We shall raise him blind on the Day of Resurrection.[4]

We understand that returning to that world of happiness, luxury, and ease does not come through anything other than worship. God says,

$$\text{فَاصْبِرْ عَلَىٰ مَا يَقُولُونَ وَسَبِّحْ بِحَمْدِ رَبِّكَ قَبْلَ طُلُوعِ الشَّمْسِ وَقَبْلَ غُرُوبِهَا وَمِنْ آنَاءِ اللَّيْلِ فَسَبِّحْ وَأَطْرَافَ النَّهَارِ لَعَلَّكَ تَرْضَىٰ}$$

Be patient with what they say, and celebrate the praise of your Lord before the rising of the sun and before the sunset, and glorify Him in watches of the night and at the day's ends, that you may be pleased.[5]

God blessed mankind when He set for us the numerous types of worship. Each of these worships fulfills a specific need and allows us to reach towards a particular aspect of excellence in our

---

[4] The Holy Quran, 20:124.

[5] The Holy Quran, 20:130.

lives. Each type of worship has its material and metaphysical effects. Prayer, fasting, Hajj, and all other worship each have their distinct purpose. We must not belittle any of these worships or approach them with a sense of indifference or lethargy. They are divine blessings, the pleasure of which we cannot taste until we steep ourselves in them.

Worship and the Good Life

Each of God's creatures is created and fashioned in such a way as to best suit their purpose. The same holds true for humankind, whose purpose is to worship the Almighty. Thus, our body, soul, and every aspect of our being are perfectly compatible with the worships prescribed by God.

It is when we veer astray from this divine goal that we experience a life of hardship and misery. This is because we would be going against the innate instincts that God endowed us with. Each creature must live in accordance with its purpose. Otherwise, it would not be able to live and flourish, just as a fish cannot live out of water or the sun cannot veer out of its orbit.

لَا الشَّمْسُ يَنْبَغِي لَهَا أَن تُدْرِكَ الْقَمَرَ وَلَا اللَّيْلُ سَابِقُ النَّهَارِ ۚ وَكُلٌّ فِي فَلَكٍ يَسْبَحُونَ

Neither it behooves the sun to overtake the moon, nor may the night outrun the day, and each swims in an orbit.[6]

---

[6] The Holy Quran, 36:40.

Like all other creatures, mankind was created with a purpose and can fulfill its highest potential when it lives up to that purpose. What differentiates us from all other creatures is that we were given moral agency and the responsibility of making choices. We may make the choice to go astray or remain steadfast on the course drawn for us by God. It is only when we remain steadfast and reach our goal – to manifest true servitude to God – that we realize the highest levels of our being and can live the good life that we were promised. God says in the Holy Quran,

$$\text{مَنْ عَمِلَ صَالِحًا مِّن ذَكَرٍ أَوْ أُنثَىٰ وَهُوَ مُؤْمِنٌ فَلَنُحْيِيَنَّهُ حَيَاةً طَيِّبَةً ۖ وَلَنَجْزِيَنَّهُمْ أَجْرَهُم بِأَحْسَنِ مَا كَانُوا يَعْمَلُونَ}$$

> Whoever acts righteously, [whether] male or female, should he be faithful, We shall revive him with a good life and pay them their reward by the best of what they used to do.[7]

When an individual veers away from this path, they will live a life of hardship and discontent. God says:

$$\text{فَمَن يُرِدِ اللَّهُ أَن يَهْدِيَهُ يَشْرَحْ صَدْرَهُ لِلْإِسْلَامِ ۖ وَمَن يُرِدْ أَن يُضِلَّهُ يَجْعَلْ صَدْرَهُ ضَيِّقًا حَرَجًا كَأَنَّمَا يَصَّعَّدُ فِي السَّمَاءِ ۚ كَذَٰلِكَ يَجْعَلُ اللَّهُ الرِّجْسَ عَلَى الَّذِينَ لَا يُؤْمِنُونَ}$$

> Whomever God desires to guide, He opens his breast to Islam, and whomever He desires to lead astray, He makes his breast narrow and straitened, as if he were

---

[7] The Holy Quran, 16:97.

climbing to a height. Thus does God lay [spiritual] defilement on those who do not have faith.[8]

An individual who lives a life of servitude to the Almighty lives in comfort, contentment, and tranquility, despite all the hardships of this world. This is true for several reasons, including:

Harmony

Everything in this world is created by God and guided towards a purpose revolving around obedience and servitude to Him. God says in the Holy Quran:

تُسَبِّحُ لَهُ السَّمَاوَاتُ السَّبْعُ وَالْأَرْضُ وَمَن فِيهِنَّ ۚ وَإِن مِّن شَيْءٍ إِلَّا يُسَبِّحُ بِحَمْدِهِ وَلَٰكِن لَّا تَفْقَهُونَ تَسْبِيحَهُمْ ۗ إِنَّهُ كَانَ حَلِيمًا غَفُورًا

The seven heavens glorify Him, and the Earth [too], and whoever is in them. There is not a thing that does not celebrate His praise, but you do not understand their glorification. Indeed, He is all-forbearing, all-forgiving.[9]

God also says:

أَلَمْ تَرَ أَنَّ اللَّهَ يَسْجُدُ لَهُ مَن فِي السَّمَاوَاتِ وَمَن فِي الْأَرْضِ وَالشَّمْسُ وَالْقَمَرُ وَالنُّجُومُ وَالْجِبَالُ وَالشَّجَرُ وَالدَّوَابُّ وَكَثِيرٌ مِّنَ النَّاسِ ۖ وَكَثِيرٌ حَقَّ عَلَيْهِ الْعَذَابُ ۗ وَمَن يُهِنِ اللَّهُ فَمَا لَهُ مِن مُّكْرِمٍ ۚ إِنَّ اللَّهَ يَفْعَلُ مَا يَشَاءُ

Have you not regarded that whoever is in the heavens and whoever is on the Earth prostrates to God, as well as the sun, the moon, and the stars, the mountains, the

---

[8] The Holy Quran, 6:125.
[9] The Holy Quran, 17:44.

trees, and the animals and many humans? And many have come to deserve the punishment. Whomever God humiliates will find no one who may bring him honor. Indeed, God does whatever He wishes.[10]

There are several other verses that describe the world in a similar way. The bottom line is that this world was created with servitude to the Almighty at its core and as its purpose. An individual who embodies servitude to God falls in full harmony with the rest of creation. When a person rebels against God's commands, they stand against the powerful current of creation, thus living a life of disharmony and discontentment.

Fulfilling Material and Spiritual Needs

Worship also leads to the material and spiritual excellence of mankind. We must realize that the soul needs to be properly nourished, just like the body. Just as the body may fall ill if it is not nourished or is nourished improperly, the same is true for the soul. Malnourishment of the soul leads to its degeneration, at which point the individual will not be able to lead a good life, but will rather continue on a path of wretchedness. It is through worship and servitude to God that we lead a good and tranquil life. God says:

$$\text{الَّذِينَ آمَنُوا وَتَطْمَئِنُّ قُلُوبُهُم بِذِكْرِ اللَّهِ ۗ أَلَا بِذِكْرِ اللَّهِ تَطْمَئِنُّ الْقُلُوبُ}$$

---

[10] The Holy Quran, 22:18.

Those who have faith and whose hearts find rest in the remembrance of God, behold! The hearts find rest in God's remembrance![11]

WORSHIP AND IDENTITY

As individuals, by virtue of the nature of our creation, we always seek to belong and identify with things outside of ourselves. We see and face so much in this world, but the more we study the world around us, the more we come to realize its vastness. All this drives a sense of fear and anxiety in us, leading us to seek something to hold on to. A sense of belonging allows us to make sense of some of the world around us. Our identity gives us a lens through which we see the world.

Worship is a means for us to create the appropriate identity for ourselves – one which is built on a sense of belonging to the Absolute. This sense of belonging is incomparable to any other identity. It is far beyond attachment to any limited and fleeting creation. God speaks of the need for us to create this identity in the Holy Quran. He says:

اللَّهُ وَلِيُّ الَّذِينَ آمَنُوا يُخْرِجُهُم مِّنَ الظُّلُمَاتِ إِلَى النُّورِ ۖ وَالَّذِينَ كَفَرُوا أَوْلِيَاؤُهُمُ الطَّاغُوتُ يُخْرِجُونَهُم مِّنَ النُّورِ إِلَى الظُّلُمَاتِ ۗ أُولَٰئِكَ أَصْحَابُ النَّارِ ۖ هُمْ فِيهَا خَالِدُونَ

God is the master of the faithful: He brings them out of darkness into light. As for the faithless, their masters are

---

[11] The Holy Quran, 13:28.

the fake deities, who drive them out of light into darkness. They shall be the inmates of the Fire, and they will remain in it [forever].[12]

We should never underestimate the value of identity and belonging. It builds an individual's character and allows them to see the world with an end goal in mind. An individual who identifies with God will always feel a sense of honor and might:

وَلِلَّهِ الْعِزَّةُ وَلِرَسُولِهِ وَلِلْمُؤْمِنِينَ وَلَكِنَّ الْمُنَافِقِينَ لَا يَعْلَمُونَ ... إِنَّ اللَّهَ هُوَ الرَّزَّاقُ ذُو الْقُوَّةِ الْمَتِينُ

All might belongs to God and His Apostle and the faithful, but the hypocrites do not know...[13] *Indeed it is God who is the All-provider, Powerful and All-strong.*[14]

That is why the companions of the Holy Prophet (s) would chant in their battles against the transgressors of Quraysh, "Our master is God, and you have no master!" Indeed, a person who has a sense of belonging to the Almighty cannot be equated with an individual who does not. This is in addition to the fact that this sense of belonging eases the troubles of our journey in this world. God says,

إِن تَكُونُوا تَأْلَمُونَ فَإِنَّهُمْ يَأْلَمُونَ كَمَا تَأْلَمُونَ ۖ وَتَرْجُونَ مِنَ اللَّهِ مَا لَا يَرْجُونَ ۗ وَكَانَ اللَّهُ عَلِيمًا حَكِيمًا

---

[12] The Holy Quran, 2:257.

[13] The Holy Quran, 63:8.

[14] The Holy Quran, 51:58.

> *If you are suffering, they are also suffering like you, but you expect from God what they do not expect, and God is all-knowing, all-wise.*[15]

The traditions of the Holy Household (a) also emphasize this point. It is narrated that Imam al-Sadiq (a) said:

في التوارة مكتوب: يا ابن آدم تفرغ لعبادتي أملاقلبك غنى ولا أكلك إلى طلبك وعلي أن أسد فاقتك، وأملا قلبك خوفا مني ؛ وإن لا تفرغ لعبادتي أملا قلبك شغلا بالدنيا ثم لا أسد فاقتك وأكلك إلى طلبك.

> *It is written in the Torah, 'O' son of Adam, worship Me and I shall fill your heart with contentedness and I shall not leave you to your wants. I shall suffice your needs and fill your heart with fear of Me. If you do not set time to worship Me, I shall fill your heart with desire for this world. I shall not suffice your needs and I shall leave you to your wants.'*[16]

Worship plays a role by instilling in us that sense of belonging and identifying with God. This, in turn, strengthens the individual's soul and character. On the other hand, an individual who does not identify with the absolute will remain weak. They will seek to identify with fleeting and inconsequential things, which in turn will only make them weaker and fickler. Such an individ-

---

[15] The Holy Quran, 4:104.
[16] Al-Kulayni, *al-Kafi*, 2:83.

ual will need to spend their power and energy in pursuit of whatever they identify with, whereas those who identify with the Almighty will draw strength and honor from Him.

True Worship

Many of us do not engage properly with our acts of worship. We see them as obligations that we need to get out of our way, simply to satisfy the obligation and avoid any punishment. There are also some individuals who look at the recommended acts of worship and see them as too stringent and extreme. That is because many of us do not know and have not tasted the sweetness of worship. We do not recognize the reality and effects of worship, so we view it superficially. Few of us have delved deep into the spirit of worship.

If we take the time to contemplate on worship, we will see that it is one of the greatest of God's blessings to His servants. For us to fully understand it, we must first recognize its essential components and the factors that allow it to have a significant effect on our being.

Knowledge and Certainty

Worship is not a set of rites and rituals that we must perform without thinking and understand. Rather, we must seek to understand their deeper meaning. Our acts of worship cannot simply be empty rituals. Indeed, the rituals of worship were set by God so that His servants may manifest their relationship to Him and grow closer to Him.

Worship cannot be a set of ritualistic actions without a deeper understanding of their role and meaning. There must be a level of contemplation and understanding for the worshipping servant. The more a servant knows of his Lord and understands his worship, the greater the value of his worship will be. That is why we find knowledge of God as the centerpiece of the Holy Household's (a) wisdom when explaining the holy verse:

وَمَا خَلَقْتُ الْجِنَّ وَالْإِنسَ إِلَّا لِيَعْبُدُونِ

I did not create the jinn and the humans except that they may worship Me.[17]

It is narrated that Imam al-Rida (a) said:

أول عبادة الله معرفته وأصل معرفة الله توحيده

The first step in worshipping God is to know Him. The pillar of knowing God is believing in His Oneness.[18]

Other narrations highlight the fact that mankind was created to know of God. It is this knowledge that allows a servant to rise higher in the levels of worship. It is narrated that Imam Hussain (a) said:

أيّها الناس ! إنّ الله جلّ ذكره ما خلق العباد إلاّ ليعرفوه، فإذا عرفوه عبدوه، فإذا عبدوه استغنوا بعبادته عن عبادة ما سواه

O' people, God Almighty did not create His servants excepts so that they may know Him. Once they know Him,

---

[17] The Holy Quran, 51:56.
[18] Al-Sadouq, 'Oyoun Akhbar al-Rida (a), 2:135.

they worship Him. Once they worship Him, they suffice themselves by His worship from worshipping anything else.

A man asked him, "May my parents be your ransom, what is it to know God?" He replied,

معرفة أهل كلّ زمان إمامهم الذي يجب عليهم طاعته

It is for the people of each era to know their Imam, who they are obligated to obey.[19]

There are countless other narrations that emphasize the importance of understanding, knowledge, and certainty when it comes to worship. The Commander of the Faithful (a) said,

لا خير في عبادة ليس فيها تفقه

There is no use to worship without understanding.[20]

He also said,

لا خير في عبادة لا فقه فيها

There is no use to worship without knowledge.[21]

It is narrated that the Holy Prophet (s) said,

لا عبادة إلا بيقين

There is no [true] worship without certainty.[22]

---

[19] Al-Sadouq, *'Ilal al-Sharai'*, 1:90.

[20] Al-Sadouq, *Ma'ani al-Akhbar*, 226.

[21] Al-Kulayni, *al-Kafi*, 1:36.

[22] Al-Nouri, *Mustadrak al-Wasa'el*, 11:196.

Certainty is a high level of knowledge and understanding that allows a clear and excellent vision.

Worship cannot have its true impact on the individual if they do not properly engage in it through having an adequate understanding. The higher an individual's level of understanding, the higher the level of worship, and the greater its benefits. This is clear in the words of Imam Ali (a) when he said,

سكنوا في أنفسكم معرفة ما تعبدون، حتى ينفعكم ما تحركون من الجوارح بعبادة من تعرفون.

> *Secure in yourselves knowledge of what you worship, so that you may reap the benefits of the movements of your limbs through worship of the One whom you know.*[23]

By understanding this relationship between worship and understanding, we can see why the apostles, messengers, and the Holy Prophet (s) and his Immaculate Household (a) were so engaged in their worships. Their worship is built on true understanding and certainty, so they taste its sweetness and observe its affects. They also continuously feel that they have not fulfilled their obligations toward God and have fallen short in fulfilling His rights upon them. They understand how little our worship is before the majesty, generosity, and blessings of God.

We, on the other hand, do not have that level of understanding and so cannot reap the same benefits from our worship. Each of us thinks that our acts of worship are enough to fulfill God's due

---

[23] Al-Majlisi, *Bihar al-Anwar*, 75:63.

rights, and that we can rest easy after we offer whatever little we do.

Because of this important role that understanding plays in our acts of worship, we see that our noble traditions continuously emphasize the importance of thought and reflection. In one narration, Imam al-Rida (a) said:

> ليس العبادة كثرة الصيام والصلاة، إنما العبادة كثرة التفكر في أمر الله

> *Worship does not come with excessive fasting of prayer. Rather, it is to constantly think about the matter of God.*[24]

Physical and Spiritual Purity

Worship is a process of purification. One of its most important goals is to purify the individual from the corruption of sin and disobedience. At the same time, worship is a means of prevention, as it guards the worshipper from falling into sin. This is what the Holy Quran refers to in some of its verses. For example:

> اتْلُ مَا أُوحِيَ إِلَيْكَ مِنَ الْكِتَابِ وَأَقِمِ الصَّلَاةَ ۖ إِنَّ الصَّلَاةَ تَنْهَىٰ عَنِ الْفَحْشَاءِ وَالْمُنكَرِ ۗ وَلَذِكْرُ اللَّهِ أَكْبَرُ ۗ وَاللَّهُ يَعْلَمُ مَا تَصْنَعُونَ

> *Recite what has been revealed to you of the Book, and maintain the prayer. Indeed, the prayer restrains from indecent and wrongful conduct, and the remembrance*

---

[24] Al-Harrani, *Tuhaf al-'Oqool*, 442.

of God is surely greater. And God knows whatever you do.[25]

Along with the important effect of restraining the individual from sin, prayer is also a means of purification for us. Our beloved Imam Ali (a) relays a beautiful narration in this regard. He said that the Holy Prophet (s) once read this holy verse:

وَأَقِمِ الصَّلَاةَ طَرَفَيِ النَّهَارِ وَزُلَفًا مِّنَ اللَّيْلِ ۚ إِنَّ الْحَسَنَاتِ يُذْهِبْنَ السَّيِّئَاتِ ۚ ذَٰلِكَ ذِكْرَىٰ لِلذَّاكِرِينَ

Maintain the prayer at the two ends of the day, and during the early hours of the night. Indeed, good deeds efface misdeeds. That is an admonition for the mindful.[26]

By way of explaining the verse, the Holy Prophet (s) said:

يا علي والذي بعثني بالحق بشيراً ونذيراً إن أحدكُم ليقوم إلى وضوئه فيتساقط عن جوارحه الذنوب، فإذا استقبل الله بوجهه وقلبه لم ينفتل عن صلاته وعليه من ذنوبه شيءٌ كما ولدته أمه

O' Ali, I swear by the One who sent me with the truth as a bearer of good news and as a warner, that whenever any of you performs his wudhu, his sins fall off of his limbs. If he turns his face and his heart to God, he will not leave his prayer except that he has shed all his sins [and become pure] like the day his mother gave birth to him.[27]

---

[25] The Holy Quran, 29:45.
[26] The Holy Quran, 11:114.
[27] Al-Majlisi, *Bihar al-Anwar*, 79:220.

We find a similar command in the Holy Quran when it comes to fasting. God says:

$$\text{يَا أَيُّهَا الَّذِينَ آمَنُوا كُتِبَ عَلَيْكُمُ الصِّيَامُ كَمَا كُتِبَ عَلَى الَّذِينَ مِن قَبْلِكُمْ لَعَلَّكُمْ تَتَّقُونَ}$$

> *O you who have faith! Prescribed for you is fasting, as it was prescribed for those who were before you, so that you may be Godwary.*[28]

At the same time, fasting also purifies an individual from sin. As the Holy Prophet (s) said,

$$\text{الصوم جنة من النار}$$

> *Fasting is a haven from Hellfire.*[29]

The same goes for almsgiving, Hajj, and any other form of worship. They play an important role in purifying the individual spiritually.

As we realize this, we must also recognize that these purifiers cannot be mixed with corruption, as they would not be able to have the proper effect. You cannot maintain two contradictory opposites at the same time. Worship will not have its effect on an individual who constantly engages in sin, for example. Such an individual will not be capable of understanding and tasting the sweetness of their worship. For these acts of worship to have

---

[28] The Holy Quran, 2:183.
[29] Al-Barqi, *al-Mahasin*, 1:287.

their full effect on our being, we must strive to remove any form of corruption from our hearts that would impede our worship.

This corruption that hampers the effects of worship can be either physical or spiritual. Physical corruptions, for example, include the consumption of impermissible foods and drinks. It is narrated that the Holy Prophet (s) said,

$$لعبادة مع أكل الحرام كالبناء على الرمل$$

> *Worship while eating what is impermissible (Haram) is like building on sand.*[30]

He is also reported to have said,

$$إن لله ملكا ينادي على بيت المقدس كل ليلة، من أكل حراما لم يقبل الله منه صرفا ولا عدلا والصرف النافلة والعدل الفريضة$$

> *God has an angel who cries out every night over the Sacred House, 'Whoever eats Haram, God will not except from him a [recommended prayer] nor a [mandatory prayer].'*[31]

There are also narrations that speak of the spiritual forms of corruption that can hamper the effects of worship. The Commander of the Faithful (a) said,

$$كيف يجد لذة العبادة من لا يصوم عن الهوى$$

---

[30] Al-Majlisi, *Bihar al-Anwar*, 100:16.

[31] Al-Majlisi, *Bihar al-Anwar*, 100:16.

How can a person who does not fast from [obeying his] desire taste the beauty of worship?[32]

It is also narrated that Prophet Jesus (a) once said,

بحق أقول لكم إنه كما ينظر المريض الى طيب الطعام فلا يلتذه مع ما يجده من شدة الوجع، كذلك صاحب الدنيا لا يلتذ بالعبادة ولا يجد حلاوتها مع ما يجد من حب المال

Surely, just as the ill looks at good food but is not able to taste its joy due to his severe pain, so too is the seeker of this world unable to feel the pleasure of worship or taste its sweetness due to his love of wealth.[33]

An individual who wishes to taste the sweetness of worship and realize all its effects must work to purify themselves from anything that would prevent them from their goal. If the physical and spiritual opposites to worship remain a part of an individual, they cannot fully utilize the acts of worship that God prescribed. As Imam Hassan (a) said,

إن من طلب العبادة تزكى لها

Whoever seeks worship will purify himself for it.[34]

Making Time

One of the primary factors for becoming engaged in worship and realizing its effects is to set aside time dedicated to it. Of course,

---

[32] Al-Wasiti, *'Oyoun al-Hikam*, 384.

[33] Al-Harrani, *Tuhaf al-'Oqool*, 507.

[34] Al-Harrani, *Tuhaf al-'Oqool*, 236.

this does not mean that an individual should neglect this world entirely and forget about their career and education. All of that, when done properly, can be considered a means of worship. God says,

$$هُوَ الَّذِي جَعَلَ لَكُمُ الْأَرْضَ ذَلُولًا فَامْشُوا فِي مَنَاكِبِهَا وَكُلُوا مِن رِّزْقِهِ ۖ وَإِلَيْهِ النُّشُورُ$$

> *It is He who made the Earth tractable for you; so walk on its flanks and eat of His provision, and towards Him is the resurrection.*[35]

We must make worship a priority in our lives. We must make sure that everything we do in this world is in accord with the purpose for which we were created. Whenever we make the effort and set aside the time in dedication to worship, we will surely taste its sweetness and feel its effects. If we do not dedicate the time and effort, and approach worship simply as an obligation to get through, then we will never realize its true meaning.

We see that many individuals do not give much importance to worship. We have many priorities in life – including our wealth, work, family, luxury, and other matters – all of which are given greater priority than worship. Many of us delay our prayers with the excuse of being busy with work. Many of us delay our Hajj with the excuse that we are busy with other aspects of our lives. How many of us do not even know the meaning of recommended prayers and Salat al-Layl? We suffice ourselves with the minimum that we are obligated with, because we look at our

---

[35] The Holy Quran, 67:15.

prayers as something that consumes time we could be spending somewhere else.

All of this reflects our poor relationship with worship and how we see it at the bottom of our list of priorities. How can we expect to properly engage in worship and reap its benefits when this is our outlook? That is why God commands us to be patient when it comes to worship. He says,

$$وَاسْتَعِينُوا بِالصَّبْرِ وَالصَّلَاةِ ۚ وَإِنَّهَا لَكَبِيرَةٌ إِلَّا عَلَى الْخَاشِعِينَ$$

Take recourse in patience and prayer, and it is indeed hard, except for the humble.[36]

Worship is hard for everyone but the humble. The humble are the ones who understand the meaning of worship and dedicate their time and energy to it.

When we dedicate ourselves to worship and make it a priority and focal point in our lives, we can begin to realize its true meaning. Every day, we will taste something new of its sweetness. Every day, we will reap a new benefit and a take an extra step on our journey towards God.

But if we put a greater priority on every endeavor, goal, whim, and desire, we will not be able to properly engage in worship. We will not be able to taste its sweetness and reap its benefits.

We see that the teachings of our faith always put an emphasis on worship and setting aside time for these rituals and placing them at the top of our list of priorities. Only then can we taste the

---

[36] The Holy Quran, 2:45.

pleasure of worship – a pleasure that cannot be compared to any worldly pleasure. Only then can we taste the sweetness and pleasure of growing closer to God's Majesty. We must set aside time for our worship and yearn for it out of a true and sincere love. Imam Hussain (a) narrates that the Holy Prophet (s) once said:

أفضل الناس من عشق العبادة فعانقها وأحبها بقلبه وباشرها بجسده وتفرغ لها، فهو لا يبالي على ما أصبح من الدنيا على عسر أم على يسر

The best of people is the one who loves worship and embraces it, yearning for it in his heart, proceeding towards it with his body, and setting aside time for it. He shall not care for the matters of the world and whether he is at hardship or at ease.[37]

It is also narrated that the Commander of the Faithful (a) said,

دوام العبادة برهان الظفر بالسعادة

Continuous worship is a mark of attainment of [true] happiness.[38]

Practical Application

After all we have discussed about the nature and beauty of worship, we must now turn to address a couple of practical methods by which we can implement some of what we discussed.

---

[37] Al-Kulayni, *al-Kafi*, 2:83.
[38] Al-Wasiti, *'Oyoun al-Hikam*, 251.

There is no doubt that when a person who forms a certain habit, their habitual routine will be an integral part of their day. We find comfort in these habits and are discomforted when we are unable to engage in them for one reason or another. This is true whether the actual habit is good or bad.

The same analysis is true of worship. The more an individual habituates themself to engage in worship, the more attached they will become to it and the more comfort they will find in it. This habituation of worship is something that is rationally desirable, as everyone agrees that forming good habits is a positive thing. We even find narrations that support this approach, such as the narration of the Holy Prophet (s) who said,

$$\text{الخير عادة}$$

Virtue is a habit.[39]

We must also realize that an important aspect of worship is its effect in purifying our soul and clearing our vision. With a clear vision, we can see more plainly the value and importance of worship, and we will be more inclined to engage ourselves in it.

We must also be cognizant not to force ourselves to worship. This would naturally create an opposite effect that would repel our hearts from worship. That is why we find in the narrations of the Holy Household (a) a constant emphasis on worship, but with a realization that these rituals must be approached freely

---

[39] Al-Hindi, *Kanz al-'Ommal*, 16:119.

and with a yearning. It is narrated that the Commander of the Faithful (a) said:

وَخَادِعْ نَفْسَكَ فِي الْعِبَادَةِ، وَارْفُقْ بِهَا وَلاَ تَقْهَرْهَا، وَخُذْ عَفْوَهَا وَنَشَاطَهَا، إِلاَّ مَا كَانَ مَكْتُوباً عَلَيْكَ مِنَ الْفَرِيضَةِ، فَإِنَّهُ لاَ بُدَّ مِنْ قَضَائِهَا وَتَعَاهُدِهَا عِنْدَ مَحَلِّهَا.

> *Deceive your heart into worshipping; persuade it and do not force it. Engage it when it is free and merry. This is except as regards the obligations enjoined upon you, for they should not be neglected and must be performed at their due times.*[40]

We see that our beloved Imams (a) would continually remind their companions of the importance of worship. Imam al-Kadhim (a) once told some of his sons:

عليك بالجد ولا تخرجن نفسك من حد التقصير في عبادة الله تعالى وطاعته فإن الله لا يعبد حق عبادته

> *Be diligent and do not think that you can evade shortcoming in the worship and obedience of God. Surely, God is never worshiped as He truly deserves.*[41]

On the other hand, they realized the need for balance in approaching worship. Imam al-Sadiq (a) would say,

لا تكرهوا الى أنفسكم العبادة

---

[40] Al-Radi, *Nahj al-Balagha*, 3:130, Letter 69.
[41] Al-Kulayni, *al-Kafi*, 2:72.

> *Do not make worship abhorrent to yourselves.*[42]

The balance is in giving the proper importance and priority to worship, but doing so freely and with desire, rather than doing it sluggishly and without the proper state of mind.

We cannot all at once reach a level of full engagement with worship, where we taste its true pleasure. The process will be gradual, and we must put in the time and effort required for us to reach that state. There should be no doubt that this is a great goal that deserves our time and energy. Only then can we reap the true benefits of these divinely prescribed rituals.

---

[42] Al-Kulayni, *al-Kafi*, 2:86.

REMEMBRANCE OF GOD

In the Name of God, the Most Beneficent, the Most Merciful

اتْلُ مَا أُوحِيَ إِلَيْكَ مِنَ الْكِتَابِ وَأَقِمِ الصَّلَاةَ ۖ إِنَّ الصَّلَاةَ تَنْهَىٰ عَنِ الْفَحْشَاءِ وَالْمُنكَرِ ۗ وَلَذِكْرُ اللَّهِ أَكْبَرُ ۗ وَاللَّهُ يَعْلَمُ مَا تَصْنَعُونَ

Recite what has been revealed to you of the Book, and maintain the prayer. Indeed, the prayer restrains from indecent and wrongful conduct, and the remembrance of God is surely greater. And God knows whatever you do.[1]

God's blessings upon humanity are too many to be counted or limited. God says,

وَإِن تَعُدُّوا نِعْمَةَ اللَّهِ لَا تُحْصُوهَا ۗ إِنَّ اللَّهَ لَغَفُورٌ رَّحِيمٌ

If you enumerate God's blessings, you will not be able to count them. Indeed God is all-forgiving, all-merciful.[2]

The most important of God's blessings is the blessing of guidance. It is through His guidance that we can elevate in the levels of closeness to His Majesty. It is the path of achieving true eternal happiness in this world and the next. Without this guidance, we would be left to our own devices and our souls would continue

---

[1] The Holy Quran, 29:45.
[2] The Holy Quran, 16:18.

to degenerate in the levels of corruption. When an individual loses all attachment to this guidance, they become like an animal or worse. God says:

$$\text{أَمْ تَحْسَبُ أَنَّ أَكْثَرَهُمْ يَسْمَعُونَ أَوْ يَعْقِلُونَ ۚ إِنْ هُمْ إِلَّا كَالْأَنْعَامِ ۖ بَلْ هُمْ أَضَلُّ سَبِيلًا}$$

Do you suppose that most of them listen or exercise their reason? They are just like cattle; indeed, they are further astray from the way.[3]

The means of guidance are numerous and vary in their degrees. When we go back to the blessed verse we mentioned at the outset of the chapter, we see that God lists a number of those means of guidance. God first mentions recitation of the Holy Book and the maintenance of prayers, both of which we know to be important aspects of our faith and integral to our journey towards God. He then mentions remembrance of Him, and states that it is surely greater. Even with everything we know about prayer and its importance, the remembrance of God is still greater. After all, prayer is only one method by which we remember God.

Remembrance of God is thus the greatest means by which we can elevate ourselves in nearness to Him. Without remembrance, we only sink further in deviance and corruption, becoming worse than any of His other creatures. God says:

---

[3] The Holy Quran, 25:44.

> وَلَقَدْ ذَرَأْنَا لِجَهَنَّمَ كَثِيرًا مِّنَ الْجِنِّ وَالْإِنسِ ۖ لَهُمْ قُلُوبٌ لَّا يَفْقَهُونَ بِهَا وَلَهُمْ أَعْيُنٌ لَّا يُبْصِرُونَ بِهَا وَلَهُمْ آذَانٌ لَّا يَسْمَعُونَ بِهَا ۚ أُولَٰئِكَ كَالْأَنْعَامِ بَلْ هُمْ أَضَلُّ ۚ أُولَٰئِكَ هُمُ الْغَافِلُونَ

Certainly We have winnowed out for Hell many of the jinn and humans: they have hearts with which they do not understand, they have eyes with which they do not see, they have ears with which they do not hear. They are like cattle; indeed, they are more astray. It is they who are the heedless.[4]

Such individuals fall to a level below the beasts, due to their heedlessness. It is heedlessness of God that makes in individual degenerate in this manner and makes their life a wretched one in this world and in the hereafter.

Here we must mention a few important points.

WHAT IS REMEMBRANCE?

Some people may think of remembrance of God simply as glorifying Him and mentioning His names and attributes. While this may be one form of remembrance, the term could encompass much more than just that. Remembrance has many levels, and the remembrance of the tongue is the lowest of these levels.

The more important aspect of remembrance is turning toward God. Words uttered by the tongue should reflect the state of the

---

[4] The Holy Quran, 7:179.

heart and its engagement with God. In one narration Moses asked God,

$$\text{إلهي ما جزاؤ من ذكرك بلسانه وقلبه؟}$$

> O' Lord, what is reward of the one who remembers you with his tongue and his heart?

God says,

$$\text{يا موسى أظلله يوم القيامة بظل عرشي وأجعله في كنفي}$$

> O' Moses, I shall shade him in the shade of my Throne and have him at my side.[5]

An individual should live their life with God's remembrance constantly in their heart and on their tongue. Yet, there are even higher levels of remembrance we should aspire to. An individual's remembrance can rise to such a level that they are constantly aware of God's presence – knowing that God is constantly with them and sees them. God is never absent from the heart and mind of such an individual. Even within this level, there is a great variety of degrees among those who have achieved it, based on their level of closeness to the Almighty. The closer an individual grows to God, the stronger their remembrance will be, until they dissolve completely in the love of their Lord.

---

[5] Al-Sadouq, *Fada'el al-Ashhor al-Thalath*, 88.

The Commander of the Faithful (a) teaches us of these levels and how we should aspire for that complete level of devotion. He taught us in the whispered prayers of the Month of Sha'ban:

إلهي هَب لي كمال الانقطاع إليك ، وأنر أبصار قلوبنا بضياء نظرها إليك حتى تخرق أبصار القلوب حُجُب النور ، فتصل إلى معدن العظمة ، وتصير أرواحنا مُعلقة بعزّ قدسك

> O' Lord, grant me excellence in devotion to you and brighten the foresight of our hearts with the light of looking on to you, so that the foresight of the hearts can breach the veils of light and reach the mettle of greatness. And so our souls will become attached to the honor of Your Majesty.[6]

When a person reaches this level of devotion and remembrance, they will see nothing in existence but God. As our beloved Imam (a) says,

ما رأيت شيئا إلا ورأيت الله قبله وبعده ومعه

> I have not seen anything except that I have seen God before, after, and alongside it.[7]

This is the greatest level of remembering God, where the individual lives with God in every instance of their being. Of course, God is always present and continues to bless and sustain us. The

---

[6] Ibn Tawus, *Iqbal al-A'mal*, 3:299.

[7] Al-Ameeni, *Tazkiyat al-Nafs*, 151. Al-Sayyid al-Ameeni did not provide a source for the narration, however it is relayed with some discrepancy by al-Mazandarani as, "I have not seen anything except that I have seen God before it." See: al-Mazandarani, *Sharh Usool al-Kafi*, 3:83.

problem is with us when we are heedless of Him. That is why our Creator stressed the importance of remembrance in many verses of His Holy Book. He says,

$$\text{وَاذْكُر رَّبَّكَ إِذَا نَسِيتَ وَقُلْ عَسَىٰ أَن يَهْدِيَنِ رَبِّي لِأَقْرَبَ مِنْ هَٰذَا رَشَدًا}$$

When you forget, remember your Lord, and say, 'Maybe my Lord will guide me to [something] more akin to rectitude than this.'[8]

This verse asks us to remember God whenever we fall from a higher level of awareness to a lower one through forgetfulness. The verse clearly indicates the existence of levels in terms of remembrance of the heart.

God – out of His boundless love for us and favor upon us – wants us to continue to grow closer to Him. We must be constantly aware of Him, just as He is constantly aware of us. He is constantly blessing and sustaining us and never forgetting about us. We exist and live out of God's constant attention towards us. We must be aware of this constant attention and meet it with constant remembrance. We must not forget about our Creator and Sustainer and must see Him before our eyes wherever we turn. We must seek to strengthen our relationship with Him day after day. We should realize that ultimately, we are the ones benefitting from this relationship. The more we grow in remembrance of, closeness to, and love for God, the more we prepare ourselves for greater blessings and rewards.

---

[8] The Holy Quran, 18:24.

Al-Faidh al-Kashani, a renowned scholar, says that the path to attaining and strengthening the love of God, to prepare to see and meet with Him, is through attainment and strengthening of knowledge. The path of attaining knowledge is through purification of the heart and removal of all worldly preoccupations; only then can one reach a complete level of devotion to God through remembrance and reflection. The heart is like a vessel: if filled with water it has no room for vinegar. It must be emptied of the water to have room for the vinegar. God did not create anyone with two hearts. Perfect love is for an individual to love their Lord with their whole heart. Therefore, if a person is attendant to anything other than God, there will be a corner of their heart that is preoccupied with that thing, rather than God. So, if an individual is preoccupied with something other than God, the result is an incomplete love of God – unless that attention given to what is besides God is given to it because it is an effect and creation of God and a manifestation of His names and attributes.

How Much to Remember?

Now that we know the importance of remembrance, is there a specific amount of remembrance that we need to maintain to grow spiritually? When we look at the verses of the Holy Quran and the noble traditions, we see that they emphasize the need for constant remembrance and that we should not suffice ourselves with only a little. Remembrance is a means to growing closer to God, so we must utilize our short lives on this Earth to grow closer and closer to Him. The verses of the Holy Quran emphasize this concept. God says,

$$\text{يَا أَيُّهَا الَّذِينَ آمَنُوا اذْكُرُوا اللَّهَ ذِكْرًا كَثِيرًا}$$

> O you who have faith! Remember God with frequent remembrance.[9]

The Holy Quran asks us to remember God, no matter what we are going through in our lives. God says of the believers:

$$\text{الَّذِينَ يَذْكُرُونَ اللَّهَ قِيَامًا وَقُعُودًا وَعَلَىٰ جُنُوبِهِمْ وَيَتَفَكَّرُونَ فِي خَلْقِ السَّمَاوَاتِ وَالْأَرْضِ رَبَّنَا مَا خَلَقْتَ هَٰذَا بَاطِلًا سُبْحَانَكَ فَقِنَا عَذَابَ النَّارِ}$$

> Those who remember God standing, sitting, and lying on their sides, and reflect on the creation of the heavens and the Earth [and say], 'Our Lord, You have not created this in vain! Immaculate are You! Save us from the punishment of the Fire.[10]

The noble verses also tell us that we need to be in the state of remembrance constantly, at all times of the day. God says,

$$\text{وَاذْكُرِ اسْمَ رَبِّكَ بُكْرَةً وَأَصِيلًا ﴿٢٥﴾ وَمِنَ اللَّيْلِ فَاسْجُدْ لَهُ وَسَبِّحْهُ لَيْلًا طَوِيلًا ﴿٢٦﴾}$$

> Celebrate the Name of your Lord morning and evening, and worship Him for a watch of the night and glorify Him the night long.[11]

---

[9] The Holy Quran, 33:41.
[10] The Holy Quran, 3:191.
[11] The Holy Quran, 76:25-26.

We see the same emphasis on the need for constant remembrance when we turn to the noble traditions. In one letter by Imam al-Sadiq (a) to his companions, he said:

فَأَكْثِرُوا ذِكْرَ اللهِ ما استطعتم في كل ساعة من ساعات الليل والنهار فإن الله أمر بكثرة الذكر له والله ذاكر لمن ذكره من المؤمنين، واعلموا أن الله لم يذكره أحد من عباده المؤمنين إلا ذكره بخير

> *Remember God whenever you can in the hours of night and day. Surely, God commanded remembrance and He will remember any believer who remembers him. Know that God is never remembered by any one of his believing servants except that He shall remember him well.* [12]

In another narration, Imam al-Sadiq (a) said:

ما من شئ إلا وله حد ينتهي إليه إلا الذكر فليس له حد ينتهي إليه، فرض الله عز وجل الفرائض فمن أداهن فهو حدهن و شهر رمضان فمن صامه فهو حده والحج فمن حج فهو حده إلا الذكر فإن الله عز وجل لم يرض منه بالقليل ولم يجعل له حدا ينتهي إليه

> *Everything has a limit at which it must end, except for remembrance, which does not have a limit and end. God Almighty has mandated the obligatory worship, so whoever fulfills this has reached their limit. The month of Ramadan [has a limit], so whoever fasts during the month reaches its limit. The Hajj [also has a limit] so*

---

[12] Al-Kulayni, *al-Kafi*, 8:7.

that whomever performs the Hajj has reached its limit. The exception is remembrance. Surely, God will not be content with little of it and has not made a limit at which it ends.

(يا أيها الذين آمنوا اذكروا الله ذكرا كثيرا وسبحوه بكرة وأصيلا) لم يجعل الله عزوجل له حد اينتهي إليه، وكان أبي عليه السلام كثير الذكر لقد كنت أمشي معه وإنه ليذكر الله وآكل معه الطعام وإنه ليذكر الله ولقد كان يحدث القوم وما يشغله ذلك عن ذكر الله

[God says,] 'O you who have faith! Remember God with frequent remembrance, and glorify Him morning and evening.'[13] [...] My father was a man of constant remembrance. I would walk alongside him and he would remember God. I would eat with him and he would remember God. He would talk to people, but that would not preoccupy him from remembering God.[14]

These noble traditions always encourage us to remember God, and not to fall short and become preoccupied. If we wish to gain eternal happiness in this world and the next, we must take the Holy Household (a) of the Prophet (s) as role models in this regard. We must study their lives and see their dedication in remembrance of God, and attempt to implement their teachings in our lives.

---

[13] The Holy Quran, 33:41-42.
[14] Al-Kulayni, al-Kafi, 2:498.

When to Remember?

When we go back to the noble traditions, we find that they specify situations when remembrance is especially important. Let us take a small sample of these significant times of remembrance:

In Ease and Hardship

When an individual is at ease – being blessed in every aspect of his life and not feeling that they need anything – they may tend to forget about their creator. We may forget that the origin and sustainer of these blessings is none other than the Almighty God. We should never think that the blessings we receive are due to our own merit or because we are in some way better than others. Rather, we must constantly remind ourselves that all blessings are ultimately gifts from God, for which we must always be grateful and thankful.

On the other hand, poverty and hardship may also lead an individual to forget about their Lord. When we face hardship in our lives, we must realize our ultimate need for the Almighty and seek refuge in Him from all the evils of this world.

We see the importance of remembering God in ease and in hardship when we read the noble traditions of our Immaculate Imams (a). Imam al-Jawad (a) narrates that the Holy Prophet (s) said:

من تظاهرت عليه النعم فليقل: الحمد لله رب العالمين، ومن ألح عليه الفقر فليكثر من قول: لا حول ولا قوة إلا بالله العلي العظيم، فإنه كنز من كنوز الجنة، وفيه شفاء من اثنين وسبعين داء أدناها الهم

Whoever is showered with blessings should say, 'Praise be to God, Lord of the realms!' Whoever is plagued by poverty should say, 'There is no power nor might except through God, the Most High and Great!' Surely, this is a treasure of paradise and contains the cure to seventy two ailments, the least of which is worry.[15]

In Times of Doubt

We may find ourselves facing some doubts at times about God's attributes and actions. Over time, these doubts may erode an individual's faith and undermine their acts of worship. We must seek refuge in God at these times and do what we can to dispel these doubts.

Imam al-Baqir (a) once relayed a relevant story from the time of the Holy Prophet (s). He said that some of the believers once complained to the Holy Prophet (s) about the misconceptions being presented to them. They said that they would evade these doubts and would rather face the worst of punishments rather than speak of them. The Holy Prophet (s) said to them:

والذي نفسي بيده إن ذلك لصريح الايمان، فإذا وجد تموه فقولوا: آمنا بالله ورسوله ولا حول ولا قوة إلا بالله

By Him who holds my soul in His hands! That is surely the most manifest faith! Whenever you come across [such sins] say, 'We believe in God and His Messenger!

---

[15] Al-Sadouq, *al-Amali*, 651.

> *Surely, there is no power nor might except through God!*[16]

In Times of Heedlessness

The noble traditions speak of a situation that we may go through from time to time. Sometimes we may feel that our hearts are empty – we feel neither the warmth of faith nor the chill of disbelief. In that state, we are heedless of where we are and where we are going. This state should not be underestimated, as it could lead to a state of loss, weakness, and despair. At that point, we must seek refuge in remembering God before our hearts die and can never return to a spiritual life.

The noble traditions mention this state and prescribe remembrance as the cure. One day, Abu Osama was accompanying Imam al-Sadiq (a). The Imam asked him to read from the Holy Quran, so he began reciting. Suddenly he began crying and said:

يا أبا أسامة ادعوا قلوبكم بذكر الله عز وجل واحذروا النكت فإنه يأتي على القلب تارات الشك.

> *O' Abu Osama, call your hearts by the remembrance of God Almighty. Beware of lethargy, as it comes over the heart at times of doubt.*[17]

In Worldly Matters

Becoming preoccupied with worldly matters is one of the main reasons for an individual becoming heedless of God. Generally,

---

[16] Al-Kulayni, *al-Kafi*, 2:425.
[17] Al-Kulayni, *al-Kafi*, 8:167.

this preoccupation weakens an individual's spiritual connection. That is why we find at times that individuals who are successful in their lives – in terms of career, business, and wealth – tend to become arrogant and forget about God's continued blessings upon them.

That is why we find many narrations that stress the importance of remembrance at times when our connection to this world may be strongest. For example, the narrations stress the importance of remembering God when entering a market and going shopping. There is also an emphasis on remembering God when looking at the mirror and taking care of your looks.[18]

True Remembrance

From the above discussion, we can see the importance of remembering God in any state we may be in. If we think about it, we spend most of our lives in the states discussed above. We must be with God and cognizant of Him at all times. We must ensure that these short lives of ours are invested well as "the farmland of the Hereafter."[19] Only then can we achieve eternal happiness in Paradise alongside the prophets, messengers, and righteous servants of God.

Some of us may think that if we mention God, pray, fast, and recite the Holy Quran, we are remembering God. All these actions, with their great benefits, are a part of remembrance of

---

[18] For example, see: Al-'Amili, *Wasa'el al-Shia*, 4:1177 to the remainder of the volume.

[19] Al-Ihsa'ei, *'Awali al-La'ali*, 1:267.

God. However, we do not truly remember Him through these actions if we perform them mindlessly and without awareness of their true meaning and the true meaning of remembrance.

To remember God is not just to pray and recite the Holy Quran. To remember God is to truly obey Him, seeing Him all around and feeling His presence in everything. To remember Him is to follow His commands and refrain from what He has forbidden. As the Holy Prophet (s) said:

من أطاع الله عز وجل فقد ذكر الله وإن قلت صلاته وصيامه وتلاوته، ومن عصى الله فقد نسي الله وإن كثرت صلاته وصيامه وتلاوته للقرآن.

Whoever obeys God Almighty has surely remembered Him, even if his prayers, fasting, and recitation were little. Whoever disobeys God has surely forgotten Him, even if he continuously prays, fasts, and recites the Quran.[20]

How much we pray and recite is not the measure of true remembrance. Remembrance is to obey God's every command and follow His guiding light. We need to cognizant of the quality of our actions and not be preoccupied with quantity. As Imam al-Baqir (a) said:

ثلاث من أشد ما عمل العباد: انصاف المؤمن من نفسه، ومواساة المرء أخاه، وذكر الله على كل حال، وهو أن يذكر الله عز وجل عند المعصية

---

[20] Al-Sadouq, *Ma'ani al-Akhbar*, 399.

يهم بها فيحول ذكر الله بينه وبين تلك المعصية وهو قول الله عز وجل (إن الذين اتقوا إذا مسهم طائف من الشيطان تذكروا فإذا هم مبصرون)

> *Three actions are the greatest that a servant may undertake; to give justice to a believer even against himself, to condole one another, and to remember God in every circumstance – to remember God Almighty while endeavoring to sin so that this remembrance acts as a deterrence from the intended act of disobedience. This is the meaning of the word of God, 'When those who are God-wary are touched by a visitation of Satan, they remember [God] and, behold, they perceive.'*[21]

True remembrance is to remember God when an opportunity to sin and disobey is presented, such that His remembrance drives us away from disobedience. That is remembrance that has a true effect on an individual. Otherwise, simply reciting and glorifying the names of God without reflection cannot be called remembrance; if we think that mindless worship is adequate remembrance, then we are fooling no one but ourselves. As Imam al-Rida (a) said,

من ذكر الله ولم يستبق الى لقائه فقد استهزأ بنفسه

> *Whoever remembers God but does not prepare to meet him has surely deceived himself.*[22]

---

[21] Al-Sadouq, *al-Khisal*, 131. Citing: The Holy Quran, 7:201.
[22] Al-Majlisi, *Bihar al-Anwar*, 75:356.

We ask God Almighty to make us amongst those who truly remember and obey Him.

GUIDANCE AND MISGUIDANCE

In the Name of God, the Most Beneficent, the Most Merciful

وَمَا أَرْسَلْنَا مِن رَّسُولٍ إِلَّا بِلِسَانِ قَوْمِهِ لِيُبَيِّنَ لَهُمْ ۖ فَيُضِلُّ اللَّهُ مَن يَشَاءُ وَيَهْدِي مَن يَشَاءُ ۚ وَهُوَ الْعَزِيزُ الْحَكِيمُ

We did not send any apostle except with the language of his people, so that he might make [Our messages] clear to them. Then God leads astray whomever He wishes, and He guides whomsoever He wishes, and He is the All-mighty, the All-wise.[1]

One of the great issues discussed in theology is the so-called paradox of free will. Is an individual free to choose their own actions despite the existence of any power that can stop them from undertaking those decisions? Or are we predestined by an external force to act the way we do, such that we have no choice in our behaviors?

---

[1] The Holy Quran, 14:4.

This debate has concerned thinkers across various religions and philosophies. In terms of Muslim theologians, there are three different philosophies presented:

First, there are those who believe in complete predestination. These thinkers and theologians believe that we are all destined to undertake the actions that we do. Any action or behavior is thus a manifestation of God's will, without the involvement of human will or decision making in the process. All acts are the acts of God, as He is the creator of all actors and all action.

Second, there is a group of theologians who believe in complete free will. They believe that God created mankind and delegated to us the complete authority to make our choices and undertake our actions. The action of any individual is theirs alone, without the involvement of divine will anywhere in the process.

The final group believes in a combination of human free will and divine predestination. This is the belief adopted by Shia scholars in accordance with the traditions of the Progeny of the Holy Prophet (s). As Imam al-Sadiq (a) said:

لا جبر ولا تفويض ولكن أمر بين أمرين

> There is no [complete] predestination and no [complete] delegation [i.e. free will]. Rather, it is a matter between the two.[2]

This is an issue of great debate amongst Muslim theologians and thinkers, currently and historically. We do not wish to debate the

---

[2] Al-Kulayni, *al-Kafi*, 1:160.

issue now and explain the philosophical and theological evidence in support of the third view. We simply lay out these opinions to make the point that this issue plays a significant role in formulating an individual's world view. The view that we adopt affects many other aspects of our lives – it can impact our view of the importance or worship, the role of ethics, and the significance of jurisprudence, to name just a few areas.

One of the important issues in Islamic theology – and one with great relevance to the paradox of free will and predestination – is the issue of divine guidance. Does God guide whomever He wishes and misguide others? Does He select who will receive the divine light of His guidance and who will remain in the shadows of deviance?

Guidance from God

When we turn to the Holy Quran, we see it clearly states that both guidance and misguidance are from God. In the verse we see at the beginning of this chapter, God also says:

وَلَوْ شَاءَ اللَّهُ لَجَعَلَكُمْ أُمَّةً وَاحِدَةً وَلَٰكِن يُضِلُّ مَن يَشَاءُ وَيَهْدِي مَن يَشَاءُ ۚ وَلَتُسْأَلُنَّ عَمَّا كُنتُمْ تَعْمَلُونَ

Had God wished, He would have made you one community, but He leads astray whomever He wishes and guides whomever He wishes, and you will surely be questioned concerning what you used to do.[3]

---

[3] The Holy Quran, 16:93.

God also says:

$$\text{فَإِنَّ اللَّهَ يُضِلُّ مَن يَشَاءُ وَيَهْدِي مَن يَشَاءُ ۖ فَلَا تَذْهَبْ نَفْسُكَ عَلَيْهِمْ حَسَرَاتٍ ۚ إِنَّ اللَّهَ عَلِيمٌ بِمَا يَصْنَعُونَ}$$

Indeed, God leads astray whomever He wishes, and guides whomever He wishes. So do not fret yourself to death regretting for them. Indeed, God knows best what they do.[4]

There are numerous other verses that hold a similar meaning. We see that whoever adopted the belief of predestination used these verses as evidence of their claims. They say that God created all creatures and has full ownership and authority over them all. He has complete authority to do with them whatever He pleases. As God says in the Holy Quran,

$$\text{لَا يُسْأَلُ عَمَّا يَفْعَلُ وَهُمْ يُسْأَلُونَ}$$

He is not questioned concerning what He does, but they are questioned.[5]

He guides and misguides as He wishes. He chooses to guide some people towards eternal Paradise and to misguide others toward Hellfire.

Many Muslim scholars and thinkers disagree with the above stated explanation of these verses. They provide the following evidence in support of their views:

---

[4] The Holy Quran, 35:8.
[5] The Holy Quran, 21:23.

First, we cannot read these verses and use them as evidence in support of a worldview without reading the Holy Quran in its totality. We must read the remainder of God's Book and see if it allows for the purported idea. We must read and take into consideration verses like the following:

مَّنِ اهْتَدَىٰ فَإِنَّمَا يَهْتَدِي لِنَفْسِهِ ۖ وَمَن ضَلَّ فَإِنَّمَا يَضِلُّ عَلَيْهَا ۚ وَلَا تَزِرُ وَازِرَةٌ وِزْرَ أُخْرَىٰ ۗ وَمَا كُنَّا مُعَذِّبِينَ حَتَّىٰ نَبْعَثَ رَسُولًا

Whoever is guided is guided only for [the good of] his own soul, and whoever goes astray, goes astray only to its detriment. No bearer shall bear another's burden.[6]

This verse and several others clearly state that guidance and misguidance is to be attributed to mankind and not to God.

Second, when we study the Holy Quran, we find that its verses can be divided into two categories – definitive and metaphorical. One verse clearly states this fact:

هُوَ الَّذِي أَنزَلَ عَلَيْكَ الْكِتَابَ مِنْهُ آيَاتٌ مُّحْكَمَاتٌ هُنَّ أُمُّ الْكِتَابِ وَأُخَرُ مُتَشَابِهَاتٌ ۖ فَأَمَّا الَّذِينَ فِي قُلُوبِهِمْ زَيْغٌ فَيَتَّبِعُونَ مَا تَشَابَهَ مِنْهُ ابْتِغَاءَ الْفِتْنَةِ وَابْتِغَاءَ تَأْوِيلِهِ

It is He who has sent down to you the Book. Parts of it are definitive verses, which are the mother of the Book, while others are metaphorical. As for those in whose

---

[6] The Holy Quran, 17:15.

hearts is deviance, they pursue what is metaphorical in it, courting temptation, and seeking its interpretation.[7]

There is no doubt that the verses attributing guidance and misguidance to God are of the metaphorical verses. As we will see in the remainder of this chapter, this attribution could have numerous meanings. We must turn back to the definitive verses that have a bearing on the issue, such us the verses indicating His divine wisdom and justice.

We cannot accept any description of our Creator that paints Him as capricious or oppressive. He is sublime above any such fault or shortcoming. That is why we see God describing to us His wisdom in the very same verses where He attributes to Himself guidance and misguidance. He does this to remind us before our thoughts carry us to think ill of Him. He says,

$$\text{فَيُضِلُّ اللَّهُ مَن يَشَاءُ وَيَهْدِي مَن يَشَاءُ ۚ وَهُوَ الْعَزِيزُ الْحَكِيمُ}$$

God leads astray whomever He wishes, and He guides whomsoever He wishes, and He is the All-mighty, the All-wise.[8]

In the verse, He reminds us of His wisdom, which is incompatible with a random selection of who to save and who to misguide. In another verse, He says,

$$\text{يُضِلُّ مَن يَشَاءُ وَيَهْدِي مَن يَشَاءُ ۚ وَلَتُسْأَلُنَّ عَمَّا كُنتُمْ تَعْمَلُونَ}$$

---

[7] The Holy Quran, 3:7.
[8] The Holy Quran, 14:4.

> *He leads astray whomever He wishes and guides whomever He wishes, and you will surely be questioned concerning what you used to do.*[9]

We will be questioned for our choices and punished or rewarded based on them. This is a testament to His justice, which is incompatible with the claim of predetermination.

A careful reader of the verses will thus see that they do not fully support the alleged claim of predestination. We must therefore try to find the correct meaning of these verses by better understanding the issue of divine guidance.

What is Guidance?

Looking back at the linguistic meaning of guidance can be helpful at this point. The Oxford Dictionary defines guidance as "advice or information aimed at resolving a problem or difficulty, especially as given by someone in authority."[10] Guidance can thus be described as showing someone the path or taking them towards it. Similar meaning is found in the Arabic equivalent of guidance found in the mentioned verses.

When we look at guidance in the Holy Quran, we also see several different meanings for the word.

First, we see there is a form of formative guidance, such as guidance of every creature towards its perfection, for which it was created. This form of guidance is not just for every human being,

---

[9] The Holy Quran, 16:93.
[10] *Oxford Dictionaries, s.v.* "Guidance."

but for every single one of His creations. He says in the Holy Quran,

$$\text{قَالَ رَبُّنَا الَّذِي أَعْطَىٰ كُلَّ شَيْءٍ خَلْقَهُ ثُمَّ هَدَىٰ}$$

Our Lord is He who gave everything its creation and then guided it.[11]

He also says,

$$\text{سَبِّحِ اسْمَ رَبِّكَ الْأَعْلَى ﴿١﴾ الَّذِي خَلَقَ فَسَوَّىٰ ﴿٢﴾ وَالَّذِي قَدَّرَ فَهَدَىٰ ﴿٣﴾}$$

Celebrate the Name of your Lord, the Most Exalted, who created and proportioned, who determined and guided.[12]

In other words, God creates every one of His creatures with whatever that creature needs to reach its highest potential. Divine guidance can thus be seen in the ability for bees to build hives out of wax and make honey out of nectar. God gives this as an example in the Holy Quran when He says:

$$\text{وَأَوْحَىٰ رَبُّكَ إِلَى النَّحْلِ أَنِ اتَّخِذِي مِنَ الْجِبَالِ بُيُوتًا وَمِنَ الشَّجَرِ وَمِمَّا يَعْرِشُونَ ﴿٦٨﴾ ثُمَّ كُلِي مِن كُلِّ الثَّمَرَاتِ فَاسْلُكِي سُبُلَ رَبِّكِ ذُلُلًا ۚ يَخْرُجُ مِن بُطُونِهَا شَرَابٌ مُّخْتَلِفٌ أَلْوَانُهُ فِيهِ شِفَاءٌ لِّلنَّاسِ ۗ إِنَّ فِي ذَٰلِكَ لَآيَةً لِّقَوْمٍ يَتَفَكَّرُونَ ﴿٦٩﴾}$$

---

[11] The Holy Quran, 20:50.
[12] The Holy Quran, 87:1-3.

> *Your Lord inspired the bee [saying]: 'Make your home in the mountains, and on the trees and the trellises that they erect. Then eat from every [kind of] fruit and follow meekly the ways of your Lord.' There issues from its belly a juice of diverse hues, in which there is a cure for the people. There is indeed a sign in that for a people who reflect.*[13]

The ability of a small embryo in a woman's womb to form into a fully grown human baby is also a form of divine guidance. These examples and others portray the formative guidance that God grants to every one of His creatures.

We can see that formative guidance is a divine blessing to every creature, albeit one that differs from one to another. When it comes to humankind, God gave us the intellect, which allows us to reach our highest levels of excellence. In that vein, we see the verses of the Holy Quran often reminding us to think, ponder, and contemplate.

Second, God has given us – humankind – a form of guidance suited to our moral agency. God outlined for us everything that may bring us closer to eternal happiness and further away from desolation. He provided this guidance through messengers, prophets, Imams, and scholars – all of whom fall within the line of God's legislative guidance, which God mentioned in the verse:

---

[13] The Holy Quran, 16:68-69.

$$\text{لَقَدْ أَرْسَلْنَا رُسُلَنَا بِالْبَيِّنَاتِ وَأَنزَلْنَا مَعَهُمُ الْكِتَابَ وَالْمِيزَانَ لِيَقُومَ النَّاسُ بِالْقِسْطِ}$$

> *Certainly We sent Our apostles with manifest proofs, and We sent down with them the Book and the Balance, so that mankind may maintain justice.*[14]

God Almighty also said,

$$\text{ذَٰلِكَ الْكِتَابُ لَا رَيْبَ ۛ فِيهِ ۛ هُدًى لِّلْمُتَّقِينَ}$$

> *This is the Book, there is no doubt in it, a guidance to the Godwary.*[15]

In another verse, God says:

$$\text{وَمَا أَرْسَلْنَا قَبْلَكَ إِلَّا رِجَالًا نُّوحِي إِلَيْهِمْ ۚ فَاسْأَلُوا أَهْلَ الذِّكْرِ إِن كُنتُمْ لَا تَعْلَمُونَ}$$

> *We did not send [any apostles] before you except as men to whom We revealed. Ask the People of the Reminder if you do not know.*[16]

This legislative guidance was sent to all of mankind and not to some people over others. Still, there are two steps required for an individual to receive this guidance. The first step took place when God sent messengers and revealed scriptures to guide us. The second step is for us to follow the guidance that God sent.

---

[14] The Holy Quran, 57:25.

[15] The Holy Quran, 2:2.

[16] The Holy Quran, 21:7.

Guidance and Misguidance

God told our Holy Prophet in one verse, "Indeed, you guide to a straight path."[17]

God also commanded us to follow those guides. God says:

$$\text{يَا أَيُّهَا الَّذِينَ آمَنُوا أَطِيعُوا اللَّهَ وَأَطِيعُوا الرَّسُولَ وَأُولِي الْأَمْرِ مِنكُمْ}$$

O you who have faith! Obey God and obey the Apostle and those vested with authority among you.[18]

He also says:

$$\text{قُلْ أَطِيعُوا اللَّهَ وَأَطِيعُوا الرَّسُولَ ۖ فَإِن تَوَلَّوْا فَإِنَّمَا عَلَيْهِ مَا حُمِّلَ وَعَلَيْكُم مَّا حُمِّلْتُمْ ۖ وَإِن تُطِيعُوهُ تَهْتَدُوا ۚ وَمَا عَلَى الرَّسُولِ إِلَّا الْبَلَاغُ الْمُبِينُ}$$

Say, 'Obey God, and obey the Apostle.' But if you turn your backs, [you should know that] he is only responsible for his burden and you are responsible for your own burden, and if you obey him, you will be guided, and the Apostle's duty is only to communicate in clear terms.[19]

This form of guidance, being sent to all mankind without preference, is also unproblematic and does not raise the issue of predestination.

Finally, there may be a form of guidance that we can label as special guidance. God may bless some individuals by guiding them to greater and greater levels of proximity to Him, after they

---

[17] The Holy Quran, 42:52.
[18] The Holy Quran, 4:59.
[19] The Holy Quran, 24:54.

made full use of His formative and legislative guidance. God mentions this guidance in several verses. He says,

$$\text{إِنَّ اللَّهَ يُضِلُّ مَن يَشَاءُ وَيَهْدِي إِلَيْهِ مَنْ أَنَابَ}$$

Indeed God leads astray whomever He wishes, and guides to Himself those who turn penitently [to Him].[20]

In another verse He says,

$$\text{وَالَّذِينَ جَاهَدُوا فِينَا لَنَهْدِيَنَّهُمْ سُبُلَنَا ۚ وَإِنَّ اللَّهَ لَمَعَ الْمُحْسِنِينَ}$$

As for those who strive in Us, We shall surely guide them in Our ways, and God is indeed with the virtuous.[21]

God also speaks of some of His righteous servants, saying:

$$\text{إِنَّهُمْ فِتْيَةٌ آمَنُوا بِرَبِّهِمْ وَزِدْنَاهُمْ هُدًى ﴿١٣﴾ وَرَبَطْنَا عَلَىٰ قُلُوبِهِمْ إِذْ قَامُوا فَقَالُوا رَبُّنَا رَبُّ السَّمَاوَاتِ وَالْأَرْضِ لَن نَّدْعُوَ مِن دُونِهِ إِلَٰهًا ۖ لَّقَدْ قُلْنَا إِذًا شَطَطًا ﴿١٤﴾}$$

They were indeed youths who had faith in their Lord, and We had enhanced them in guidance, and fortified their hearts, when they stood up and said, 'Our Lord is the Lord of the heavens and the Earth. We will never invoke any god besides Him, for then we shall certainly have said an atrocious lie.'[22]

We see that the verses that speak of God guiding some individuals and not others are speaking of this form of guidance. In

---

[20] The Holy Quran, 13:27.

[21] The Holy Quran, 29:69.

[22] The Holy Quran, 18:13-14.

other words, God's special guidance is reserved for those who made full use of the other forms of guidance that He provided.

This form of guidance is also unproblematic. It does not raise the problem of predestination, because neither guidance nor misguidance is predetermined. Rather, this guidance is a blessing granted to those who utilized their free will and moral agency in worship and obedience to Him. This form of guidance does not contradict God's justice or wisdom, as it is not given without reason. God only grants it to those who earned it by their choices and their following of His formative and legislative guidance.

Similarly, God does not randomly or unjustly misguide his creation. As we said, God has granted His formative and legislative guidance to all, without exception. The verses that refer to misguidance are also references to the special guidance, which God grants only to those who work to earn it. When some verses mention that God misguides some people, they mean that He excludes them from His special guidance.

When we read the verses that speak of misguidance, we find that this exclusion is also tied to a reason rooted in the individual's actions and choices. God says,

$$\text{وَيُضِلُّ اللَّهُ الظَّالِمِينَ ۚ وَيَفْعَلُ اللَّهُ مَا يَشَاءُ}$$

> God leads astray the wrongdoers, and God does whatever He wishes.[23]

God also says,

---

[23] The Holy Quran, 14:27.

$$إِنَّ الَّذِينَ كَفَرُوا وَظَلَمُوا لَمْ يَكُنِ اللَّهُ لِيَغْفِرَ لَهُمْ وَلَا لِيَهْدِيَهُمْ طَرِيقًا$$

Indeed, those who are faithless and do wrong, God shall never forgive them, nor shall He guide them to any way.[24]

In a third verse, God says,

$$فَلَمَّا زَاغُوا أَزَاغَ اللَّهُ قُلُوبَهُمْ ۚ وَاللَّهُ لَا يَهْدِي الْقَوْمَ الْفَاسِقِينَ$$

So when they swerved [from the right path], God made their hearts swerve, and God does not guide the transgressing lot.[25]

There are other, similar verses that speak of God misguiding the wretched among His creation, and clearly indicating that it is not out of caprice or transgression on His part. The theme in all these verses is that special guidance and misguidance are earned through the actions and choices of an individual.

Therefore, it should be clear that these multiple layers of guidance – the formative, legislative, and special – are all part of a singular truth of divine guidance. All creatures were blessed with formative guidance, which brings them closer to excellence in the purpose for which they were created. For mankind, this means guidance through intellect and the various other faculties that God has granted us.

God also blessed us with legislative guidance by means of His messengers, prophets, and chosen servants. He outlined for us

---

[24] The Holy Quran, 4:168.
[25] The Holy Quran, 61:5.

a clear path through which we can make the choice to grow closer in proximity to Him. Whoever utilizes these two forms of guidance to the fullest will be blessed with the third layer of guidance, which God reserved for his selected servants. As for those who do not follow the first two layers of guidance that God granted, they will be excluded from this third layer. That is the meaning of misguidance as mentioned in the verses of the Holy Quran.

In one narration, Imam al-Sadiq (a) explained to us in detail the process of guidance. He said:

إن الله عزوجل إذا أراد بعبد خيرا نكت في قلبه نكتة من نور وفتح مسامع قلبه ووكل به ملكا يسدده، وإذا أراد بعبد سوءا نكت في قلبه نكتة سوداء وسد مسامع قلبه ووكل به شيطانا يضله، (فمن يرد الله أن يهديه يشرح صدره للاسلام ومن يرد أن يضله يجعل صدره ضيقا حرجا كأنما يصعد في السماء)

Surely, if God Almighty wishes well for a servant, He will pelt in his heart a pellet of light, open his ears and heart, and appoint for him an angel to support him. If He wishes ill for a servant, He will pelt in his heart a black pellet, close his ears and heart, and appoint for him a daemon to misguide him. [God Almighty says,] 'Whomever God desires to guide, He opens his breast to Islam, and whomever He desires to lead astray, He makes his breast narrow and straitened, as if he were climbing to a height. Thus does God lay [spiritual] defilement on those who do not have faith.'[26]

THE REASONS FOR GUIDANCE

Guidance and misguidance are not predestined and imposed upon us by God. They are rather based on our own choices and willingness to seek and earn His guidance. This is clear in some of the verses of the Holy Quran. These verses include:

إِنَّ اللَّهَ يُضِلُّ مَن يَشَاءُ وَيَهْدِي إِلَيْهِ مَنْ أَنَابَ

Indeed, God leads astray whomever He wishes, and guides to Himself those who turn penitently [to Him].[27]

وَالَّذِينَ جَاهَدُوا فِينَا لَنَهْدِيَنَّهُمْ سُبُلَنَا ۚ وَإِنَّ اللَّهَ لَمَعَ الْمُحْسِنِينَ

As for those who strive in Us, We shall surely guide them in Our ways, and God is indeed with the virtuous.[28]

وَالَّذِينَ اهْتَدَوْا زَادَهُمْ هُدًى وَآتَاهُمْ تَقْوَاهُمْ

As for those who are [rightly] guided, He enhances their guidance and invests them with their Godwariness.[29]

يَهْدِي بِهِ اللَّهُ مَنِ اتَّبَعَ رِضْوَانَهُ سُبُلَ السَّلَامِ وَيُخْرِجُهُم مِّنَ الظُّلُمَاتِ إِلَى النُّورِ بِإِذْنِهِ وَيَهْدِيهِمْ إِلَىٰ صِرَاطٍ مُّسْتَقِيمٍ

---

[26] Al-Kulayni, *al-Kafi*, 1:166. Citing: The Holy Quran, 6:125.
[27] The Holy Quran, 13:27.
[28] The Holy Quran, 29:69.
[29] The Holy Quran, 47:17.

Guidance and Misguidance

With it [i.e. the Holy Book], God guides those who follow [the course of] His pleasure to the ways of peace, and brings them out from darkness into light by His will, and guides them to a straight path.[30]

We can therefore achieve guidance by turning penitently to God and striving in His way. On the other hand, there are clear verses that mention how some people fall into misguidance, including:

وَاللَّهُ لَا يَهْدِي الْقَوْمَ الظَّالِمِينَ

God does not guide the wrongdoing lot.[31]

وَاللَّهُ لَا يَهْدِي الْقَوْمَ الْكَافِرِينَ

God does not guide the faithless lot.[32]

إِنَّ اللَّهَ لَا يَهْدِي مَنْ هُوَ كَاذِبٌ كَفَّارٌ

Indeed, God does not guide someone who is a liar and an ingrate.[33]

إِنَّ اللَّهَ لَا يَهْدِي مَنْ هُوَ مُسْرِفٌ كَذَّابٌ

Indeed, God does not guide someone who is a transgressor and liar.[34]

---

[30] The Holy Quran, 5:16.
[31] The Holy Quran, 2:258.
[32] The Holy Quran, 2:264.
[33] The Holy Quran, 39:3.
[34] The Holy Quran, 40:28.

It should thus be clear that misguidance is only earned when an individual transgresses against the boundaries that God drew for us and guided us towards.

How do we achieve guidance and avoid misguidance? The answer should be clear by now. Anyone who wishes to receive God's special guidance should work to earn it by following the other types of guidance which are already in their hands. We must first follow the formative guidance, which God granted us to listen to His words and believe in them. We must then follow His legislative guidance by obeying His commands and devoting ourselves to Him. Only then will we be eligible to receive the grace of His selective guidance.

Ill Outcomes

In the Name of God, the Most Beneficent, the Most Merciful

سَلْ بَنِي إِسْرَائِيلَ كَمْ آتَيْنَاهُم مِّنْ آيَةٍ بَيِّنَةٍ ۗ وَمَن يُبَدِّلْ نِعْمَةَ اللَّهِ مِن بَعْدِ مَا جَاءَتْهُ فَإِنَّ اللَّهَ شَدِيدُ الْعِقَابِ

Ask the Children of Israel how many a manifest sign We had given them. Whoever changes God's blessing after it has come to him, indeed God is severe in retribution.[1]

We discussed in the previous chapter the nature of guidance and how we may be able to earn it. If we read some of the parables in the Holy Quran and look at some of the examples we see in our lives, we find that there are people who strive to earn guidance, but then somehow end up losing it.

We find that the Holy Quran and the blessed narrations emphasize that no one is immune to losing the blessing of guidance. In other words, once a level of spirituality and closeness to God is achieved, there is still much work involved in maintaining it.

---

[1] The Holy Quran, 2:211.

An example of how this great blessing can be lost is provided throughout the Holy Quran in the story of Satan. Our narrations tell us that before becoming the vile and damned creature that he would become, Satan was one of God's closest worshipers. Imam Ali (a) explained how and why Satan lost that status:

فَاعْتَبِرُوا بِمَا كَانَ مِنْ فِعْلِ اللهِ بِإِبْلِيسَ، إِذْ أَحْبَطَ عَمَلَهُ الطَّوِيلَ، وَجَهْدَهُ الْجَهِيدَ، وَكَانَ قَدْ عَبَدَ اللهَ سِتَّةَ آلَافِ سَنَة، لاَ يُدْرَى أَمِنْ سِنِي الدُّنْيَا أَمْ مِنْ سِنِي الْآخِرَةِ، عَنْ كِبْرِ سَاعَة وَاحِدَة. فَمَنْ بَعْدَ إِبْلِيسَ يَسْلَمُ عَلَى اللهِ بِمِثْلِ مَعْصِيَتِهِ؟

You should take a lesson from what God did with Satan! He nullified his great acts and extensive efforts on account of the vanity of one moment, although Satan had worshipped God for six thousand years – whether that is by the reckoning of this world or of the next world is not known. Who now can remain safe from God after Satan by committing a similar disobedience?

كَلَّا، مَا كَانَ اللهُ سُبْحَانَهُ لِيُدْخِلَ الْجَنَّةَ بَشَراً بِأَمْرٍ أَخْرَجَ بِهِ مِنْهَا مَلَكاً، إِنَّ حُكْمَهُ فِي أَهْلِ السَّمَاءِ وَأَهْلِ الْأَرْضِ لَوَاحِدٌ، وَمَا بَيْنَ اللهِ وَبَيْنَ أَحَدٍ مِنْ خَلْقِهِ هَوَادَةٌ فِي إِبَاحَةِ حِمَى حَرَّمَهُ عَلَى الْعَالَمِينَ.

None at all. God, the Glorified, would not let a human being enter Paradise if he does the same thing for which God turned out from it an angel. His command for the inhabitants of the heavens and the Earth is the same.

Ill Outcomes

> *There is no friendship between God and any of His creatures so as to give him license for a forbidden thing which He has held unlawful for all creation.*[2]

The relationship with God is governed by the criteria that He set, without any favor given to any individual. Even our Holy Prophet (s) would have fallen from his great status as the most beloved of God's creation, had he disobeyed any of God's commands. That is why God speaks to the Prophet (s) and the believers in the Holy Quran, saying,

$$\text{وَلَقَدْ أُوحِيَ إِلَيْكَ وَإِلَى الَّذِينَ مِن قَبْلِكَ لَئِنْ أَشْرَكْتَ لَيَحْبَطَنَّ عَمَلُكَ وَلَتَكُونَنَّ مِنَ الْخَاسِرِينَ}$$

Certainly it has been revealed to you and to those [who have been] before you: If you ascribe a partner to God, your works shall fail and you shall surely be among the losers.[3]

God knows that the Holy Prophet (s) or any of His other Immaculate servants would not disobey Him or transgress in any way. However, He makes such statements to show all His creatures that no matter how much they excel, they are not immune from falling into deviance and reaping ill consequences.

---

[2] Al-Radi, *Nahj al-Balagha*, 2:139, Sermon 192.
[3] The Holy Quran, 39:65.

The Reasons for Ill Outcomes

There are many reasons why a person may fall out of guidance into misguidance and reach an ill outcome in his or her life. We will list a few of the important things that we should look out for, but generally, we should always live our lives in conscious awareness that we may at some point slip up. We need to be aware that whatever level of spirituality we attain is not guaranteed for us, but that we must continue to work to maintain our standing and reach higher levels. To that effect, the Holy Prophet (s) said,

لا يزال المؤمن خائفا من سوء العاقبة لا يتيقن الوصول الى رضوان الله حتى يكون وقت نزع روحه وظهور ملك الموت له

> *A believer will surely remain in fear of ill outcomes uncertain that he has pleased God, until it is time for the departing of his soul and the appearance of the angel of death.*[4]

The Holy Quran and blessed narrations have pointed out for us a number of factors that may lead to ill outcomes. They include the following:

Insincerity

There are many people who go about living their lives in this world with duplicity and hypocrisy. They put on a show for everyone around them, persuading their friends and associates that they are the best of people. But, these individuals may harbor the

---

[4] Al-Majlisi, *Bihar al-Anwar*, 68:366.

Ill Outcomes

most wretched of thoughts and commit the greatest of sins. These individuals may be able to fool the people around them, but they can never fool the Omniscient Lord, who sees the most secret of their actions and hears the deepest of their thoughts.

Even if a person keeps their actions secret, the consequences of these actions will manifest in the individual. Imam al-Sadiq (a) once recited this verse to a companion:

$$بَلِ الْإِنسَانُ عَلَىٰ نَفْسِهِ بَصِيرَةٌ$$

Indeed, man is a witness to himself.[5]

He explained the verse and said,

$$ما يصنع الإنسان أن يعتذر الى الناس خلاف ما يعلم الله منه، إن رسول الله كان يقول: من أسر سريرة رداه الله ردائها إن خيرا فخير وإن شرا فشر.$$

Why would an individual show to people the opposite of what God knows of him? Surely, the Messenger of God (s) used to say, 'Whoever keeps [his actions] secret, God will endow him with their effects – good for good and ill for ill.'[6]

Such individuals were not among the pious in the first place. Their duplicity allowed them to show a face to others that was not what they really are. When such individuals continue in their

---

[5] The Holy Quran, 75:14.
[6] Al-'Amili, *Wasa'el al-Shia*, 1:38.

deviance, God unmasks them in this world and readies for them an appropriate punishment in the hereafter.

We must look at ourselves and ask ourselves if we are of these people. Do we put on a show of spirituality, while we are in fact far away from real piety? Each one of us must investigate our own thoughts and beliefs and see if this applies to us.

The most important thing is always to be truthful with God. He knows any secret that we may try to keep. We know that we have faults and shortcomings. We must not try to hide them from God and train our conscience to ignore them. We must turn penitently to Him and confide in Him what we cannot reveal to others. We must seek His support to overcome our shortcomings. Imam Ali (a) said:

مَنْ أَصْلَحَ سَرِيرَتَهُ أَصْلَحَ اللهُ عَلاَنِيَتَهُ، وَمَنْ عَمِلَ لِدِينِهِ كَفَاهُ اللهُ أَمْرَ دُنْيَاهُ، وَمَنْ أَحْسَنَ فِيمَا بَيْنَهُ وبَيْنَ اللهِ كَفَاهُ اللهُ مَا بَيْنَهُ وَبَيْنَ النَّاسِ.

Whoever set right his inward self, God sets right his outward self. Whoever acts for his religion, God will suffice him in the matters of this world. Whoever perfects his dealings between himself and God, God will suffice him in his dealings between him and other people.[7]

Misconceptions

It is hard for Satan and the whispers of desire to lure into deviance an individual who has devoted their life to worship and spirituality. When a person reaches such a high level, their test

---

[7] Al-Radi, *Nahj al-Balagha*, 4:99, Saying 423.

becomes one of belief. Satan attempts to eat at the core of an individual's creed to demolish everything that the individual built. As we are reminded in the Holy Quran, Satan exclaims to God:

$$\text{قَالَ فَبِمَا أَغْوَيْتَنِي لَأَقْعُدَنَّ لَهُمْ صِرَاطَكَ الْمُسْتَقِيمَ ﴿١٦﴾ ثُمَّ لَآتِيَنَّهُم مِّن بَيْنِ أَيْدِيهِمْ وَمِنْ خَلْفِهِمْ وَعَنْ أَيْمَانِهِمْ وَعَن شَمَائِلِهِمْ ۖ وَلَا تَجِدُ أَكْثَرَهُمْ شَاكِرِينَ ﴿١٧﴾}$$

> *I will surely lie in wait for them on Your straight path. Then I will come at them from their front and from their rear, and from their right and their left, and You will not find most of them to be grateful.*[8]

This is why we see some individuals, currently and historically, who may seem to have devoted themselves to the service of God, but are in fact a force of corruption in the land, due to a misconception that they could not properly resolve. The best historical example for such a group is the Kharijites, who emerged during the time of Imam Ali (a).[9]

To summarize the anecdote of the Kharijites, they were a group that opposed Imam Ali (a), because he agreed to their demands and appointed an arbitrator between him and Muawiya. When

---

[8] The Holy Quran, 7:16, 17.

[9] The Kharijites were a group of Muslims who believed that both Imam Ali (a) and Muawiya should be removed because they went against established tradition when they appointed arbiters to decide their dispute after the Battle of Siffin. The Kharijites amassed an army and prepared to attack Imam Ali (a). Although Imam Ali (a) was victorious against the Kharijite army in the Battle of Nahrawan, the remnants of the Kharijites would continue to cause trouble and would ultimately succeed in assassinating Imam Ali (a). –Eds.

they realized that their initial demand was misguided, they accused Imam Ali (a) of apostasy and continued to wage several battles against him, ultimately succeeding in assassinating our beloved Imam (a).

If we look at the historical accounts of who the Kharijites were, we find them to be some of the most spiritual Muslims of their time. They lived in constant devotion and prayer, with marks stamped on their foreheads out of their prolonged prostration. Yet, because their faith was weak, a misconception was able to steer them off the path and make them amongst the most infamous deviants of Islamic history. They thought that their wretched actions were sanctioned by Islam and they committed their crimes in the name of the religion. They were indeed amongst the deviants whom God addressed in the verse:

قُلْ هَلْ نُنَبِّئُكُم بِالْأَخْسَرِينَ أَعْمَالًا ﴿١٠٣﴾ الَّذِينَ ضَلَّ سَعْيُهُمْ فِي الْحَيَاةِ الدُّنْيَا وَهُمْ يَحْسَبُونَ أَنَّهُمْ يُحْسِنُونَ صُنْعًا ﴿١٠٤﴾

Say, 'Shall we inform you who are the biggest losers in their works? Those whose efforts are misguided in the life of the world, while they suppose they are doing good.'[10]

The moral of the story is that even the most pious of worshippers can fall into misguidance if they are not well-rooted in their knowledge and faith.

---

[10] The Holy Quran, 18:103-04.

Self-interest

Self-interest doubtlessly plays a large role in the deviance of many. Vices such as jealousy, greed, and vanity were always among the most corrupting, whether the individual is a pious Muslim or not. They also play a significant role in corrupting a believer who was once guided but falls to the vileness of their own base desires.

Relevant anecdotes can be seen in the stories of some of the followers of our Immaculate Imams (a) who corrupted their faith by their self-interest. One such individual was known as Muhammad ibn Ali al-Shalmaghani, who was a confidant and messenger between the representatives of Imam Mahdi (a) during the Minor Occultation and the rest of the Shia. But despite his high status, al-Shalmaghani became envious and began to fabricate lies to boost his own status, as opposed to the real representative appointed by the Imam (a). He became so corrupt that Imam Mahdi (a) signed a letter informing the Shia of his deviance, saying:

إن محمّد بن علي المعروف بالشلمغاني... ادّعى ما كفر معه بالخالق جلّ وتعالى وافترى كذباً وزوراً ... وإننا قد برئنا إلى الله تعالى وإلى رسوله وآله - صلوات الله وسلامه ورحمته وبركاته عليهم - بمّته ....

Muhammad ibn Ali, known as al-Shalmaghani... has claimed that with which he has denied the Creator, Glo-

rious and Majestic, and has fabricated lies and fallacies... We repudiate him in front of God and His Messenger (s)....[11]

Even an individual who was so close to the Imams (a) and had lived in their presence and heard their words could turn on them and become corrupted by his desires. The Holy Quran speaks to us of such individuals and says:

وَاتْلُ عَلَيْهِمْ نَبَأَ الَّذِي آتَيْنَاهُ آيَاتِنَا فَانسَلَخَ مِنْهَا فَأَتْبَعَهُ الشَّيْطَانُ فَكَانَ مِنَ الْغَاوِينَ

Relate to them an account of him to whom We gave Our signs, but he cast them off. Thereupon Satan pursued him, and he became one of the perverse. Had We wished, We would have surely raised him by their means, but he clung to the Earth and followed his [base] desires.[12]

Falling into Sin

The most important factor in facilitating an individual's salvation in the hereafter is their faith in God. Through adhering to the correct creed, we can insure our eternal happiness and bliss. Alongside our faith, our actions and deeds are another factor that plays an important role in this journey. The relationship between faith and action is like the relationship between a valuable gemstone and its protective case. We need to safeguard the gem

---

[11] Al-Tabrasi, *al-Ihtijaj*, 2:290.
[12] The Holy Quran, 7:175-76.

and make sure it is not damaged. The case allows us to ensure that we do not lose or damage it.

Even an individual who has full certainty in their faith and a great understanding of their creed can find themselves corrupted if they fall into sin. Transgression against the boundaries that God drew for us can lead to us rejecting the faith that we once had. God draws to us the example of such an individual when He says in the Holy Quran,

$$ثُمَّ كَانَ عَاقِبَةَ الَّذِينَ أَسَاءُوا السُّوأَىٰ أَن كَذَّبُوا بِآيَاتِ اللَّهِ وَكَانُوا بِهَا يَسْتَهْزِئُونَ$$

Then the fate of those who committed misdeeds was that they denied the signs of God and they used to deride them.[13]

Imam al-Baqir (a) also has a beautiful narration in this regard. He said:

$$ما من عبد إلا وفي قلبه نكتة بيضاء، فإذا أذنب ذنبا خرج في النكتة نكتة سوداء، فإن تاب ذهب ذلك السواد وإن تمادى في الذنوب زاد ذلك السواد حتى يغطي البياض فإذا غطى البياض لم يرجع صاحبه إلى خير أبدا وهو قول الله عزوجل (كلا بل ران على قلوبهم ما كانوا يكسبون)$$

Every servant has a light spot in his heart. Whenever he transgresses with a sin, a dark spot will emerge out of the light spot. If he repents, that darkness will recede. If

---

[13] The Holy Quran, 30:10.

he continues to transgress with sin, the darkness will expand until it covers the light. Once the light has been covered, the individual will never turn back. That is the word of God Almighty, 'No, that is not the case! Rather, their hearts have been sullied by what they have been earning.'[14]

Preventing Ill Outcomes

After addressing some of the reasons why an individual may become misguided after a life of piety and devotion, we should now turn to some of the means by which we can protect ourselves from ill outcomes.

Reliance on God

For a person to safeguard themselves from ill outcomes and maintain their piety and rectitude, they must always live in a state of awareness of their need for God. We must always understand that God is the giver of everything, and that without Him, we have nothing. We must put our trust in Him that He will continue to give, sustain, bless, and guide us in all our affairs. If we can realize the importance of this aspect of our being, we can safeguard ourselves from deviating away from God's straight path. God says:

$$\text{وَمَن يَتَوَكَّلْ عَلَى اللَّهِ فَهُوَ حَسْبُهُ ۚ إِنَّ اللَّهَ بَالِغُ أَمْرِهِ ۚ قَدْ جَعَلَ اللَّهُ لِكُلِّ شَيْءٍ قَدْرًا}$$

---

[14] Al-Majlisi, *Bihar al-Anwar*, 70:332. Citing: The Holy Quran, 83:14.

Whoever puts his trust in God, He will suffice him. Indeed, God carries through His commands. Certainly, God has ordained a measure [and extent] for everything.[15]

We must also realize that our need for God is not just a material thing. We need Him to support us in our journey toward Him. We need Him to continue to bless us with the right beliefs and to help us make the right choices. Therefore, our Immaculate Imams (a) continuously emphasized the importance of feeling this state of need towards God. As Imam Ali (a) said:

إن أردت أن يؤمنك الله سوء العاقبة فاعلم أن ما تأتيه من خير فبفضل الله وتوفيقه، وما تأتيه من سوء فبإمهال الله وإنظاره إياك وحلمه وعفوه عنك.

If you wish that God safeguard you from ill outcomes, know that any good that you may do is by the grace and blessing of God. Whatever evil you may undertake, then it is by God's indulgence and reprieve and by His forbearance and forgiveness towards you.[16]

Even when we are in disobedience to God, we must continue to feel our need for Him. We must realize that no matter what we do and how we transgress, it is He who keeps on sustaining us and granting us the very breath that we take. No matter how much we transgress, we cannot overpower or escape Him. Any

---

[15] The Holy Quran, 65:3.
[16] Al-Majlisi, *Bihar al-Anwar*, 67:392.

sin that we commit is by His patience towards us, always giving us a chance to right the wrongs that we do. Any righteous deed that we undertake is by His power and blessing, without which we would continue to behave like any other wretch.

Using Reason

God granted us reason and distinguished us with it over all other creatures. Through reason, we can reach the highest levels of our excellence. By ignoring our reason and acting based on our passions, jealousies, and desires, we stoop to a level lower than wild beasts. We find many Quranic verses and noble traditions emphasizing the importance of using reason and safeguarding it as a tool to reach towards God.

We see many historical examples of people who let go of their reason and followed their passions to the edge of a cliff and into the pits of damnation. One such group were the fanatics that lived during the time of Imam Ali (a) and who believed him to be a god. Their love for him clouded their minds and they could not think clearly about his role.

Was he not a servant of God who devoted his entire life to Him? Was he not a pupil of God's Messenger (s)? Is God, who created these individuals and endowed them with such attributes, not greater than His creation?

The answers may seem clear to us, but an individual who abandons reason will not see them so clearly. We give this example to draw a point and reflect on our own lives and frames of mind. We may not be fanatics of Imam Ali (a) who ascribe him as a partner to God, but do we let our reverence for some individuals in our lives get in the way of our reason? Do we revere a friend, family member, or role model so much as to have that undue reverence cloud our intellect? These are points to ponder on.

We must not allow ourselves to look at other fallible human beings like us as the standard by which we measure things. This is a trend that God warned of in the Holy Quran, and we must take it seriously and ensure that it does not get in the way of our journey towards God. God says:

اتَّخَذُوا أَحْبَارَهُمْ وَرُهْبَانَهُمْ أَرْبَابًا مِّن دُونِ اللَّهِ وَالْمَسِيحَ ابْنَ مَرْيَمَ وَمَا أُمِرُوا إِلَّا لِيَعْبُدُوا إِلَٰهًا وَاحِدًا ۖ لَّا إِلَٰهَ إِلَّا هُوَ ۚ سُبْحَانَهُ عَمَّا يُشْرِكُونَ

They have taken their scribes and their monks as lords besides God, and also Christ, Mary's son; though they were commanded to worship only the One God, there is no god except Him; He is far too immaculate to have any partners that they ascribe [to Him]![17]

Our narrations expound on this verse and explain to us how some people took the scribes of their time as gods. The people of those times did not consciously worship these scribes, but they listened to their teachings as opposed to what God had laid out for them in the scripture. Imam al-Sadiq (a) says:

---

[17] The Holy Quran, 9:31.

أما والله ما دعوهم الى عبادة أنفسهم ولو دعوهم إلى عبادة أنفسهم لما أجابوهم ولكن أحلوا لهم حراما وحرموا عليهم حلالا فعبدوهم كم حيث لا يشعرون.

> *By God, they [the scribes] did not call the people to worship them, and if they had done so the people would not have answered their calls. Rather, they permitted for them what is forbidden and forbade what is permitted, such that they began to worship them unwittingly.*[18]

We must not let such individuals stand in the way of our reason and cloud our judgment. We should look at the principles and teachings of our faith and use these teachings as the standard. This is what our Imams (a) taught us to do, rather than to follow others based on whimsy. Imam Ali (a) said:

لا يعرف الحق بالرجال، إعرف الحق تعرف أهله

> *Truth is not known through people. Know the truth and you shall know the truthful!*[19]

Our intellect is therefore a safeguard for us against deviance and allows us to avoid ill outcomes. This may be what Imam al-Sadiq (a) meant when he said,

من كان عاقلا ختم الله له بالجنة إن شاء الله

---

[18] Al-Huwaizi, *Tafseer Noor al-Thaqalayn*, 2:209.
[19] Ibn Tawus, *Al-Tara'ef*, 136.

Whoever makes use of his intellect, God will make Paradise his final destination – God willing.[20]

Observing Religious Doctrine

Each one of us is accountable for all of our actions, no matter how small. God says,

$$وَلَا تَقْفُ مَا لَيْسَ لَكَ بِهِ عِلْمٌ ۚ إِنَّ السَّمْعَ وَالْبَصَرَ وَالْفُؤَادَ كُلُّ أُولَٰئِكَ كَانَ عَنْهُ مَسْئُولًا$$

Indeed hearing, eyesight, and the heart – all of these are accountable.[21]

We must make sure that any action that we take is justified in the eyes of God. That is why we must always be aware and keep in mind the boundaries that God drew for us through the prescriptions of *Halal* and *Haram*. He delivered those prescriptions to us through the Holy Prophet Muhammad (s), who is the perfect guide and role model for us on this journey. After the Holy Prophet (s), we follow his Immaculate Progeny (a), who taught us the details of our faith in both their words and their actions.

After the Immaculate Imams (a), and during the time of the Occultation of our Twelfth Imam (a), we must continue to learn about and understand these teachings that God commanded us to stick by. We must seek those who the Imams (a) appointed as their representatives when their followers could not reach them. Historically, these representatives were the ones who studied

---

[20] Al-Majlisi, *Bihar al-Anwar*, 1:91.
[21] The Holy Quran, 17:36.

and taught the narrations of the Holy Household (a). In contemporary terms, it means that we must follow the scholars of the seminary, especially the most learned amongst them, who are best suited to lead us in this journey of ours. Therefore, so much emphasis is placed on the issue of *marjaeya* and why it is so important to choose a *marja* in accordance with the correct guidelines and standards.

We cannot simply choose to follow whoever our parents follow, or to follow someone because he speaks the same language or is from the same ethnic background. These are irrational standards that do not have any bearing on whether this individual is most suited to lead us on our journey toward God. We cannot follow our passions in this regard, but must look to the religious rulings that outline the correct method of choosing an individual to follow.

We must turn back to ourselves and double-check our actions and our intent, not just in this issue, but in every issue. We must make sure that we are acting out of a sincere intention of seeking closeness to God, and not just as a form of duplicity and hypocrisy. We must make sure that we hold the correct beliefs as taught to us by our Immaculate Imams (a) and that we do not have any misconceptions or misgivings about our faith. We must make sure that we are not following our own self-interest and desires, as that will only lead us down the path of deviance.

We must observe the teachings of our religion and use reason in making the best choices for ourselves and our hereafter. We

Ill Outcomes

must realize our complete need of God, who is the giver and sustainer of all things.

Through all this, we can avoid the ill outcome of misguidance, after having put time and effort into seeking closeness to our Lord. We pray to God to support us on this journey and help us reach our goal.

SEEKING CLOSENESS TO GOD

In the Name of God, the Most Beneficent, the Most Merciful

ثُمَّ أَوْرَثْنَا الْكِتَابَ الَّذِينَ اصْطَفَيْنَا مِنْ عِبَادِنَا ۖ فَمِنْهُمْ ظَالِمٌ لِّنَفْسِهِ وَمِنْهُم مُّقْتَصِدٌ وَمِنْهُمْ سَابِقٌ بِالْخَيْرَاتِ بِإِذْنِ اللَّهِ ۚ ذَٰلِكَ هُوَ الْفَضْلُ الْكَبِيرُ

Then We made those whom We chose from Our servants [to be] heirs to the Book. Yet, some of them are those who wrong themselves, and some of them are average, and some of them are those who take the lead in all the good works by God's will. That is the greatest grace [of God]![1]

God created mankind with two dimensions – the physical and the spiritual. The physical dimension is one that we share with the beasts and much of creation. In terms of reaching our excellence as human beings, the physical dimension does not play a large role. One individual may be more fit and athletic, excelling in the physical aspects of life. But that does not grant them any form of superiority over others. The true measure of excellence among mankind is in terms of the spiritual dimension of their

---

[1] The Holy Quran, 35:32.

lives. That is why we see that the best of creation – the Holy Prophet (s) – and the worst of creation – people such as Abu Lahab – both have physical bodies that are similar in many respects. But when it comes to the meaningful measure of our lives, the two do not compare.

A human being cannot reach excellence in their human nature, without the spiritual dimension. A person who does not pay any heed to spiritual life is therefore worse than the beast who cannot heed that dimension. That is why God says in the Holy Quran:

وَلَقَدْ ذَرَأْنَا لِجَهَنَّمَ كَثِيرًا مِّنَ الْجِنِّ وَالْإِنسِ ۖ لَهُمْ قُلُوبٌ لَّا يَفْقَهُونَ بِهَا وَلَهُمْ أَعْيُنٌ لَّا يُبْصِرُونَ بِهَا وَلَهُمْ آذَانٌ لَّا يَسْمَعُونَ بِهَا ۚ أُولَٰئِكَ كَالْأَنْعَامِ بَلْ هُمْ أَضَلُّ ۚ أُولَٰئِكَ هُمُ الْغَافِلُونَ

Certainly We have winnowed out for Hell many of the jinn and humans: they have hearts with which they do not understand, they have eyes with which they do not see, they have ears with which they do not hear. They are like cattle; indeed, they are more astray. It is they who are the heedless.[2]

Mankind was given greater faculties and abilities than all other creation. Our abilities are even greater than the angels. That is why when the best of God's creation, the Holy Prophet Muhammad (s), ascended to the heavens and continued to ascend, he reached a point where Gabriel could no longer accompany him and the angel said:

---

[2] The Holy Quran, 7:179.

تقدم يا رسول الله ليس لي أن أجوز هذا المكان ولو دنوت أنملة لاحترقت

Go forth, O' Messenger of God (s)! It is not permitted for me to proceed beyond this point, and if I transgress just an inch, I will surely be burned.[3]

The spiritual dimension and our ability as human beings to reach closer to God is thus the ultimate purpose of our lives. It is this closeness to God that can bestow upon us the attributes of excellence as we draw closer and closer to the spring of excellence. This is the meaning of the supplication taught to us by Imam Ali (a), who said:

إلهي هَب لي كمال الانقطاع إليك ، وأنر أبصار قلوبنا بضياء نظرها إليك حتى تخرق أبصار القلوب حُجُب النور ، فتصل إلى معدن العظمة ، وتصير أرواحنا مُعلقة بعزّ قدسك

O' Lord, grant me excellence in devotion to you and brighten the foresight of our hearts with the light of looking on to You, so that the foresight of the hearts can breach the veils of light and reach the mettle of greatness. And so our souls will become attached to the honor of Your Majesty.[4]

How to Seek Closeness to God?

There is no doubt that each of us can dedicate all of our actions toward seeking closeness to God. Whether it is an act of worship

---

[3] Al-Majlisi, *Bihar al-Anwar*, 18:382.
[4] Ibn Tawus, *Iqbal al-A'mal*, 3:299.

or simple acts of subsistence, so long as the intent behind our actions is seeking His pleasure, we will always grow closer to Him. There are, however, a few things which are especially helpful in this regard, as we will outline below.

True Monotheistic Faith

God made faith as the best means to grow closer to Him. The more an individual grows in faith, the closer they grow to God. As the Commander of the Faithful (a) said,

أقرب الناس الى الله أحسنهم إيمانا

The closest of people to God is the best of them in faith.[5]

Still, we must recognize that faith is an issue that is much more involved than spoken words. It is something that must be rooted deep in the hearts. That why God says in the Holy Quran:

قَالَتِ الْأَعْرَابُ آمَنَّا ۖ قُل لَّمْ تُؤْمِنُوا وَلَٰكِن قُولُوا أَسْلَمْنَا وَلَمَّا يَدْخُلِ الْإِيمَانُ فِي قُلُوبِكُمْ ۖ وَإِن تُطِيعُوا اللَّهَ وَرَسُولَهُ لَا يَلِتْكُم مِّنْ أَعْمَالِكُمْ شَيْئًا ۚ إِنَّ اللَّهَ غَفُورٌ رَّحِيمٌ

The Bedouins say, 'We have faith.' Say, 'You do not have faith yet; rather, say, "We have embraced Islam," for faith has not yet entered into your hearts. Yet if you obey God and His Apostle, He will not stint anything of [the reward of] your works. Indeed God is all-forgiving, all-merciful.'[6]

---

[5] Al-Wasiti, *'Oyoun al-Hikam*, 121.
[6] The Holy Quran, 49:14.

Faith is therefore a level higher than simply adhering to the doctrines of the religion. The Holy Prophet (s) said:

الإيمان ما وقر في القلوب وصدقته الأعمال والإسلام ما جرى على اللسان

Faith is what settles in the hearts and is confirmed by action. Islam is what is spoken by the tongue.[7]

Imam al-Baqir (a) added,

واجتمعوا على الصلاة والزكاة والصوم والحج فخرجوا بذلك من الكفر وأضيفوا إلى الإيمان

[Because of Islam, people] were united in prayer, zakat, fasting and Hajj, and thus were taken from disbelief and into belief.[8]

Islam is therefore a general classification applied to anyone who witnesses that there is no god but God and that the Holy Prophet Muhammad (s) is His messenger. This gives Muslims rights and obligations toward one another in issues such as marriage, inheritance, and other social issues. It unites us in our prayers, Hajj, and other acts of worship. But it is not the measure by which God distinguishes one individual over another. We are all equally Muslim, albeit some of us may be more faithful than others.

What is true faith? If we look at the noble narrations, we can deduce a common, defining theme for what true faith means. Let

---

[7] Al-Majlisi, *Bihar al-Anwar*, 47:208.
[8] Al-Kulayni, *al-Kafi*, 2:26-27

us first go through some of these narrations. The Holy Prophet (s) is reported to have said:

ما بلغ عبد حقيقة الإيمان حتى يعلم أن ما أصابه لم يكن ليخطئه وما أخطأه لم يكن يصيبه

> A servant does not reach the true faith until he is certain that what befell him would never have missed him, and that what has passed him up would never have reached him.[9]

Imam Ali (a) said,

لاَ يَصْدُقُ إِيمَانُ عَبْدٍ، حَتَّى يَكُونَ بِمَا فِي يَدِ اللهِ سُبْحَانَهُ أَوْثَقَ مِنهُ بِمَا فِي يَدِهِ

> A servant does not realize true faith unless his trust in what is with God is more than his trust in what he himself has.[10]

Imam al-Sadiq (a) also said,

اعلموا أنه لا يؤمن عبد من عبيده حتى يرضى عن الله فيما صنع الله إليه وصنع به على ما أحب وكره

> Know that a servant has not reached [true] faith until he is content with what God has done to and for him, whether it is as he desires or not."[11]

---

[9] Al-Hindi, *Kanz al-'Ommal*, 1:25.
[10] Al-Radi, *Nahj al-Balagha*, 4:74, Saying 310.
[11] Al-Kulayni, *al-Kafi*, 8:8.

All these narrations in fact refer to one common understanding of faith – that is, to believe that everything in the world is by and at the command of God. This is true monotheism. This is why Imam Ali (a) is reported to have said,

ما رَأَيْتُ شَيْئًا إلا ورَأَيْتُ الله قَبْلَه

> I have not seen anything except that I have seen God before it.[12]

When an individual reaches true certainty in God, they will turn wholeheartedly toward Him. They will not see anything but God. They will not seek anything except God's pleasure. This is true monotheistic faith – true *tawheed*.

Some people have the misconception that *tawheed* means that we should turn to God directly, without seeking any means to reach closer to Him. This fallacy is clearly erroneous, especially considering the verses of the Holy Quran. True tawheed is to obey God's every command. When God commands us to seek Him through the means which He set, we do not step outside the boundaries of our faith. God says in the Holy Quran:

يَا أَيُّهَا الَّذِينَ آمَنُوا اتَّقُوا اللَّهَ وَابْتَغُوا إِلَيْهِ الْوَسِيلَةَ وَجَاهِدُوا فِي سَبِيلِهِ لَعَلَّكُمْ تُفْلِحُونَ

> O' you who have faith! Be wary of God, and seek the means of recourse to Him.[13]

---

[12] Al-Mazandarani, *Sharh Usool al-Kafi*, 3:83.
[13] The Holy Quran, 5:35.

Therefore, not seeking the proper means to Him is a form of disobedience of His commands. As Lady Fatima (a) emphasized in her famous sermon after the passing of the Holy Prophet (s), we must follow God's command by following the messengers and guides which He chose for us. She said:

فاتقوا الله حق تقاته و لاتموتن إلا وأنتم مسلمون و لاتتولوا مدبرين وأطيعوه فيما أمركم ونهاكم فإنما يخشي الله من عباده العلماء فاحمدوا الله ألذي بنوره وعظمته ابتغي من في السماوات و من في الأرض إليه الوسيلة فنحن وسيلته في خلقه ونحن آل رسوله ونحن حجة غيبه وورثة أنبيائ

So, be wary of God as He truly deserves and do not die except as Muslims. Do not turn on your heels. Obey Him in all His commands and inhibitions, for surely only those of God's servants having knowledge fear Him. Praise God who, by His greatness and light, the denizens of the heavens and the Earth have sought the means to Him. Surely, we are His means amongst His creations and we are the family of His Messenger. We are His proof to what is unseen and the inheritors of His prophets.[14]

True *tawheed* is built on following the commands of God and seeking the means to Him. The true means to God are His chosen Prophet (s) and the Immaculate guides after him. We must follow this path that God drew for us. God says:

---

[14] Al-Tabari, *Dala'el al-Imama*, 113.

> وَأَنَّ هَٰذَا صِرَاطِي مُسْتَقِيمًا فَاتَّبِعُوهُ ۖ وَلَا تَتَّبِعُوا السُّبُلَ فَتَفَرَّقَ بِكُمْ عَن سَبِيلِهِ ۚ ذَٰلِكُمْ وَصَّاكُم بِهِ لَعَلَّكُمْ تَتَّقُونَ

This indeed is my straight path, so follow it, and do not follow [other] ways, for they will separate you from His way. This is what He enjoins upon you so that you may be Godwary.[15]

That is why Imam al-Hadi (a) taught us to say in visitation of our beloved Imams (a):

> مَنْ أَرَادَ اللَّهَ بَدَأَ بِكُمْ، وَمَنْ وَحَّدَهُ قَبِلَ عَنْكُمْ، وَمَنْ قَصَدَهُ تَوَجَّهَ بِكُمْ

Whoever seeks God starts with you! Whoever believes in His oneness takes [his religion] from you! Whoever pursues Him will turn to Him with you [as his intercessors]![16]

Seeking any means beside this will not bring us closer to God. Rather, it will only drive us further away from Him, because it is a form of disobedience of His commands. We must therefore take God's prescribed means to be able to perfect our faith and reach toward Him.

Good Work

Closeness to God cannot be attained without expending effort and striving toward that goal. We cannot expect to grow spiritually without putting the time and making the tough decisions

---

[15] The Holy Quran, 6:153.

[16] Al-Tusi, *Tahtheeb al-Ahkam*, 6:99.

that are entailed. God did not grant closeness to Him to His prophets and messengers before He tested them, and so He does the same to us. God says,

$$وَجَعَلْنَا مِنْهُمْ أَئِمَّةً يَهْدُونَ بِأَمْرِنَا لَمَّا صَبَرُوا ۖ وَكَانُوا بِآيَاتِنَا يُوقِنُونَ$$

When they had been patient and had conviction in Our signs, We appointed amongst them imams to guide [the people] by Our command.[17]

God continues to emphasize the righteous deeds of His close servants in many verses of the Holy Quran. For example, He says,

$$وَجَعَلْنَاهُمْ أَئِمَّةً يَهْدُونَ بِأَمْرِنَا وَأَوْحَيْنَا إِلَيْهِمْ فِعْلَ الْخَيْرَاتِ وَإِقَامَ الصَّلَاةِ وَإِيتَاءَ الزَّكَاةِ ۖ وَكَانُوا لَنَا عَابِدِينَ$$

We made them imams, guiding by Our command, and We revealed to them [concerning] the performance of good deeds, the maintenance of prayers, and the giving of zakat, and they used to worship Us.[18]

The best example of the great effort that the pious put in seeking closeness to God can be seen in our beloved Prophet Muhammad (s). Even though "he drew nearer and nearer [to God] until he was within two bows' length or even nearer,"[19] he continued to strive in seeking the pleasure of God and closeness to Him. In fact, he was so consumed in his devotion that he began to wear

---

[17] The Holy Quran, 32:24.

[18] The Holy Quran, 21:73.

[19] The Holy Quran, 53:8-9.

himself out. That is why God revealed the verse speaking to the Holy Prophet (s),

طه ﴿١﴾ مَا أَنزَلْنَا عَلَيْكَ الْقُرْآنَ لِتَشْقَىٰ ﴿٢﴾

[O' Muhammad!] We did not send down to you the Quran that you should be miserable.[20]

The point is that seeking closeness to God does not come without effort. Imam Ali al-Sajjad (a) teaches us to supplicate and say,

اللهم اجعلني من الذين جدوا في قصدك فلم ينكلوا وسلكوا الطريق إليك فلم يعدلوا، واعتمدوا عليك في الوصول حتى وصلوا

O' God, make me one of those individuals who diligently sought You and did not slack, who walked the path to You and did not stray, and who relied on You to reach You until he did....[21]

In another supplication he taught us to say:

وألحقنا بعبادك الذين هم بالبدار إليك يسارعون، وبابك على الدوام يطرقون، وإياك في الليل والنهار يعبدون... قد انقطعت إليك همتي، وانصرفت نحوك رغبتي، فأنت لا غيرك مرادي، ولك لا لسواك سهري وسهادي ولقاؤك قرة عيني، ووصلك منى نفسي، وإليك شوقي، وفي محبتك ولهي وإلى هواك صبابتي ورضاك بغيتي، ورؤيتك حاجتي، وجوارك طلبتي، وقربك غاية سؤلي

---

[20] The Holy Quran, 20:1-2.
[21] Al-Majlisi, *Bihar al-Anwar*, 91:156.

> *Join us with your servants who proactively rush towards You, continuously knock Your doors, and worship You day and night... Indeed, my endeavors are devoted to You and my will is directed at You. For You, and no one else, are my vigil and wakefulness. To meet You is the apple of my eye and to be at Your service is the hope of my soul. To You I yearn and with Your love I am engrossed. It is Your love that I long for and Your satisfaction that I desire. My need is that I see You. My request is that I be at Your side. To be close to You is my ultimate plea.*[22]

There are several other points that we should also keep in mind.

First, when we look at the books of jurisprudence, we find that all acts of worship are conditioned on the intent of seeking closeness to God. Our faith does not see any spiritual value to acts done without that intent. Any act done with the intention of gaining recognition or appeasing a personal guilt does not hold any weight in this regard.

Second, the actions that we undertake to seek closeness to God must be acts that He asked us for and sanctioned. We cannot seek closeness to God by means of worship that we fabricate ourselves. We must always turn back to the Holy Prophet (s) and the Immaculate Imams (a) and learn from them how we can grow closer to our Lord.

---

[22] Al-Majlisi, *Bihar al-Anwar*, 91:147-48.

Third, we must realize that first and foremost in our journey of closeness to God, we must observe the acts which He made obligatory and keep away from what He forbade. No amount of extra fasting or prayer can do us any good if we do not maintain our daily prayers. What value will our acts of worship hold if we continue to transgress against our Lord? Imam al-Sadiq (a) relays that God once told Prophet Moses:

يا موسى ما تقرب الي المتقربون بمثل الورع عن محارمي فإني أمنحهم جنات عدن لا أشرك معهم أحدا

O' Moses, no one can seek closeness to me through anything like forsaking what I have forbidden. Indeed, I shall grant them the Gardens of Eden and not join any alongside them![23]

Devotion

It is not enough to undertake the type of actions that we generally regard as righteous. For our actions to count and to bring us closer to God, they must be performed with sincerity and devotion. Imam al-Baqir (a) said:

لا يكون العبد عابدا لله حق عبادته حتى ينقطع عن الخلق كلهم إليه فحينئذ يقول: هذا خالص لي فيقبله بكرمه

A servant is not truly a worshipper of God until he devotes himself to Him and not to any of His creatures.

---

[23] Al-Majlisi, *Bihar al-Anwar*, 67:307.

This is when God will say, 'This is purely for me,' and accepts him with His grace.[24]

Indeed, God commands us to be devoted to Him in our faith. He says:

$$\text{وَمَا أُمِرُوا إِلَّا لِيَعْبُدُوا اللَّهَ مُخْلِصِينَ لَهُ الدِّينَ حُنَفَاءَ وَيُقِيمُوا الصَّلَاةَ وَيُؤْتُوا الزَّكَاةَ ۚ وَذَٰلِكَ دِينُ الْقَيِّمَةِ}$$

Though they were not commanded except to worship God, dedicating their faith to Him as men of pure faith, and to maintain the prayer and pay the zakat. That is the upright religion.[25]

There are multiple levels of devotion that a person can attain in regard to his acts of worship. The lowest level is to clear their intent from all forms of duplicity or ascribing any partner to God. There is no lower level than this, as an act undertaken with the intention of gaining closeness to anyone besides God is invalid and corrupt.

A person can gradually rise in levels of devotion to reach the apex when they devote every aspect of their being their creator. At this level, nothing besides God can enter the heart of the believer. This is what Imam Ali (a) described when he said,

$$\text{طوبى لمن أخلص لله عمله وعلمه وحبه وبغضه وأخذه وتركه وكلامه وصمته}$$

---

[24] Al-Hilli, *'Oddat al-Daa'i*, 219.
[25] The Holy Quran, 98:5.

> *Blessed is the one who devotes to God his actions and knowledge, what he loves and what he hates, what he takes and what he leaves, and his speech and silence.*[26]

How can an individual reach these high levels of devotion? Our noble traditions describe to us a few methods that we can utilize in training ourselves to gain this devotion.

There is an evident correlation between devotion and worship. An individual more dedicated to worshipping God will more quickly rise in devotion to Him. Worship purifies the soul and allows it to excel further and further in this regard. As Imam Ali (a) said,

الإخلاص ثمرة العبادة

Devotion is the fruit of worship.[27]

Faith is another factor that plays into an individual's devotion to God. Imam Ali (a) said,

الإخلاص ثمرة اليقين

Devotion is the fruit of certitude.[28]

Certitude is a level of faith that can be achieved through worship. God says,

وَاعْبُدْ رَبَّكَ حَتَّىٰ يَأْتِيَكَ الْيَقِينُ

---

[26] Al-Harrani, *Tohaf al-'Oqool*, 91.
[27] Al-Wasiti, *'Oyoun al-Hikam*, 38.
[28] Al-Wasiti, *'Oyoun al-Hikam*, 23.

Worship your Lord until certainty comes to you.[29]

Devotion is also related to God's love for any of His servants. A companion of the Holy Prophet Muhammad (s) once asked about devotion. The Prophet (s) in turn asked Gabriel, who asked God. God's reply was,

الإخلاص سر من سري أودعه في قلب من أحببته

Devotion is a secret amongst My secrets. I entrust it in the hearts of those whom I love.[30]

Therefore, if God loves a servant, He will grant them devotion. But how does someone earn God's love? If we look at the noble tradition, we find that this too is tied back to worship. The Holy Prophet (s) relays that God says:

ما تقرب إلي عبد بشيء أحب ألي مما افترضت عليه وإنه ليتقرب إلي بالنافلة حتى أحبه

No servant can seek closeness to Me by a means better than what I have prescribed. He shall grow closer to Me through recommended prayers until I love him.[31]

It should be clear at this point that all these factors we are speaking of are very intertwined. Worship leads to closeness, which leads to divine love, which leads to devotion, which also leads to closeness, and so on.

---

[29] The Holy Quran, 15:99.

[30] Al-Borojourdi, *Jami' Ahadeeth al-Shia*, 1:375.

[31] Al-Kulayni, *al-Kafi*, 2:352.

The moral is that so long as the individual gets on the straight path and makes a conscious effort to grow closer to God, God will take their hand and lead them closer and closer to Him. This is indeed a sign of God's ultimate generosity. Indeed,

وَمَا كَانَ عَطَاءُ رَبِّكَ مَحْظُورًا

The bounty of your Lord is not confined.[32]

The important thing to realize is that guidance and closeness to God is not something that God gives out haphazardly. Rather, an individual must work to earn the level of closeness that they seek. God says,

فَأَمَّا مَنْ أَعْطَىٰ وَاتَّقَىٰ ﴿٥﴾ وَصَدَّقَ بِالْحُسْنَىٰ ﴿٦﴾ فَسَنُيَسِّرُهُ لِلْيُسْرَىٰ ﴿٧﴾

As for him who gives and is Godwary and confirms the best promise, We will surely ease him toward felicity.[33]

He also says,

وَالَّذِينَ جَاهَدُوا فِينَا لَنَهْدِيَنَّهُمْ سُبُلَنَا ۚ وَإِنَّ اللَّهَ لَمَعَ الْمُحْسِنِينَ

As for those who strive in Us, We shall surely guide them in Our ways, and God is indeed with the virtuous.[34]

---

[32] The Holy Quran, 17:20.

[33] The Holy Quran, 92:5-7.

[34] The Holy Quran, 29:69.

The Fruits of Closeness

When we observe how mankind functions in society, we find that an individual is greatly influenced by those who they associates with. An individual who associates with a group who have adopted a certain vice will likely end up committing the vice themself. An individual who associates with the affluent in society will more likely be able to climb the social ladder. An individual who associates with scholars and professors will more easily become a learned individual. All these individuals draw upon the attributes of whomever they associate with.

This is all in terms of worldly affairs and attributes. But what happens when an individual draws closer to God, the One of supreme attributes? There is no doubt that becoming closer to God will allow us to manifest more and more of the divine qualities. For example, we are all dependent creations who need our sustainer. God tells us:

يَا أَيُّهَا النَّاسُ أَنتُمُ الْفُقَرَاءُ إِلَى اللَّهِ ۖ وَاللَّهُ هُوَ الْغَنِيُّ الْحَمِيدُ

O mankind! You are the ones who stand in need of God, and God – He is the All-sufficient, the All-laudable.[35]

The closer we grow to Him, the more sufficient we will be. God's attributes go much further. He says:

هُوَ اللَّهُ الَّذِي لَا إِلَٰهَ إِلَّا هُوَ ۖ عَالِمُ الْغَيْبِ وَالشَّهَادَةِ ۖ هُوَ الرَّحْمَٰنُ الرَّحِيمُ ﴿٢٢﴾ هُوَ اللَّهُ الَّذِي لَا إِلَٰهَ إِلَّا هُوَ الْمَلِكُ الْقُدُّوسُ السَّلَامُ الْمُؤْمِنُ

---

[35] The Holy Quran, 35:15.

> الْمُهَيْمِنُ الْعَزِيزُ الْجَبَّارُ الْمُتَكَبِّرُ ۚ سُبْحَانَ اللَّهِ عَمَّا يُشْرِكُونَ ﴿٢٣﴾ هُوَ اللَّهُ الْخَالِقُ الْبَارِئُ الْمُصَوِّرُ ۖ لَهُ الْأَسْمَاءُ الْحُسْنَىٰ ۚ يُسَبِّحُ لَهُ مَا فِي السَّمَاوَاتِ وَالْأَرْضِ ۖ وَهُوَ الْعَزِيزُ الْحَكِيمُ ﴿٢٤﴾

He is God – there is no god except Him – Knower of the sensible and the Unseen, He is the All-beneficent, the All-merciful. He is God – there is no god except Him – the Sovereign, the All-holy, the All-benign, the Securer, the All-conserver, the All-mighty, the All-compeller, and the All-magnanimous. Clear is God of any partners that they may ascribe [to Him]! He is God, the Creator, the Maker, and the Former. To Him belong the Best Names. Whatever there is in the heavens and the Earth glorifies Him and He is the All-mighty, the All-wise.[36]

How does growing closer to God affect us human beings? There are countless ways in which this closeness will allow us to grow for the better. For the sake of brevity, let us address a few prominent examples.

Achieving Excellence

Any individual seeking excellence knows that they have a long road ahead. Self-betterment is a long and arduous journey. But those who have achieved closeness to God undertake this journey with ease. Divine care for such individuals allows them to reach the highest levels of greatness in a shorter time span than others.

---

[36] The Holy Quran, 59:22-24.

This aspect of closeness to God is evident in our Holy Prophet (s) and his blessed Progeny (a). God also speaks of others in the Holy Quran who were able to receive the greatest of divine blessings in their infancy, due to what God knows of their devotion and closeness to Him. God bestowed great blessings on Jesus, son of Mary, while he was still an infant. God says:

إِذْ قَالَتِ الْمَلَائِكَةُ يَا مَرْيَمُ إِنَّ اللَّهَ يُبَشِّرُكِ بِكَلِمَةٍ مِنْهُ اسْمُهُ الْمَسِيحُ عِيسَى ابْنُ مَرْيَمَ وَجِيهًا فِي الدُّنْيَا وَالْآخِرَةِ وَمِنَ الْمُقَرَّبِينَ ﴿٤٥﴾ وَيُكَلِّمُ النَّاسَ فِي الْمَهْدِ وَكَهْلًا وَمِنَ الصَّالِحِينَ ﴿٤٦﴾

> *When the angels said, 'O Mary, God gives you the good news of a Word from Him whose name is Messiah, Jesus, son of Mary, distinguished in the world and the Hereafter and one of those brought near [to God]. He will speak to the people in the cradle and in adulthood, and will be one of the righteous.'*[37]

Divine Love

Attaining closeness to God can also lead to receiving more and more of His divine love. This takes the servant further along the journey of excellence. Imam al-Baqir (a) narrates that when the Holy Prophet Muhammad (s) ascended to the heavens, God told him:

ما تقرب إلي عبد بشيء أحب إلي مما افترضت عليه وإنه ليتقرب إلي بالنافلة حتى أحبه فإذا أحببته كنت سمعه الذي يسمع به وبصره الذي

---

[37] The Holy Quran, 3:45-46.

يبصر به ولسانه الذي ينطق به ويده التي يبطش بها، إن دعاني أجبته وإن سألني أعطيته

> *No servant can seek closeness to Me by a means better than what I have prescribed. He shall grow closer to Me through recommended prayers until I love him. Once I love him, I shall be the ear by which he hears, the eye by which he sees, the tongue by which he speaks, and the hand by which he strikes. If he supplicates to Me, I shall answer him, and if he asks Me, I shall give [to] him.*[38]

God tells the Holy Prophet (s) about the great capabilities that He gives to whomever He loves. He becomes the servant's eyes, ears, and hands, granting him knowledge and ability. An individual who gains closeness to God therefore has no limit to how much they can grow in excellence on their spiritual journey.

We see several examples in the Holy Quran and in our history of individuals who gained extraordinary capability through their closeness to God and His love for them. One of the best examples of this is Jesus, son of Mary, who was given so many capabilities by God that people began to think of him as a god, rather than as a righteous servant of the One Lord. God says:

وَيُعَلِّمُهُ الْكِتَابَ وَالْحِكْمَةَ وَالتَّوْرَاةَ وَالْإِنجِيلَ ﴿٤٨﴾ وَرَسُولًا إِلَىٰ بَنِي إِسْرَائِيلَ أَنِّي قَدْ جِئْتُكُم بِآيَةٍ مِّن رَّبِّكُمْ ۖ أَنِّي أَخْلُقُ لَكُم مِّنَ الطِّينِ كَهَيْئَةِ الطَّيْرِ فَأَنفُخُ فِيهِ فَيَكُونُ طَيْرًا بِإِذْنِ اللَّهِ ۖ وَأُبْرِئُ الْأَكْمَهَ وَالْأَبْرَصَ وَأُحْيِي الْمَوْتَىٰ

---

[38] Al-Kulayni, *al-Kafi*, 2:352.

$$\text{بِإِذْنِ اللَّهِ ۖ وَأُنَبِّئُكُم بِمَا تَأْكُلُونَ وَمَا تَدَّخِرُونَ فِي بُيُوتِكُمْ ۚ إِنَّ فِي ذَٰلِكَ لَآيَةً لَّكُمْ إِن كُنتُم مُّؤْمِنِينَ ﴿٤٩﴾}$$

> *He will teach him the Book and wisdom, the Torah and the Evangel, and [he will be] an apostle to the Children of Israel, [and he will declare,] "I have certainly brought you a sign from your Lord: I will create for you the form of a bird out of clay, then I will breathe into it, and it will become a bird by God's leave. I heal the blind and the leper and I revive the dead by God's leave. I will tell you what you have eaten and what you have stored in your houses. There is indeed a sign in that for you, should you be faithful.*[39]

Jesus was given miraculous abilities, but all his miracles were in full dependence on God's omnipotence. He himself would declare, as we saw in the verse, that whatever miracle he undertakes is only by God's leave. Yet there were individuals who did not understand the reality of true tawheed, failed to use their reason, and began to take Jesus as a lord beside God Almighty. God says:

$$\text{وَإِذْ قَالَ اللَّهُ يَا عِيسَى ابْنَ مَرْيَمَ أَأَنتَ قُلْتَ لِلنَّاسِ اتَّخِذُونِي وَأُمِّيَ إِلَٰهَيْنِ مِن دُونِ اللَّهِ ۖ قَالَ سُبْحَانَكَ مَا يَكُونُ لِي أَنْ أَقُولَ مَا لَيْسَ لِي بِحَقٍّ ۚ إِن كُنتُ قُلْتُهُ فَقَدْ عَلِمْتَهُ ۚ تَعْلَمُ مَا فِي نَفْسِي وَلَا أَعْلَمُ مَا فِي نَفْسِكَ ۚ إِنَّكَ أَنتَ عَلَّامُ الْغُيُوبِ}$$

> *When God will say, 'O Jesus, son of Mary! Was it you who said to the people, "Take me and my mother for*

---

[39] The Holy Quran, 3:48-49.

gods besides God"?' He will say, 'Immaculate are You! It does not behoove me to say what I have no right to [say]. Had I said it, You would certainly have known it: You know whatever is in my self, and I do not know what is in Your Self. Indeed, You are knower of all that is Unseen.

مَا قُلْتُ لَهُمْ إِلَّا مَا أَمَرْتَنِي بِهِ أَنِ اعْبُدُوا اللَّهَ رَبِّي وَرَبَّكُمْ ۚ وَكُنتُ عَلَيْهِمْ شَهِيدًا مَّا دُمْتُ فِيهِمْ ۖ فَلَمَّا تَوَفَّيْتَنِي كُنتَ أَنتَ الرَّقِيبَ عَلَيْهِمْ ۚ وَأَنتَ عَلَىٰ كُلِّ شَيْءٍ شَهِيدٌ

I did not say to them [anything] except what You had commanded me [to say]: "Worship God, my Lord and your Lord." And I was a witness to them so long as I was among them. But when You had taken me away, You Yourself were watchful over them, and You are witness to all things.[40]

These were all powers and capabilities that God granted to Jesus, son of Mary, but what abilities did God grant to His most beloved creations – the Holy Prophet Muhammad (s) and his Immaculate heirs (a)? These individuals, with our beloved Prophet (s) at the forefront, surpassed in their excellence any other prophet or righteous servant. That is why they were granted much more than any other prophet or righteous servant. God removed from them all impurities and purified them thoroughly. They were given unimaginable levels of excellence through their closeness to the Almighty. It is enough to read the

---

[40] The Holy Quran, 5:116-17.

following segment of *al-Ziyara al-Jami'a*, which was taught to us by Imam al-Hadi (a):

فَالرَّاغِبُ عَنْكُمْ مَارِقٌ وَاللَّازِمُ لَكُمْ لَاحِقٌ وَالْمُقَصِّرُ فِي حَقِّكُمْ زَاهِقٌ وَالْحَقُّ مَعَكُمْ وَفِيكُمْ وَمِنْكُمْ وَإِلَيْكُمْ وَأَنْتُمْ أَهْلُهُ وَمَعْدِنُهُ وَمِيرَاثُ النُّبُوَّةِ عِنْدَكُمْ وَإِيَابُ الْخَلْقِ إِلَيْكُمْ وَحِسَابُهُمْ عَلَيْكُمْ وَفَصْلُ الْخِطَابِ عِنْدَكُمْ وَآيَاتُ اللهِ لَدَيْكُمْ وَعَزَائِمُهُ فِيكُمْ وَنُورُهُ وَبُرْهَانُهُ عِنْدَكُمْ وَأَمْرُهُ إِلَيْكُمْ ...

Whosoever turns away from you deviates from the right path and whosoever closely adhere to you reaches the destination. Whosoever falls short in fulfilling his duties to you has surely lost. Verily, truth is with you, in you, from you, and unto you, as you are its people and mettle. Verily, the inheritance of Prophethood is with you. Verily, the return of creation is to you and their judgment is with you. The clearest and most precise words are with you. The signs of God are with you, His resolve is in you, His light and proof are with you, and His commands are with you....

مَوَالِيَّ لَا أُحْصِي ثَنَاءَكُمْ وَلَا أَبْلُغُ مِنَ الْمَدْحِ كُنْهَكُمْ وَمِنَ الْوَصْفِ قَدْرَكُمْ وَأَنْتُمْ نُورُ الْأَخْيَارِ وَهُدَاةُ الْأَبْرَارِ وَحُجَجُ الْجَبَّارِ بِكُمْ فَتَحَ اللهُ وَبِكُمْ يَخْتِمُ اللهُ وَبِكُمْ يُنَزِّلُ الْغَيْثَ وَبِكُمْ يُمْسِكُ السَّمَاءَ أَنْ تَقَعَ عَلَى الْأَرْضِ إِلَّا بِإِذْنِهِ وَبِكُمْ يُنَفِّسُ الْهَمَّ وَيَكْشِفُ الضُّرَّ وَعِنْدَكُمْ مَا نَزَلَتْ بِهِ رُسُلُهُ وَهَبَطَتْ بِهِ مَلَائِكَتُهُ.

O' my masters! I cannot count all your merits. Nor can I fully praise your essence or describe your status. You are the light of the virtuous, the guides to the pious, and the proofs of the Omnipotent Lord. God began creation with You and with you He sealed it. With you, He sends down abundant rains and prevents the heavens from falling upon the Earth, except by his permission. With you, He drives away troubles and dismisses hardships. With you is that with which His Messengers came down and with which His Angels descended.[41]

Their status is so high that we cannot even comprehend the greatness that they were given. We read in the supplication of the Month of Rajab, taught to us by Imam Mahdi (a):

اللهم إني أسألك بمعاني جميع ما يدعوك به ولاة أمرك، المأمونون على سرِّك، المستبشرون بأمرك، الواصفون لقدرتك، المعلنون لعظمتك، أسألك بما نطق فيهم من مشيتك، فجعلتهم معادن لكلماتك، وأركاناً لتوحيدك، وآياتك ومقاماتك التي لا تعطيل لها في كل مكان، يعرفك بها من عرفك، لا فرق بينك وبينها إلا أنهم عبادك وخلقك، فتقها ورتقها بيدك، بدؤها منك وعودها إليك

> O' God, I ask you by all that is encompassed in the supplications of Your vicegerents – whom You trusted with Your secret, who take glad tidings in Your commands, who [accurately] describe Your omnipotence, and who pronounce Your glory. I ask You by Your will, which has been pronounced through them, so that they became the mettle of Your words. [You made them] the cornerstones of [belief in] Your oneness, Your signs, and Your status – which cannot be denied. Those who know You

---

[41] Al-Tousi, *Tahtheeb al-Ahkam*, 6:97-99.

know You through them so that there is no difference between You and them except that they are your servants and creations. [The universe's] creation and destruction are with You. Its inception is from you and its return is to you.[42]

May God allow us to be followers of the righteous servants whom He chose as protectors of His message and a mercy to all creation.

---

[42] Al-Tousi, *Misbah al-Mutahajjid*, 803.

Translation Note

We must acknowledge the great difficulty that comes with attempting to translate the Holy Quran. Muslim scholars have pondered on the meanings of the holy text for centuries, and the meanings of its verses only grow deeper as time passes. The process of translation always begs us to find precise meanings for the passages that we translate. However, when we encounter the majesty of the Holy Quran, we find ourselves incapable of understanding, let alone translating, its true and deep meanings. We turned to the works of translators who have attempted to do this before. Although no translation can do justice to the Holy Quran, we found the translation of Ali Quli Qarai to be the most proper in understanding, when compared to the understanding of the text as derived by our grand scholars. As such, we decided to rely on Qarai's translations throughout this book, with some adaptations that allowed us to weave the verses more appropriately with the rest of the work.

Another great limitation came with translation of the narrations of the Grand Prophet Muhammad (s) and his Holy Household (a). Their words are ever so deep and ever so powerful. We attempted to convey these passages to the reader in a tone that is understandable, without deviating from the essence of the words of these immaculate personalities. We pray that we were successful in this endeavor.

Finally, we want to take this opportunity to thank you for your support. As students of Islam and as translators of this text, our greatest purpose is to please God by passing along these teachings to others. By picking up this book, you have lent your crucial support in this endeavor. We hope that you will continue your support throughout the rest of this book, and we ask that you keep us in prayers whenever you pick it up.

The Editorial and Translation Team,

The Mainstay Foundation

Referenced Works

Holy Scriptures

The Holy Quran.

Other Works

Al-'Amili, Muhammad ibn al-Hassan. *Wasa'el al-Shia*. Beirut: Daar Ihya al-Torath al-Arabi.

Al-'Amili, Zayn al-Deen ibn Ali. *Munyat al-Mureed*. Qum: Maktab al-I'lam al-Islami.

Al-Ameeni, Ibrahim. *Tazkiyat al-Nafs*. Daar al-Balagha, 2000.

Al-Asfahani, Al-Hussain ibn Muhammad. Al-*Mufradat*. Qum, 1983.

Al-Barqi, Ahmad ibn Muhammad. *Al-Mahasin*. Tehran: Daar al-Kutub al-Islamiya, 1950.

Al-Borojourdi, Agha Hussein. *Jami' Ahadeeth al-Shia*. Qum: al-Matba'a al-Ilmiyya, 1978.

Al-Harrani, al-Hassan ibn Ali. *Tohaf al-'Oqool*. Qum: Muasasat al-Nashr al-Islami, 1983.

Al-Haydari, Kamal. *Al-Tarbiya al-Roohiya*. Qum: Daar al-Sadiqain, 2000.

Al-Hilli, Ahmad ibn Muhammad. *'Oddat al-Daa'i*. Qum: Maktabat al-Wijdani.

Al-Hindi, Ali al-Muttaqi. *Kanz al-'Ommal*. Muasasat al-Risala, 1989.

Al-Huwaizi, Abd Ali. *Tafseer Noor al-Thaqalayn*. Qum: Ismailian.

Al-Ihsa'ei, Muhammad ibn Ali. *'Awali al-La'ali*. Qum: Sayyid al-Shuhada, 1983.

Al-Kulayni, Muhammad ibn Yaqoub. *Al-Kafi*. Tehran: Daar al-Kutub al-Islamiya, 1968.

Al-Majlisi, Muhammad Baqir. *Bihar al-Anwar*. Beirut: al-Wafaa, 1983.

Al-Mazandarani, Muhammad Salih. *Sharh Usool al-Kafi*. Beirut: Daar Ihya al-Torath al-Arabi, 2000.

Al-Mufeed, Muhammad ibn Muhammad ibn al-Nu'man. *Al-Ikhtisas*. Beirut: Daar al-Mufeed, 1993.

Al-Nouri, Mirza Hussain. *Mustadrak al-Wasa'el*. Beirut: Mu'asasat Aal al-Bayt li Ihya' al-Torath.

Al-Qayyoumi, Jawad. *Sahifat al-Mahdi (a)*. Mu'assasat al-Nashr al-Islami.

Al-Radi, Muhammad ibn Al-Hussain. *Al-Majazat al-Nabawiyya*. Qum.

Al-Radi, Muhammad ibn al-Hussain. *Nahj al-Balagha*. Beirut: Daar al-Ma'rifa.

Al-Reyshahri, Muhammad. *Mizan al-Hikma*. Cairo: Daar al-Hadith, 1995.

Al-Sadouq, Muhammad ibn Ali. *'Ilal al-Sharai'*. Najaf: al-Matbaa al-Haydaria, 1966.

Al-Sadouq, Muhammad ibn Ali. *'Oyun Akhbar al-Rida*. Beirut: al-A'lami, 1984.

Al-Sadouq, Muhammad ibn Ali. *Al-Amali*. Qum: Muassasat al-Bitha, 1996.

Al-Sadouq, Muhammad ibn Ali. *Al-Khisal*. Qum: Jama'at al-Mudarriseen, 1983.

Al-Sadouq, Muhammad ibn Ali. *Fada'el al-Ashhor al-Thalath*. Daar al-Rasul al-Akram.

Al-Sadouq, Muhammad ibn Ali. *Ma'ani al-Akhbar*. Qum: Muasasat al-Nashr al-Islami, 1942.

Al-Tabari, Muhammad ibn Jareer. *Dala'el al-Imama*. Qum: Mu'assasat al-Bi'tha.

Al-Tabatabaei, Muhammad Hussain. *Tafsir al-Mizan*. Qum: Jama'at al-Mudarriseen.

Al-Tabrasi, Ahmad ibn Ali. *Al-Ihtijaj*. Najaf: al-Nu'man, 1966.

Al-Tabrasi, Ameen al-Deen. *Majama' al-Bayan*. Beirut: al-A'lami, 1995.

Al-Tousi, Muhammad ibn al-Hassan. *Misbah al-Mutahajjid*. Beirut: Fiqh al-Shia, 1991.

Al-Tousi, Muhammad ibn al-Hassan. *Tahtheeb al-Ahkam*. Tehran: Daar al-Kutub al-Islamiya, 1970.

Al-Wasiti, Kafi al-Deen al-Laithi. *'Oyoun al-Hikam*. Qum: Daar al-Hadith.

Ibn Tawus, Ali ibn Moussa. *Al-Tara'ef*. Qum: al-Khayyam.

Ibn Tawus, Ali ibn Moussa. *Iqbaal al-A'mal*. Qum: Maktab al-I'lam al-Islami, 1993.

Printed in Great Britain
by Amazon